INDIA'S ENERGY

Essays on Sustainable Development

Institut Français de Pondichéry (French Institute of Pondicherry): Created in 1955, the IFP is a multidisciplinary research and advanced educational institute. Major research works are focussing on Sanskrit and Tamil languages and literatures—in close collaboration with the *Ecole Française d'Extrême-Orient*—ecosystems, biodiversity and sustainability, dynamics of population and socio-economic development. (Institut Français de Pondichéry, 11, Saint Louis Street, P.B. 33, Pondicherry 605 001, Tel: 91 413 41 70/33 41 68, Telex: 469224 FRAN-In, Fax: 91 413 33 95 34, E-mail: instfran@giasmd01.vsnl.net.in, Website: http://www.ifpindia.org)

Centre de Sciences Humaines (Centre for Social Sciences and Humanities): Created in New Delhi in 1989 the CSH, like its counterpart in Pondicherry, is also part of the same network of research centres of the French Ministry of Foreign Affairs. The Centre's research work is primarily oriented towards the study of issues concerning the contemporary dynamics relative to development in India and South Asia. The activities of the Centre are focused on four main themes, namely: Economic growth and sustainable development, International and regional relations, Institutional structures and political constructions of identity and Urban dynamics. (Centre de Sciences Humaines, 2, Aurangzeb Road, New Delhi 110 011, Tel: 91 11 301 62 59/301 41 73, Fax: 91 11 301 84 80, E-mail: public@csh-del.ernet.in, Website: http://www.france.diplomatic.fr/hote/delhi-csh/home.htm)

INDIA'S ENERGY

Essays on Sustainable Development

Edited by
PIERRE AUDINET
P.R. SHUKLA
FRÉDÉRIC GRARE

MANOHAR

CENTRE DE SCIENCES HUMAINES
2000

First published 2000

ISBN 81-7304-351-5

Published by
Ajay Kumar Jain for
Manohar Publishers & Distributors
4753/23 Ansari Road, Daryaganj
New Delhi 110002

Printed at
Rajkamal Electric Press
B 35/9 GT Karnal Road Indl Area
Delhi 110033

Contents

Contents

Foreword

Power Perspective

YOGINDER K. ALAGH

This is a volume on India's energy structures, performance and outlook. The Programme for Strategic and International Security Studies (Geneva) and the Centre de Sciences Humaines (New Delhi) has with its collaborators been organizing a series of meetings, based on research on this subject and this volume includes articles discussed in a meeting in Geneva in June 1998. The articles are divided into four sets. The first looks at the long-term issues. The second is sectoral, or concerns a specific issue. The third looks at strategic security concerns in a regional setting. The final set is on related subjects.

Sujata Gupta presents TERI's model forecasts for energy through the year 2050, by which time India is expected to have stabilized its population. The main features of these forecasts have been extensively discussed in different fora and so are not repeated here. CO_2 emissions have started reaching intolerable levels giving a sharp rise to energy management questions, as also lifestyle questions, embedded in 'alternative assumptions'. Sujata Gupta comes out forcefully with a conclusion which all serious long-term studies of India's energy perspectives make, but on which there is little practical concern. In her own words:

> One of the main carbon emissions mitigation strategies suggested by the model is the substitution of fossil fuels, by removable and nuclear sources of energy—hydro power generation increases as the carbon constraint becomes more stringent—in the baseline, new nuclear power generating capacity is not indicated. In the carbon constrained scenario additional nuclear based power generation becomes an alternative to reduce carbon emissions.

India's nuclear power plants have been running close to capacity levels from the last four years and are making money. The replacement of the coolant tubes with indigenous technology at Rana Pratap

Sagar and the experimental fast breeder reactor at Kalpakkam, would have given any country confidence to go ahead. In the first buyer-seller meet organized by the AEC I had shown that the long run marginal cost of nuclear power is comparable to alternatives around 800 km away from coal sources. Also as a minister, I had announced India's willingness to look at private investment from abroad as a possibility. As Pokharan cools down, this is necessary again. As regards hydro power, to begin with, the National Rehabilitation Policy, which follows a weaker variant of the Sardar Sarovar pattern is yet to see the light of day. The Hanumantha Rao Committee I had set up for Tehri should be accepted by the government. Meanwhile those who say that hydropower is unnecessary, should produce a counterfactual.

John Gale has written on coal as the 'Energy for the twenty-first century in India'. He makes the point I had made in my article on 'Fuel for Power' that in most locations, if the hydro option is not available, domestic coal is still the cheapest option in India, in terms of real costs (Alagh, 1998). Gale projects coal demand in India at 690 million tonnes by 2009-10. He makes the point, first noted way back in India's Fifth Plan that 'The average calorific value of coal used in Indian power stations has decreased from 22 GJ/t in 1970 to 15 GJ/t currently. As a result, unit consumption of coal per unit of power generated has increased and the efficiency of power generation has decreased.' Gale then discusses Circulating Fluidized Bed Combustion, Pressurized Fluidized Bed Combustion and Integrated Gassification Combined Cycles. He lists the current IGCC investments underway. I had offered that any entrepreneur, domestic or foreign, who would invest in production, based on Indian technologies for cleaner coal use would get support from the science and technology set-up. More initiatives are required in this area to take up the initial capital cost disadvantages.

The basic point is that India will not be able to burn unlimited amount of coal in an unrestrained manner as at present and this is the problem these articles trying to cope with. The study by O. Schwank, T. Von Stokar and N. North gets at this issue in a frontal manner by comparing carbon emission path options for Switzerland and India. They set the problem within the framework of an internationally harmonized carbon tax. Best available technologies and lifestyle changes are looked into. Zero energy building technologies, industrial process sector use, 'cars through transition of highly fuel efficient vehicles' are all discussed. Their projections don't show any easy convergence to Kyoto scenarios. For India they find total carbon emissions rising rapidly. However 'under a high GDP scenario India would not exceed the per capita carbon emissions of the EU or Japan in 2050 and a significant disparity in income levels would still remain'. Their projections basically make a case for early action scenarios and attention to the global aspect of the problem. On the other hand a very interesting and useful article by P. Audinet and E. Fages on climate change and allocations of GEF Funds has been included. They take a very practical approach of seeing how India, a non-Annex I country, can be made a more active participant. They find the budget, conflicting incentives, technological biases, all making the programme, have limited scope. They make a number of remedial proposals, both administrative and conceptual.

Leena Srivastava sets the problem in a long-term context but closely examines recent policy measures from the angle of adequacy. She sees the counter guarantee projects, the setting up of regulatory bodies, the liquid fuel policies and hydro and mega project policies as short-term reactions to the compelling needs of capacity additions. The counter guarantee policies or fast track projects as they were called were not clearly or particularly well thought out incentive packages at the initial phases of privatization. But the legislation in Parliament on private investment in transmission and the regulatory bills were steps in the right direction. The transmission bill was piloted through the Parliamentary Standing Committee on Energy when I was Power Minister and it was very widely discussed and debated, and the public policy concerns of various influential groups were taken into account. For example, while I started an availability tariff, at the existing stage of Indian distribution policies, it was quite sensible to agree that transmission regulation would be under public regulation, even though investment was privatized. The process of Parliamentary committee debate also meant wider acceptance of reform principles and I was allowed to introduce the CERC and SERC Bill, which my predecessor could not. But I agree with Leena Srivastava that short run considerations forced my successor to substantially water down the bill, while a more rounded strategy would have helped in saving clauses like a minimum tariff for rural areas and the mandatory nature of the original provisions. The mega power policy had its origin in the eminent persons group I had set up. This kind of mechanism emerges from the fact that different interest groups are willing to give concessions to a large market like India and there has to be an institutional mechanism to internalize these advantages.

All in all it seems a little severe to say that there are no long-term considerations underlying India's energy policies. A more balanced view probably would be that while there is a framework, details keep on being flushed out sequentially, including by groups like TERI. But Leena Srivastava makes an important point that within this framework two kinds of obstacles keep on coming up. One, short-term interests, sometimes of a rather unhealthy kind, keep on having their way. Second, the process of reform in the implementation process is itself slow and erratic. The typical pattern is to announce a policy and then to modify it under attack. Again bring up the original objectives at a more appropriate time. Sometimes as in the CERC/SERC bill the objectives are watered down. Progress in a democracy is slow but sure.

Etienne surveys the field of rural power. He makes the point that India has the largest electricity system in rural areas in the world. He documents in great detail its shortcomings. As Power Minister I announced in Parliament that electrification of around 3,000 villages had disappeared. It was difficult to channel funds to these villages to restore power, because the state government insisted on all 'arrears' being written off as a precondition. However the big bang reform approach was equally unproductive. As Power Minister, I found that thousands of farmers in villages in Ajmer, Udaipur and Chittorgarh were willing to pay Rs. 1.25/unit, but more than 50,000 connections given under such conditions were not energized, because the SEB did not have escrow leeway. Here a rule was standing in the way of genuine reform and I insisted on the loan for distribution improvements going through.

SKN Nair's paper on power demand leads to the issue of overestimation of energy survey, which is not a demand forecast, but a statement of wishes. These forecasts cannot be validated by any sensible system of income and price elasticities as seen in the mid-seventies. Nair gives alternative and sensible figures. He then gives a detailed system-wise description of trends and requirements. Is one moving to markets for power? The availability tariff that I initiated as Power Minister is I believe a first step in that direction. But it will require one to get out of the existing unit level tariff

formulas including those negotiated for IPPs. It should be possible to do so, because I believe that payment for deemed generation will at best be slow. An availability tariff will mean immediate cash. If one does not go this way and Coelho whom I had asked to look into this said one should, one will keep on facing the incongruity of asking Tatas to back down at Rs. 2 a unit or less and pay around Rs. 4 to Dabhol.

Nair also looks at the short run working of the system with PLFs. From June 1996 to April 1997 when I was a minister, a programme called PAGER was run which monitored individual plant level working. Energy growth was 7.8 per cent and deficits went down. The year before that growth was 3.8 per cent and from April 1997 to July 1998 it was again 5 per cent. So monitoring and remeding difficulties matters.

Grare's article on Central Asia's possible role in India's energy systems is a comprehensive look into a strategic issue. His conclusions will have a major impact sooner than people think. Gilles Boquérat's article looks at the South Asian context. He laments the lack of a collaborative approach at the regional level for an optimal development of the subcontinental energy resources. The article by Sundararajan on oil and gas restructuring is of interest to the sectoral specialist and makes a point that energy reform has to be general and sector specific.

All in all a very interesting selection with both questions and answers but more important, the articles keep on raising new questions. It will definitely push India's cooperation on energy with France at a higher level.

Acknowledgements

The collection of articles assembled in this book were produced on the occasion of an international seminar organized in Geneva in June 1998 by the Programme for Strategic and International Security Studies (Geneva), in collaboration with the Centre de Sciences Humaines (New Delhi), the Indian Institute of Management (Ahmadabad) and the Modern Asia Research Centre (Geneva). This first meeting was followed in September 1998 by a second workshop organised in Delhi by the CSH and the IIM.

The editors would like to thank the Direction of Development and Co-operation (Swiss Ministry of Foreign Affairs), Unocal Corporation (Houston), Petroconsultants (Geneva) and the Indian Council for Cultural Relations (New Delhi) whose financial support have made both the seminar and the book possible. They would also like to express their profound gratitude to Ms. Uma Krishnan whose work enabled the book to appear.

INDIA: SIMPLIFIED ENERGY BALANCE (1997)

(million tons of oil equivalent)

Supply and consumption	*Coal*	*Crude oil*	*Petroleum products*	*Gas*	*Nuclear*	*Hydro*	*Geothermal, solar, etc.*	*Combustible renewable and waste*	*Electricity*	*Heat*	*Total*
Indigenous production	147.2	37.6	-	17.8	2.6	6.4	N	192.8	-	-	404.5
Imports	5.8	33.1	20.1	-	-	-	-	-	0.1	-	59.2
Exports	N	-0.6	-1.7	-	-	-	-	-	N	-	-2.4
International marine bunkers	-	-	-0.5	-	-	-	-	-	-	-	-0.5
Stock changes	0.3	-	-	-	-	-	-	-	-	-	0.3
Total primary energy supply	153.3	70.1	17.9	17.8	2.6	6.4	N	192.8	0.1	-	461.0
Total final consumption	42.6	0.7	79.2	9.4	-	-	-	192.8	30.0	-	354.7
Industry sector	42.5	0.7	17.3	9.0	-	-	-	22.0	13.7	-	105.2
Transport sector	N	-	40.9	-	-	-	-	-	0.6	-	41.5
Other sectors	N	-	16.9	0.4	-	-	-	170.8	15.7	-	203.9
Non-energy use	-	-	4.1	-	-	-	-	-	-	-	4.1
Electricity generated – GWh	338887	-	12000	27583	10100	74775	57	-	-	-	463402

Source: International Energy Agency, 1999, *Energy Balances of Non-OECD Countries 1996-1997*, IEA, Paris.

Notes: N : Negligible.

\- : Not applicable, nil or not available.

Abbreviations

Abbreviation	*Full form*
bn.kWh	billion kilo Watts per hour
bn.bbl	billion barrels
bn.f^3	billion cubic feet
bn.m^3	billion cubic metres
bn.t	billion tons
bn.tC	billion tons of Carbon
bbloe	barrel oil equivalent
CHF60.-/t	60 Swiss Francs per ton
m^3	cubic metre
EJ	Exa Joule
GCA	Gross Cropped Area
GJ	Giga Joule
GJ per ton	Giga Joule per ton
Gt	Giga ton
GtC	Giga ton of Carbon
GW	Giga Watt
GWe	Giga Watt electric
kgoe	kilo of oil equivalent
kV	kilo Volt
kW	kilo Watt
kWh	kilo Watt hour
kWh per annum	kilo Watt hour per annum
mbbl	million barrels
mbbld	million barrels per day
mm^3	million cubic metres
mkWh	million kilo Watts per hour
mmt	million metric tons
mt	million tons
mtC	million tons of Carbon
mtce per annum	million tons of coal equivalent per annum
$mtCO_2$	million tons of Carbon Dioxide

mtoe	million tons oil equivalent
mt per annum	million tons per annum
MW	Mega Watt
MWd	Mega Watt per day
mWe	million Watt electric
NO_2	Nitrogen dioxide
PJ	Peta Joule
ppmv	party per million volume
SO_2	Sulphur dioxide
tC	tons of Carbon
tCO_2	tons of Carbon Dioxide
tC/cap/a	tons of Carbon per capita per annum
Tg	Tera gram
toe	ton oil equivalent
TWh	Tera Watt hour
TWh per annum	Tera Watt hour per annum
V	Volt

Introduction

PIERRE AUDINET
FRÉDÉRIC GRARE
P.R. SHUKLA

India is emerging on the world scene as a major energy consumer. Growing imports of oil, gas and coal redefine the conditions that guarantee India's energy security. India's final energy demand grows faster than the development of its national resources. Beyond, one can observe a regular growth in the intensity of polluting energy emissions of the economic activity. This is worsened by the misallocation of resources due to pricing policies and management systems that induce a lot of inefficiency and waste.

To tackle the long run constraints of the present demand and supply trends, drastic changes in the management of the sector are required. Implementation of reforms began in 1991. Some options exist but a number of bold decisions still have to be taken and implemented to fulfil the energy needs of a population that has now crossed one billion inhabitants. Hence the need to contribute to the debate on sustainable development and scenarios for the coming century.

In 1995, a government of India committee chaired by Mr. U. Sundararajan estimated that to reduce oil dependency to 60 per cent, given the present demand and supply patterns, an additional investment of US $50 billion would be needed. In total, more than 10 billion US $ a year of investments in power production, transmission and distribution, oil exploration and refining, and construction of gas terminals will be required in order to satisfy energy demand over the next decade. Which country is able to mobilize almost 4 per cent of its GDP for energy from its domestic savings alone? Foreign direct investments in energy are on the rise, thanks to a much-needed liberalization in the power generation sector that began in 1991. A similar liberalization trend is taking place in the oil and gas sector, with the progressive dismantling of the administered pricing mechanism, which had previously ruled production conditions. Despite these welcome changes, a number of questions still remain unanswered. Will investment be enough? If not, will growth be hampered?

The level of most energy prices in India is still lower than international prices (or what could be reference prices for non-traded products such as electricity). The energy economic environment will be affected by both the removal of price subsidies on power and liquid fuels, and capacity constraints, which will tend to push prices up in the short run. How will the allocation of resources improve in such an environment? Will the consumption be rationalized? What will be the technological options chosen? What are the additional incentives required to make consumption patterns more sustainable?

As in other countries, the energy sector is responsible for most of the 880 mt of CO_2 emissions produced in India (1997). Global effects now add to local ones, and India has to get more involved in global climate change negotiations. What are the terms of the environment-development equation that policy makers will have to handle? What are the choices India will make for its energy transition towards a more environmental friendly energy system given its local natural resources? What is the future of coal, oil and gas, nuclear and also renewables?

Energy demands and changes in preferences as to fuel choice modify India's import patterns, translating into more oil imports. In ten years from now, the size of India's imports will reach the equivalent of the present total oil consumption of France. How will its energy choices affect international energy prices? Moreover the increasing concentration of the world fossil fuel production in the Middle East will make India more vulnerable than ever to regional political hazards. Should India look for its energy future in an increased SAARC co-operation? Will it import energy from its neighbours: Hydropower from Nepal or gas from Bangladesh? Will the availability of oil and gas from Central Asia ease the supply of energy to India?

National choices must increasingly be made within a global or international framework that has implications far beyond the borders of India. Essential components for a sustainable energy development are and will remain the capacity to mobilize private investment (foreign and domestic), to take into account global environment and to develop India's energy resources and external linkages.

To provide a clearer picture of the future, the collection of articles presented in this book begins with a scenario exercise. It explores future demand, and technology trajectories to satisfy it at minimum costs, possibly lowering polluting emissions (Shukla). The next paper explores the particular issue of infrastructure development and the role of the state in guiding it and funding part of it (Etienne, Nair, Srivastava). The global environmental agenda is examined in the next paper, emphasizing the conceptual changes needed actually taking into consideration environment needs at the macro-economic level (Gupta, Schwank et al.) or at the project level (Audinet et al.) The appraisal of technologies available to exploit existing resources is assessed both for coal (Gale) and oil (Rogier) in the fifth article. The development of external energy linkages (both regional and international) as an integral part of energy security is analysed in the sixth paper (Dietl, Boquérat, Grare). Reforms in the Indian energy sector began to be implemented in both the liquid fuel and the electricity sector. The last chapter ends on the example of restructuring in the oil and gas sector.

The book points out to a renewed role for the state. The policy reforms implemented from 1991 are shaping a new increasingly competitive energy supply sector more able to face the present and future challenges. The role of the market is clearly much larger than in the past. While the state is withdrawing from the ownership and management of resources and from the determination of prices, it now has to help new private actors handle increasingly important dimensions such as the one of risk and uncertainty. This is not an easy task and the assessment of the energy policy followed in the past decade demonstrates that India's institutions are still in a transition period. A fragile social situation, inadequate management in the public sector and vested interests slow down the implementation of reform and the development of new behaviours. Some of the institutional elements indispensable to the smooth functioning of a market economy are now in place.[1] The energy sector has gone a long way towards more sustainability, but a lot remains to be done to actually implement policies, to improve the efficiency of the state's action and to facilitate market development and provide an affordable energy service of decent quality to all the citizens.

The emissions are reported in the book both in terms of carbon and carbon dioxide and the conversion multiplier from carbon to carbon dioxide is 3.67 (or 44/12).[2]

NOTES

1. Like the Central Electricity Regulatory Authority and the state ones in some states.
2. This is to highlight the fact that Shukla's report of emissions of around 212 million tons of carbon (from Indian energy system) and Alagh's report of 800 million tons of carbon dioxide per year are not contradictory. These two numbers are consistent since the ratio of the molecular weights of carbon dioxide and that of carbon are 44:12, which is nearly 3.67.

Future Energy Trends and Carbon Mitigation Strategies for India

P.R. SHUKLA

ENERGY AND EMISSIONS FROM INDIA: INTRODUCTION

From a relatively low economic base, the Indian economy has grown rapidly in the past few decades. Economic growth is fuelled by rapidly rising energy demand. The commercial energy demand has grown at an annual rate of over 6 per cent (Shukla, 1997a). In past two decades, domestic coal has emerged as the mainstay of primary energy in electric power and industry sectors (CMIE, 1999). The electric power sector capacity additions during the past two decades have come mainly from coal thermal plants. Rising transport demand and increased share of road transport has translated into the growing consumption of oil products. During the past decade, the natural gas consumption has grown, although its contribution in primary energy still remains very low. Growth in commercial energy consumption has also resulted from rapid substitution of traditional biomass along the conventional fuel ladder.

Rising energy demand and enhanced share of coal in primary energy has led to a rapidly rising trend of energy emissions from India and higher carbon intensity of the economy (Shukla, 1997a; Loulou et al., 1997). This trend, which is likely to continue, will enhance India's share in the global emissions in next few decades (Shukla, 1996; Fisher-Vanden et al., 1997). Although per capita emissions from India are low at present, the total annual emissions exceeds 200 million tons of carbon (Shukla, 1997a). Coal combustion also emits considerable sulfur dioxide (SO_2) which has been a grave concern for local pollution (Shukla and Pandey, 1997). Lately this has drawn the attention of the policy-makers, although no major policy initiative is formally initiated for SO_2 control.

The control of local pollutants has entered the national agenda, whereas the mitigation of greenhouse gases has attained importance due to its implications on global climate change. The United Nations

Framework Convention on Climate Change (UNFCCC, 1992) provides broad framework. The Kyoto Protocol (UNFCCC, 1997) under the UNFCCC has proposed a mitigation regime. The carbon mitigation is however complicated by the fact that India has large coal reserves, but limited gas and oil reserves. The substitution away from coal therefore would require energy imports. While India has the experience with emerging renewable energy technologies, the capital and foreign exchange constraints are likely to restrict a shift away from coal, unless the economic and fiscal policies to relax these constraints are instituted under a co-operative global regime.

This article presents an analysis of long-term energy and emissions trajectories for India using an integrated modelling framework based on bottom-up paradigm. The framework integrates an energy system model (MARKAL), fifteen end-use sector models (AIM/END-USE model), and a demand projection model that separately projects demands for thirty-seven end-use services. Twenty-two electricity generation and eighty-six demand technologies are considered. Demand-supply integration within a bottom-up framework is achieved through a soft linkage of MARKAL with the AIM/END-USE model whereby the output of each end-use modelling exercise is exogenously passed to the MARKAL model as input. The analysis spanning four decades examines a reference scenario and several carbon mitigation scenarios and provides insights into the implications of mitigation commitments on energy and technology mix, energy costs mitigation costs.

MODELLING SYSTEM AND TECHNOLOGY SPECIFICATIONS

Analysis presented here follows from an integrated modelling system (Shukla and Pandey, 1999). The system soft links two well known bottom-up models—MARKAL (Berger et al., 1987; Fishbone and Abilock, 1981; Manne and Wene, 1992; Shukla, 1996) and AIM/END-USE (Asian-Pacific Integrated Model/ End-use Component) developed in Japan (Morita et al., 1994; Morita et al., 1996; Kainuma et al., 1997). Long term sector demand projections are exogenous inputs that drive the models. Sector demands are projected using logistic regression. Technology representation in the models is fairly detailed. Technologies are specified for demand as well as supply sides. Nearly 280 present and future demand technologies are

TABLE 1: TECHNOLOGY SPECIFICATION

Sectors	*No. of Sub-Sectors*	*No. of Technologies*
Industrial	11	152
Residential	2	46
Agricultural	1	14
Transport	8	25
Services	1	9
Power Sector*	1	22
Oil Refinery*	1	12
Total	25	280

Note: *These energy supply technologies are represented in MARKAL, but not in AIM/END-USE models.

represented (Table 1). Supply technologies represented are of two types: Electricity generation technologies and oil refineries. There are 22 different types of electricity generating technologies and 12 refinery technologies representing different fuel mix and cost structure.

Technological progress in the model is assumed to be influenced mainly by three factors: Autonomous energy efficiency improvement (AEEI), alterations in present technologies and introduction of new technologies. Technology penetration on demand side is exogenously specified based on sector specific studies and expert information.

SECTOR DEMAND PROJECTIONS

End-use demand projections are made for 40 years. Since India is now in a high growth phase, whereas in the long run the growth shall have to saturate and stabilize at a lower level, logistic curve regression has been used for projecting the end-use demand for each sector. Similar representation is also commonly used for technology penetration in the energy and environment context (Edmonds and Reilly, 1983; Grubler et al., 1993). The consistency of the end-use demand projections with the macro-economy is achieved by using macro-economic parameters like sector level gross domestic products (GDP) as independent variables for demand projections. The overall consistency is achieved by using an integrated demand projection framework that accounts for all sectors at the bottom level and overall GDP, and consumption at the top level. Logistic projections are made using past sector level consumption data as well as estimates, if available, from other detailed studies for some future years. Expert opinions are used for factoring in the future expectations.

$$\Upsilon_t = \Upsilon_0 \frac{\exp\,(a+bt)}{l+\exp\,(a+bt)} \tag{1}$$

where, Y_t is the level of demand at time t, and Y_0 is the asymptotic limit for the demand Y_t, and is estimated based on expert opinion and experience of developed countries. The parameters a and b are estimated by the linear regression of the log-log form of equation (1), those given in equation (2), are based on time series data.

$$\ln\left(\frac{(\Upsilon_t/\Upsilon_0)}{(1-\Upsilon_t/\Upsilon_0)}\right) = a+bt \tag{2}$$

Demand projection for some selected industry sectors (Figure 1) and transport (Figure 2) is shown later.

REFERENCE SCENARIO ANALYSIS

The reference scenario assumes what is often called a 'business-as-usual' dynamics. Scenario presumes no policy interventions for emissions control or other than normal non-market and long-term policy interventions related to energy and technology. Main scenario assumptions are:

- Compounded annual rate of growth (CARG) in GDP of 5.5 per cent over 40 years (1995-2035), decreasing from 6.8 per cent in first five-year period to 4.1 per cent in last five-year period.
- Discount rate: 8 per cent.
- No carbon emission mitigation.

ENERGY PROJECTIONS

Energy projections for the reference scenario are shown in Figure 3. Primary energy demand rises three times (Figure 3a), from 14 EJ (Exa Joules) in 1995 to 43 EJ in 2035. Coal retains predominance in energy supply, although its share declines. Non-commercial biomass energy use stagnates, causing a decline in its present share of 35 per cent to 15 per cent in 2035. Consumption of commercial energy rises by four times. The electricity demand grows at even faster rate (Figure 3b), rising from 385 TWh (in 1995) to 2061 TWh (in 2035). Gas substitutes coal to a small extent in the power sector

INDUSTRY DEMAND PROJECTIONS

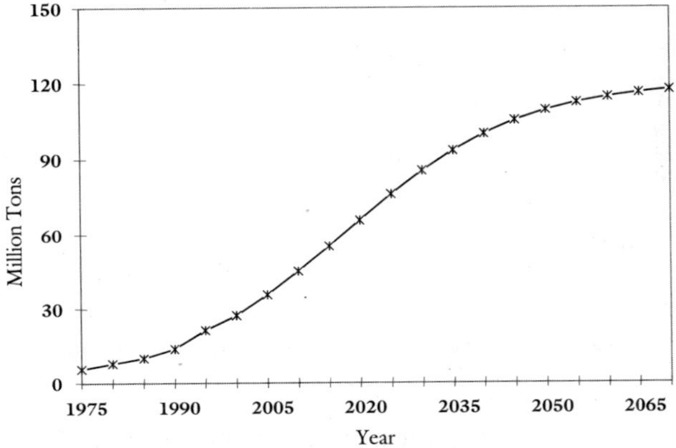

FIGURE 1A: STEEL DEMAND PROJECTION

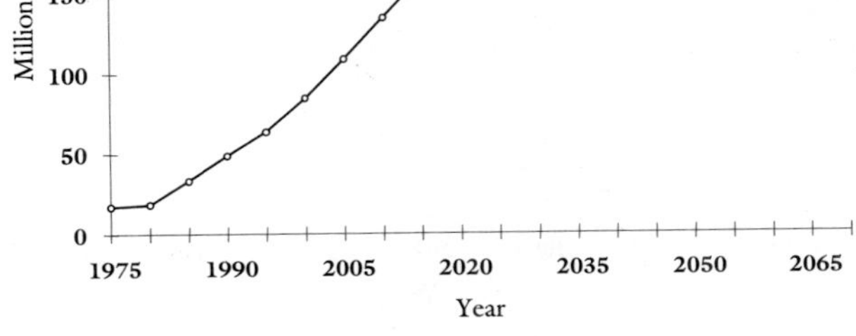

FIGURE 1B: CEMENT DEMAND PROJECTION

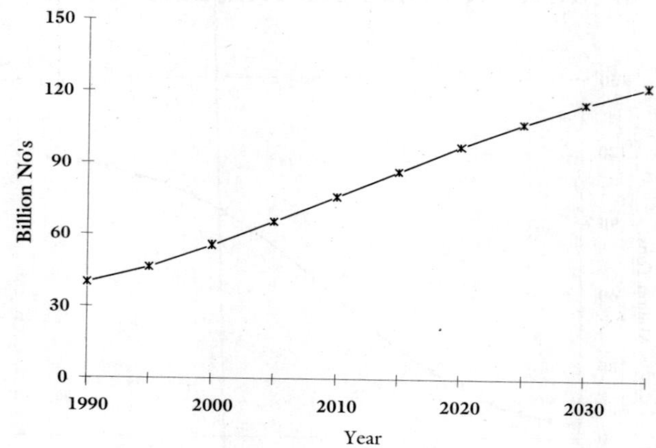

FIGURE 1C: BRICK DEMAND PROJECTION

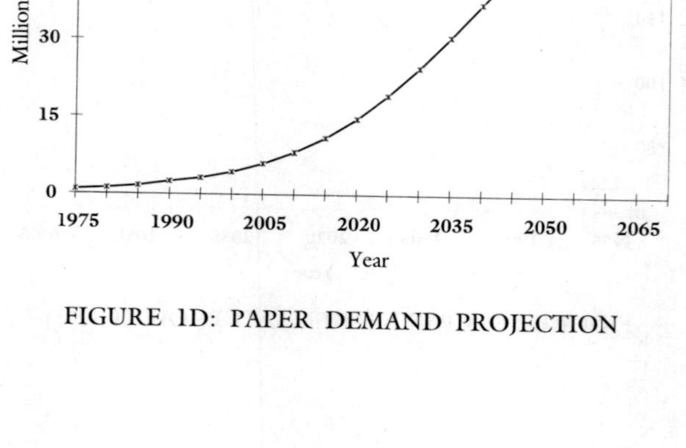

FIGURE 1D: PAPER DEMAND PROJECTION

TRANSPORT DEMAND PROJECTIONS

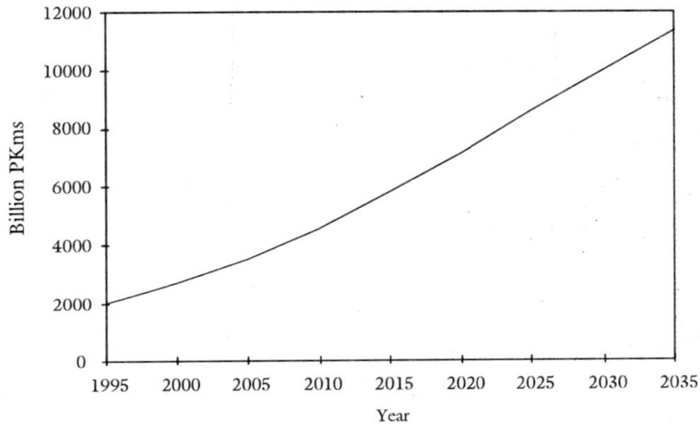

FIGURE 2A: ROAD PASSENGER DEMAND PROJECTION

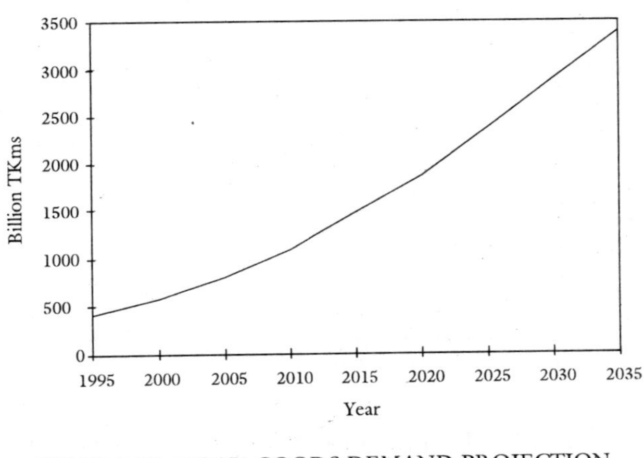

FIGURE 2B: ROAD GOODS DEMAND PROJECTION

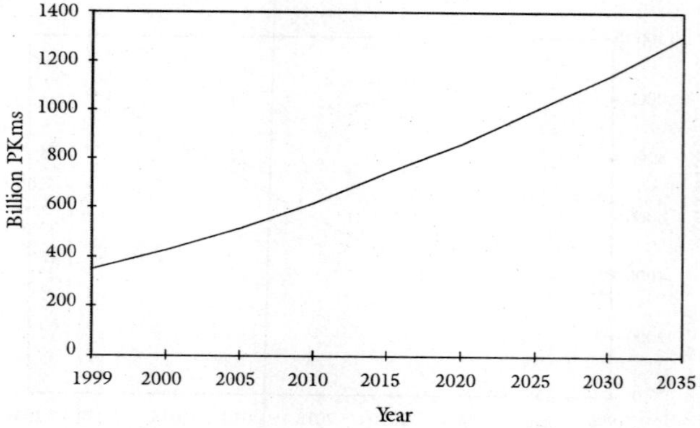

FIGURE 2C: RAIL PASSENGER DEMAND PROJECTION

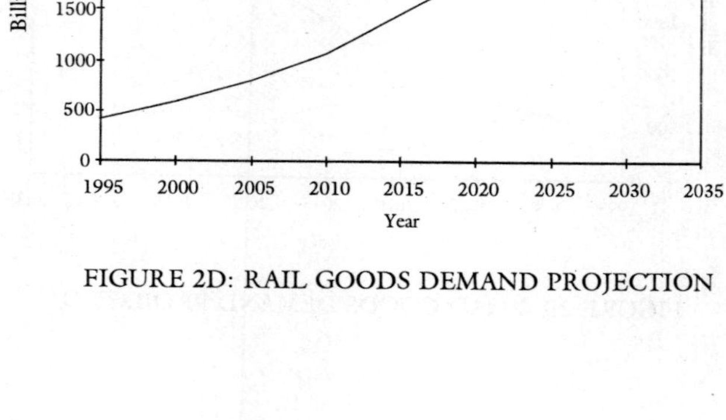

FIGURE 2D: RAIL GOODS DEMAND PROJECTION

ENERGY AND ELECTRICITY DEMAND IN REFERENCE CASE

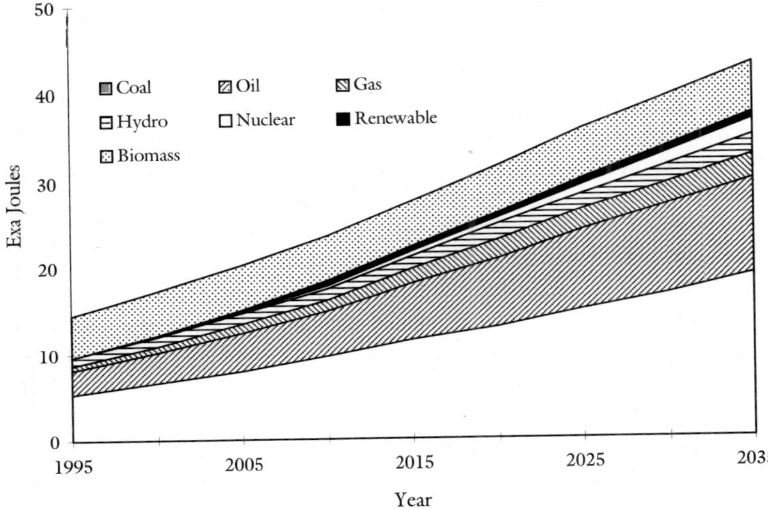

FIGURE 3A: ENERGY CONSUMPTION

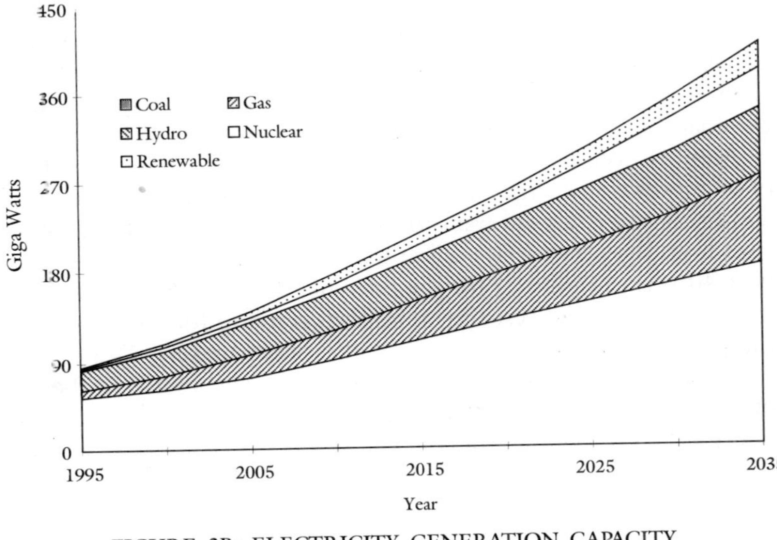

FIGURE 3B: ELECTRICITY GENERATION CAPACITY

leading to a decline in the share of coal to 58 per cent in 2035 from the present 71 per cent. Share of gas in the power sector in the same period rises from 7 to 16 per cent.

A most notable rise is in diesel and gasoline consumption due to very rapidly growing transport sector. Energy demand in industry too rises fast, raising the share of industry in primary energy to 41 per cent in 2035 from the present 29 per cent. Relatively, a slower growth is anticipated for primary energy in the household sector resulting in a decline in its share in primary energy from 56 to 28 per cent over the 40 year horizon. This however does not signify a low rate of improvement in energy services to the household sector since the households shift from an inefficient biomass to more efficient LPG for cooking, and from kerosene to much more efficient electric lighting. The share of households in electricity consumption rises from 19 to 24 per cent due to the switch to electricity from other fuels, as well as due to high penetration of new electric appliances. Agriculture and commercial sectors, being primarily electricity consumers, continue to have insignificant share in primary energy.

Coal remains the main energy resource for electric power and industries. In the past two decades, the electric power sector capacity additions have come primarily from coal based power plants. Under reference case which does not presume stringent environmental controls for pollutants and no intervention for climate change, the rapidly rising trend of coal consumption shall continue in future. The trend in coal consumption since 1975 and projections from the analysis till 2035 are shown in Figure 4. Under reference scenario, the coal consumption rises to about a billion tons in 2035.

Another noticeable aspect of future energy mix is the rising share of oil products in energy supply. An ever increasing transport demand and rising share of road transport drive the oil consumption, which rises from the present 70 million tons to nearly 300 million tons in next 40 years (Figure 5) for the reference scenario. Since India has little known oil reserves, the oil imports scenario for the future is a cause for considerable concern for the policy-makers. During the past decade, many energy consuming sectors have preferred the use of natural gas. While the share of gas in primary energy still remains low, the trends suggest a rapidly rising penetration of gas.

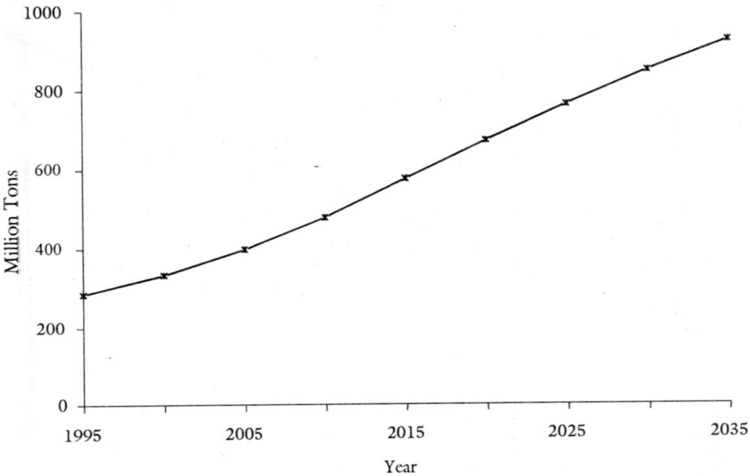

FIGURE 4: CONSUMPTION TREND FOR COAL IN INDIA

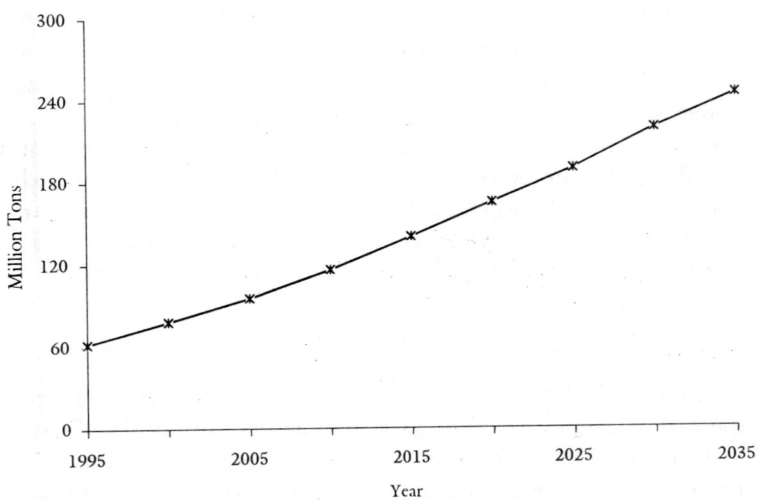

FIGURE 5: CONSUMPTION TREND FOR OIL IN INDIA

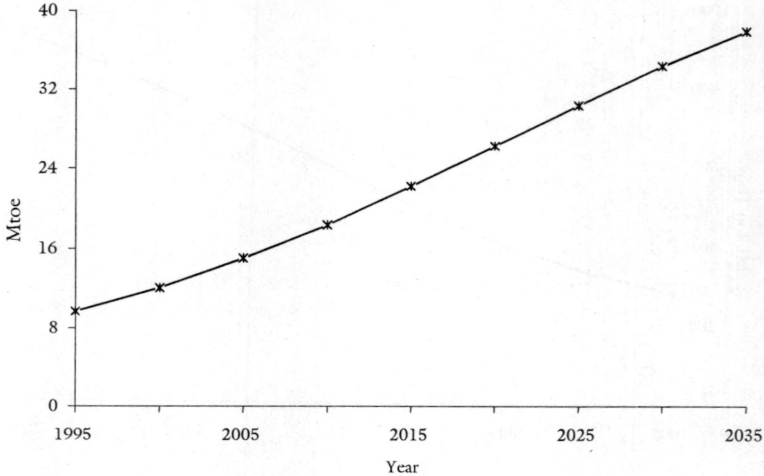

FIGURE 6: COMMERCIAL ENERGY CONSUMPTION

Energy Intensity

In the aggregate, the commercial energy demand trend suggests a fast rising trajectory (Figure 6). The energy intensity of the economy however declines (Figure 7), although at a very gradual pace. The decline in energy intensity is contributed mainly by the penetration of efficient technologies on demand and supply side. Fuel switching also contributes marginally to decline in energy intensity due to increase in share of gas in primary energy that replaces coal and continued decline in the share of traditional biomass energy.

Reference Case Carbon Emissions and Intensity

As an associate product of rising fossil fuel use (Figures 4 and 5), the carbon emissions trend also continue to rise rapidly (Figures 7 and 8) from 213 to 761 million tons of carbon from 1995 to 2035. Power sector, despite a minor switch from coal to gas, maintains the highest share of 46 per cent in total emissions (Figure 8). This is due to high growth of the sector. Coal consumption remains the main contributor to carbon emissions, although emissions from oil shall rise at a faster rate.

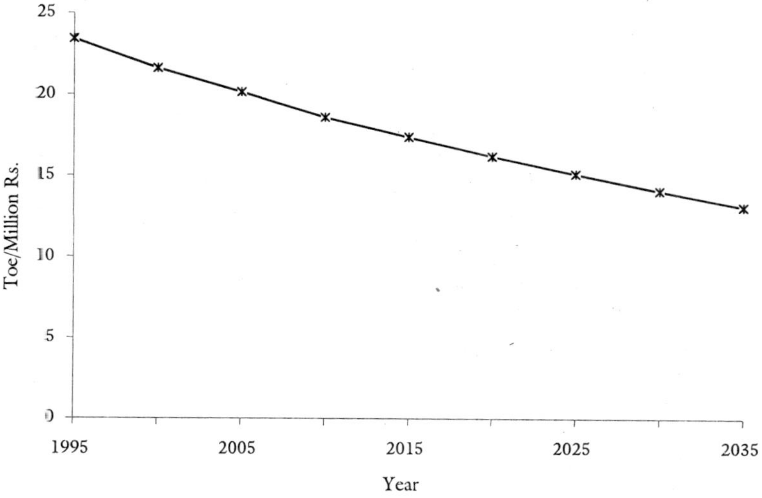

FIGURE 7: COMMERCIAL ENERGY INTENSITY

CARBON EMISSIONS IN REFERENCE CASE

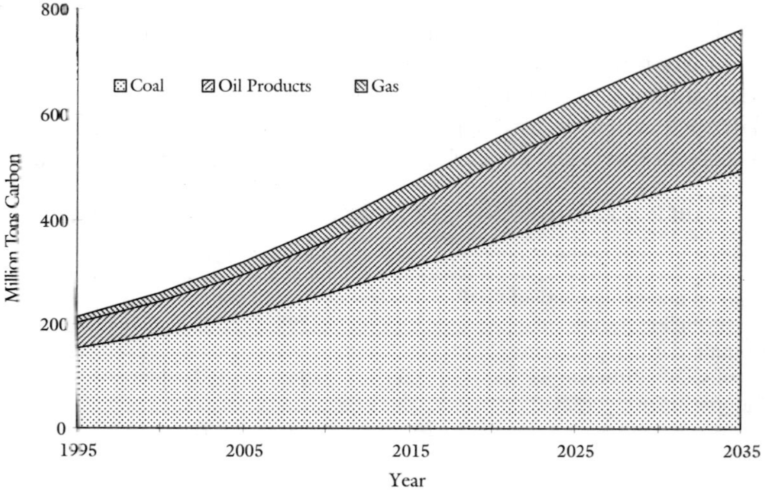

FIGURE 8A: FUEL-WISE CARBON EMISSIONS

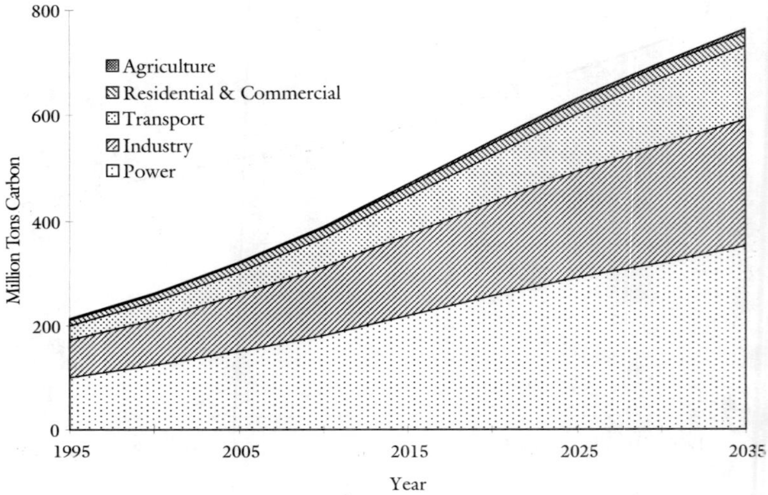

FIGURE 8B: SECTOR-WISE CARBON EMISSIONS

The carbon intensity of GDP improves by 1.7 per cent annually for the reference scenario (Table 2, Figure 9). Improvements in carbon intensity arise mainly from energy efficiency improvements and to a minor extent from the switch to lower carbon intensity fuels, e.g. substitution of coal by gas. This is evident from the fact that carbon intensity of commercial energy declines by only 0.2 per cent annually. Carbon intensity of primary energy increases by 0.46 per cent due to decline in biomass use. Carbon intensity of Indian industry, i.e. the carbon emissions per gross value added in

TABLE 2: ENERGY AND CARBON INTENSITIES (*reference scenario*)

Year	*1995*	*2005*	*2015*	*2025*	*2035*
Primary Energy Intensity of GDP (PJ/billion Rs.)	1.68	1.29	1.02	0.83	0.70
Commercial Energy Intensity of GDP (PJ/billion Rs.)	1.11	0.96	0.82	0.70	0.61
Carbon Intensity of GDP (tC/million Rs.)	24.62	20.38	17.32	14.65	12.40
Carbon Intensity of Primary Energy (mtC/EJ)	14.66	15.84	16.98	17.58	17.60
Carbon Intensity of Commercial Energy (mtC/EJ)	22.15	21.27	21.11	20.87	20.33

industry sector, drops at an annual rate of 0.8 per cent in four decades. Technological improvements in the processes as well as energy use in steel, cement, brick, paper and sugar industries contribute to this improvement.

CARBON MITIGATION ANALYSIS

For carbon mitigation analysis, five scenarios with different levels of cumulative mitigation commitment have been considered. For the reference scenario, the cumulative emissions from 1995 to 2035 adds to nearly 20 billion tons of carbon (bn.tC). Mitigation scenario (Table 3) presumes mitigation targets for the cumulative emissions over the reference scenario.

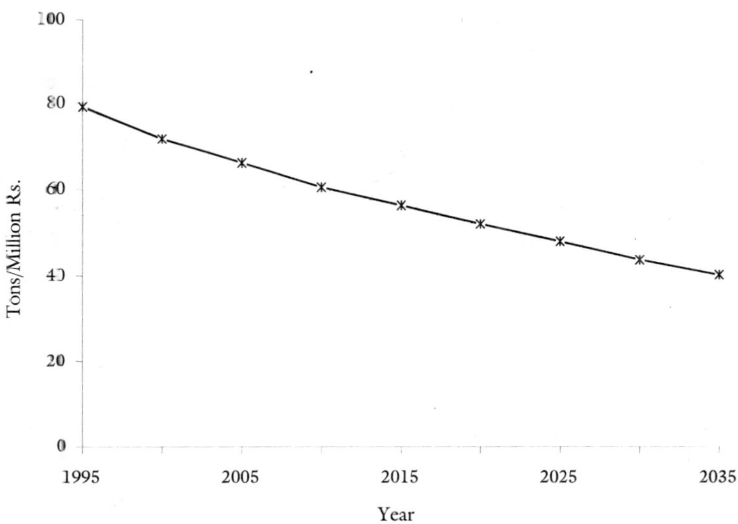

FIGURE 9: CARBON INTENSITY

TABLE 3: MITIGATION SCENARIO ASSUMPTIONS

Mitigation Scenarios	*Very High*	*High*	*Medium*	*Low*	*Very Low*	*Reference*
Cumulative Mitigation (per cent) over 2005-35	25	20	15	10	5	Nil
Emissions Mitigated (bn.tC)	5	4	3	2	1	Nil

The implications of five carbon mitigation scenarios for the future energy and technology mix suggest the following. In a cumulative mitigation strategy, the least cost mitigation strategy calls for higher mitigation in later periods due to slow turnover of energy system technology stocks and discounting. The direct impact of carbon mitigation is on the long run marginal costs (LRMC) of energy and electricity (Figure 10). Under very high (25 per cent) mitigation, the electricity cost doubles compared to the reference case in the later periods. Increasing mitigation results in a shift in power production from coal to gas and ultimately to renewable technologies. The shift in electricity mix results in substantial increase in electricity cost (Figure 10). Even a small mitigation target of 5 per cent causes a decline in share of coal in electricity generation capacity to 34 per cent in 2035, compared to 58 per cent for the reference case. A 25 per cent mitigation target requires almost total shutting down of coal power in 2035.

Gas power shows the converse trend, as it is the main substitute for declining coal power. Higher gas demand for low to medium mitigation (5 per cent to 15 per cent) can be supplied from higher domestic production and less expensive import of gas from nearby regions. Stringent mitigation targets of 20 per cent and 25 per cent however would require substantial and expensive gas imports. The

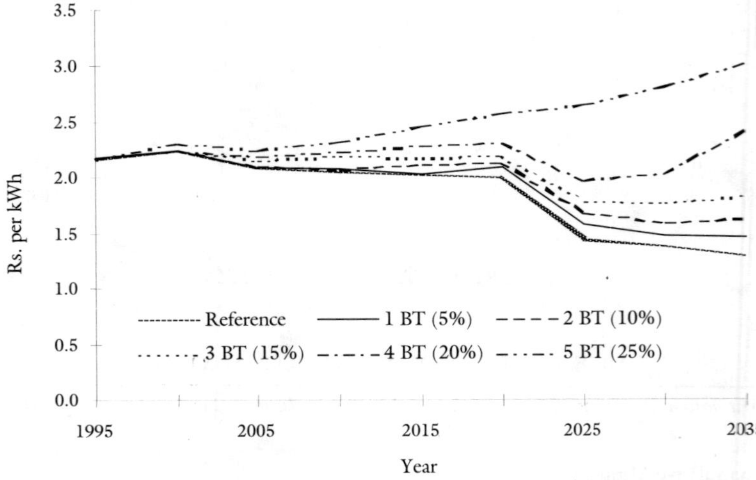

FIGURE 10: LONG RUN MARGINAL COST OF ELECTRICITY UNDER MITIGATION SCENARIOS

high mitigation target would also require early penetration of renewable power technologies; like wind, solar, biomass and large hydro, and a higher share of nuclear power. The share of renewable energy based power capacity (excluding large hydro) would be 23 per cent in 2035 for 25 per cent mitigation target.

In low mitigation scenarios, i.e. for 15 per cent or lower mitigation, the inertia of existing technological stock prevents significant fuel substitution till the year 2010. While 5 per cent mitigation leads to a drop in coal consumption by 16 per cent in 2035 over the reference case, a 25 per cent mitigation causes decline in coal consumption by 71 per cent in 2035 (Table 4). In low and medium mitigation scenarios, coal is substituted mainly by natural gas. Due to the rising gas prices with higher use of gas, the renewable energy becomes a major option for higher (20 per cent and 25 per cent) mitigation targets. In 25 per cent mitigation scenario, the penetration of renewable energy (excluding large hydro) is six times higher in 2035 over the reference case. Natural gas makes early penetration, whereas renewable energy penetrates late. This is due to higher initial investment cost of renewable energy technologies and high discount rate. Very high mitigation targets lead to greater share of large hydro and nuclear energy. Thus, any stringent mitigation target shall require substantial technological transformation of Indian energy system. Besides, this would require making investment in infrastructure to support the new technologies, and reforms to remove the barriers to the penetration of advanced technologies.

TABLE 4: IMPLICATIONS OF MITIGATION TARGETS ON PRIMARY ENERGY

(per cent change over the reference scenario)

Scenario	*Energy Resource*	*2005*	*2015*	*2025*	*2035*
1 Bn.tC mitigation	Coal	- 1.4	- 1.9	- 7.0	- 16.3
	Gas	+ 6.7	+ 6.8	+ 12.9	+ 37.8
	Renewable energy	0	0	+ 16.7	+ 62.5
3 Bn.tC mitigation	Coal	- 5.4	- 16.8	- 31.7	- 45.9
	Gas	+ 20	+ 50	+ 71	+ 97
	Renewable energy	0	+ 50	+ 100	+ 300
5 Bn.C mitigation	Coal	- 12.2	- 31.8	- 59.2	- 71.5
	Gas	+ 40	+ 81.8	+ 145.2	+ 170.3
	Renewable energy	+ 50	+ 175	+ 300	+ 575

MITIGATION COST AND COMPETITIVENESS

Mitigation cost analysis suggest that 4 billion tons of carbon can be mitigated at a marginal cost below US $10 (present value) per ton of carbon. Beyond this level, there is a steep rise in mitigation cost (Figure 11). The economic losses can be even higher due to large energy imports and additional costs of logistics and infrastructure to suit the needs of altered energy system. Energy intensive industries like sugar, steel and paper industries witness greater carbon emissions reduction under mitigation scenarios. Mitigation in industries happens due to myriad technological changes. For instance, technological changes in sugar industry arise from penetration of cogeneration technology that reduces emissions through substantial energy efficiency improvement. In steel industry, the mitigation arises from a switch to electric arc process and gas based sponge iron process. In paper industry, waste recycling and energy efficiency improvements reduce emissions.

Stringent mitigation targets impose high cost on the energy system which translate into higher production cost of energy intensive goods. A direct implication of high mitigation cost is the higher cost of energy and energy intensive commodities. The production cost of cement and steel under various mitigation scenarios are shown in

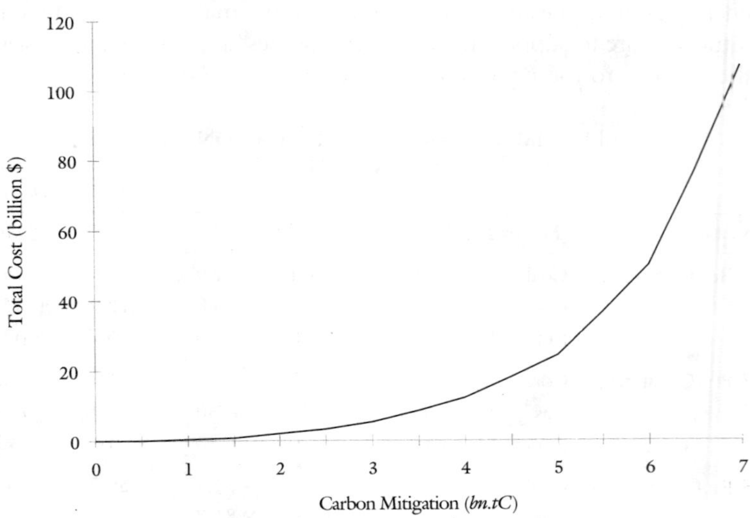

FIGURE 11: COST OF CARBON MITIGATION

Figure 12. Primarily technology and fuel switching in the power sector achieve the lower targets, till 15 per cent mitigation. End-use sectors need little change towards energy efficient and low carbon intensive technologies. Cement industry, owing to high use of coal and electricity, and little fuel substitution opportunities, exhibits very high increase in the production cost (Figure 12a). Under high

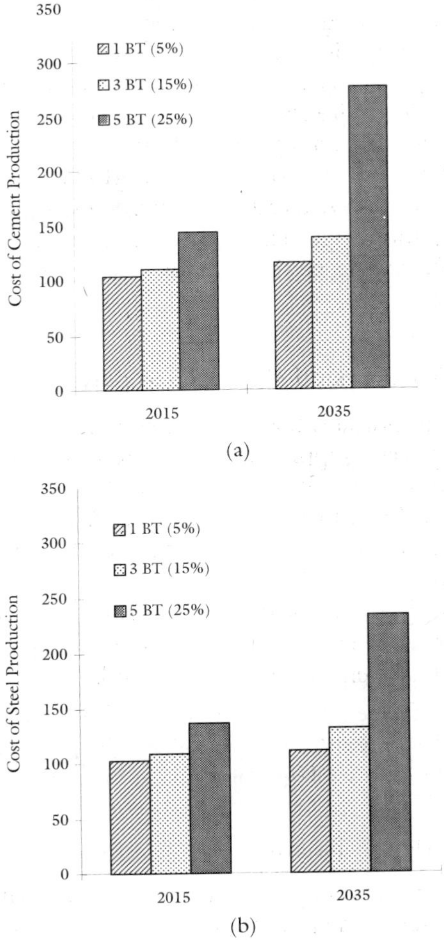

FIGURE 12: IMPLICATION OF CARBON MITIGATION ON PRODUCTION COST

(production cost in reference scenario = 100)

mitigation scenarios (25 per cent mitigation), the cost of cement rises by 48 per cent in 2015, and by 160 per cent in 2035 compared to the reference scenario. In the same scenario, the cost of steel rises by 40 per cent in 2015 and by 140 per cent in 2035 (Figure 12b). As these commodities are vital raw material inputs for manufacturing industries, the competitiveness of entire Indian industry will be adversely affected by adoption of stringent mitigation targets, unless appropriate burden sharing and revenue recycling policies are adopted.

The marginal mitigation cost for India should equal the global tradable permit price trajectory. A sound mitigation strategy for India therefore will require anticipation of global permit price trends and the burden sharing arrangement. Both of these parameters are highly dependent on the outcome of global climate change negotiation process. Unless a reasonable burden sharing arrangement is agreed upon, India's participation in emissions limitation at a globally cost effective level shall impose excessive burden on the Indian economy.

ENERGY AND TECHNOLOGY STRATEGY

The analysis so far indicates that rising energy needs of the economy, global energy prices, supply of energy resource and emissions limitation targets shall profoundly influence energy and technology choices for India. While uncertainties shroud the future, the energy and technology strategy is vital for building a robust foundation for a sustainable economic development.

Most vital set of options belong to the supply side of energy. The analysis has shown: (i) energy supply options significantly influence economic growth and energy system costs and, (ii) energy resources and technologies are the most critical options in the least cost strategy for greenhouse gas emissions mitigation. Some important aspects of energy and technology strategy for India are indicated next.

NATURAL GAS SUPPLY: PROMISE AND BARRIERS

Due to its domestic abundance, coal is the traditional mainstay of Indian energy system. The growth of electricity and industry sectors in the past two decades was fuelled mainly by coal. However this path has now raised local and global pollution concerns. Besides, the potential for the import of gas at competitive prices has improved significantly in recent years. The market has responded to the latter signal and to a minor extent the switch to gas from coal has occurred in the electricity and industry sectors. However, the use of gas remains much below the economic potential due to various barriers such as: (i) little environmental incentives, (ii) coal tariff distortions, and (iii) political problems associated with negotiations on gas supply and pipeline routes.

Implications of the first observation are evident from the earlier analysis of carbon mitigation. The immediate effect of carbon tax or emissions limitation on the Indian energy system is the substitution of coal by gas. The substitution shall be greater if the externalities from local pollution are internalized. The tariff barriers persist, but these are expected to ease in the wake of economic reforms where removal of tariff distortions is an important agenda. At present, political problems around natural gas supply remains the most obstructive and costly barrier.

Natural gas can be transported in several ways. A cost-effective means is transportation via pipelines. Another option is transport of liquid natural gas (LNG) via the sea using tankers. The offshore pipelines and onshore pipelines are cost effective compared to LNG transport at distances under 3,000 and 6,000 km respectively for a 10 billion cubic metre (bn.m^3) supply (IEA, 1995). The best sources of natural gas supply to India are the Middle East, central Asia and the newly discovered reserves off the Bangladesh coast in Bay of Bengal. In past five years, LNG import became a preferred option due to lower gestation and infrastructure needs. The LNG projects shall deliver gas at the west coast of India from the Middle East at an estimated price in the range of US $3 to US $4 per GJ (Giga Joule). Likewise, at the south coast of India, the LNG can be delivered at a similar cost from South-East Asia. The imported coal and liquid fuels also have the delivered cost at the coast in the same range as LNG.

The supply of gas to the hinterland involves added costs. At present, northern India receives gas from Bombay high via HBJ pipeline. This pipeline delivers gas to some locations in central India and north India, finally ending at Delhi. At current price of delivered gas in the north, the demand far exceeds the supply from this pipeline. The demand is rising further from the northern states of Punjab and Haryana that have the most productive agriculture in India. Their electricity consumption from agriculture as well as other sectors is rising following rising incomes, industrialization and modernization of agriculture. This region is experiencing high energy growth, fuelled at present by coal transported over 1,000 km from mines located in central and north-east India. Considerable mitigation can be achieved in north India if gas is available at a competitive price. The imported LNG from the west coast, if delivered via pipeline shall have economic cost between US $4 to US $5 per GJ, a price too high to induce substitution of domestic coal delivered at US $2 per GJ.

A viable option for north India is to import LNG from Turkmenistan. The pipeline route will then pass through Afghanistan and Pakistan, entering India through Punjab and ending near Delhi. This pipeline can also deliver at some gas locations in Pakistan. The pipeline, in absence of risk factors, can deliver gas at US $3 per GJ. At this price, a substantial market for gas exists in north India. Another cheaper option is gas imported from Bangladesh, the cost of which can be below US $3 per GJ. At this price, the analysis suggests a substantial demand for gas in India. The ultimate success of enhancing gas supply shall depend on political will and acumen to overcome the barriers, since a robust economic rational for the piped gas does exist. In fact, the annual loss to India, by not having the economical pipelines along these routes which can deliver 20 bn.m^3 gas to India annually at US $3 per GJ compared to a supply of gas via other means at US $4 per GJ, shall be US $750 million. In case of a carbon mitigation regime, which for instance may have global marginal mitigation cost of US $50 per ton of carbon, there will be an added cost of US $500 million annually from the foregone mitigation opportunities. Regional cooperation in gas supply therefore has considerable economic value for India. Rising beyond the political differences, this economic value must be realized in the interest of the economic development of the region, besides simultaneously contributing to the UNFCCC objective of cost effective GHG emissions mitigation.

RENEWABLE TECHNOLOGIES

Rapid technological advancements leading to competitive costs and reliable performance of renewable energy technologies have led to optimism about the future of renewable energy in the world (Johansson et al., 1993a; Johansson et al., 1993b). India has a history of promoting renewable energy through a technology push approach. These policies have helped the penetration of renewable

TABLE 5: WIND POWER CAPACITY (MW) ADDITIONS IN INDIA

Till March 1992	*1992-3*	*1993-4*	*1994-5*	*1995-6*	*1996-7*	*Installed Capacity March 1997*
41.180	12.700	61.090	235.535	382.113	169.032	901.650

Source: Annual Report, Ministry of Non-Conventional Energy Sources, Government of India.

technologies in niche markets. Recent success has been the wind energy in which the capacity has spurted during past few years (Table 5). However the technology push policies which helped initial penetration, needs to be supplemented by market pull policies like environmental levies on polluting technologies, to promote higher penetration of renewable energy (Shukla, 1997b).

The analysis of renewable electricity generation technologies suggests high economic potential in India for small hydro and wind power technologies in the immediate future, biomass in the medium term and solar technologies in the long run. The analysis suggests that under a strong carbon mitigation scenario, renewable energy technologies meet 15 per cent of the electricity demand in India (Shukla, 1997b) in the year 2035. One also finds a significant potential for the biomass energy under strong mitigation scenarios (Shukla, 1997c), although land supply in such a case emerges as an important issue requiring attention.

HYDRO AND NUCLEAR: THE CONVENTIONAL CARBON FREE TECHNOLOGIES

Hydro and nuclear are established energy technologies that are carbon free. Penetration of these technologies have implications for GHG mitigation. In the first two decades of India's independence, hydro projects were pushed by government policies to meet the dual needs of irrigation and electricity. Large hydro projects became showpieces of development, described by Prime Minister Nehru as 'temples of modern India'. While in the past two decades, the growth in hydropower capacity has been marginal and their share in electricity generation has steadily declined, the large hydro projects have suffered due to the growing concerns of associated social and ecological problems. Only a third of the economic hydro potential is exploited

(CMIE, 1997). An unexploited power potential of over 50,000 MW remains a viable option for energy and mitigation strategy. Lately, the penetration of small hydro projects has enhanced. However, greater exploitation of hydro potential would require addressing the concerns around large dam projects to overcome the associated barriers. This is a vital issue for India's energy and mitigation strategy.

Nuclear energy has existed in India for over two decades. However, its share in electricity generation has remained below 3 per cent (CMIE, 1997). The low operational efficiency of the existing nuclear plants and the high initial cost have been the deterrents to further penetration of nuclear energy. The safety concerns remain paramount due to inaccessible information on plant operation and waste disposal. Besides, external political barriers to nuclear energy persist. The analysis suggests that a strong GHG mitigation regime can enhance the share of nuclear power. However, to exploit the economic potential of this option, difficult social and political barriers will have to be overcome.

Electricity: Peak-Power Technology Mix and T&D

Electricity is the fastest growing energy sector. The most noticeable aspect of the electricity growth is the widening gap between the demand and supply which result in 'black outs'. While the energy gap is 9 per cent, the power or the peak electricity gap has risen to 20 per cent (CMIE, 1999), leading to frequent 'black outs' during the evening peak hours. The main cause of rising peak power deficit is the changing technology mix. Traditionally, the utilities have used hydropower for peak power capacity, whereas thermal power stations are used for base load. The power planning has followed an empirical rule of developing a third of capacity in peaking (i.e. hydro) technologies. Since the share of hydro capacity is likely to decline, the technology strategy needs to consider other technologies like peaking gas turbines.

An important area, where technology changes can provide considerable energy and mitigation benefits, is the electricity transmission and distribution (T&D). These losses in India are 23 per cent (CMIE, 1999). The investment in this area has lagged due to defective policies. Opportunities for introduction of new technologies shall be available since the power capacity is expected to rise rapidly in the coming decade.

DEMAND SIDE TECHNOLOGY CHOICES

The importance of demand side technology interventions is an oft-discussed issue. From a market perspective, the inefficiencies on the demand side in developing nations are high and persist in the wake of capital shortages, risks, high transaction costs and weak financial markets. While the removal of inefficiencies is a larger issue of development (Shukla, 1997d; Shukla 1997e) rather than an energy technology issue, identification of demand side technologies remains vital for the long-term technology strategy for India. Demand side technology strategy is classified into five thrust areas:

(*i*) *Traditional energy technologies.* In rural areas, use of very inefficient technologies like biomass stoves with 8-10 per cent combustion efficiency persists, which contribute a third of national energy use (Shukla, 1997c). These technologies cause substantial indoor air pollution and are the single largest source of mortality and morbidity from air pollution. The Human Development Report (UNDP, 1998) mentions 5,89,000 deaths in India annually from the indoor air pollution caused by household energy use. In the market sense, these technologies offer a sizeable 'no regret' potential. Although the technology policies to harness these 'low hanging fruits' have met with myriad barriers in past two decades, the need to harness these options is paramount for energy conservation, emissions mitigation and more so from the human development perspective.

(*ii*) *Technologies in the industry sector.* This sector is the largest consumer of energy in India. Demand side technology improvements need to focus on production as well as energy technologies. The analysis suggests the following to be most prominent technology options in different industry sectors: (a) cogeneration technology for improvement of energy efficiency and carbon mitigation in sugar industry, (b) electric arc process and gas based sponge iron production in steel industry, and (c) waste recycling technology in paper industry. Besides, the substantial efficiency improvements are possible in India in the generic technologies such as boilers and electric motors. The DSM programme in the electricity sector can net considerable gains from removal of inefficiencies in industries.

(*iii*) *Enhancing irrigation pump efficiency in agriculture sector.* Electric pumps used for irrigation by the farmers are among the most inefficient demand side technologies in India. The importance of this technology is evident from the fact that agriculture consumes 30 per cent electricity, most of which is for pumping. This is a well accepted 'no regret' option which has survived due to electricity tariff distortions. Improvements in pump-set efficiency can contribute to significant mitigation.

(*iv*) *DSM programme for electric appliances.* The analysis suggests that a well designed DSM (demand side management programme) is likely to generate benefits in all sectors. In the household and commercial sectors, the technology stocks are changing rapidly. This offers opportunities for introducing efficient DSM options. Major strategy issue here is not the advanced technologies, but institutional changes. Appliance standards, labelling and consumer awareness are some important DSM measures which are essential to the success of these programmes.

(*v*) *Efficiency improvements in transport sector.* Technology strategy for transport sector needs to address three broad areas: (a) share of road versus rail, (b) transport infrastructure, and (c) vehicle efficiency. Often, greater attention is paid to the latter. Studies indicate that the first two are more important for India, like in the case of most large developing nations. The share of road transport has increased dramatically over the past few years at the expense of rail transport due to the paucity of infrastructure investments. While road infrastructure has expanded, the poor maintenance of roads and increased congestion had led to lower transport efficiency. Therefore, despite improvements in vehicle efficiency, the overall efficiency of transport has lagged behind the international standards (Shukla, 1993). Sizable potential for improvement in transport efficiency thus exists, which can contribute to the mitigation of carbon emissions as well as the rising urban pollution.

CONCLUSION

Energy and emission trends from India reminds one of an urgent need to alter these trajectories, both in the interest of India's sustainable development and the global climate change. The analysis in this article provides important information for rational long-term energy and technology strategy. An important conclusion is that the near term energy and carbon mitigation strategy for India should focus on enhancing the supply of natural gas and improving efficiency of demand side technologies. The long run options are investments in rail, road and electricity transmission infrastructure and renewable energy technologies. The latter can be a consistent element of a larger national development strategy.

The mitigation analysis presumes mitigation actions to take place over a conventional reference future. However, as pointed out in the subsequent discussion, it is important to consider alternatives, which are beyond the reach of current conventional wisdom such as long distance intercountry pipeline transport of gas and development of renewable and nuclear technologies. Analysis of such bifurcation scenarios (Hourcade, 1993) provide added insights.

The Kyoto Protocol has proposed the Clean Development Mechanism (CDM), a voluntary instrument, through which developing nations can participate in greenhouse gas mitigation. Analysis in this article suggests that India has significant potential for low cost mitigation supply. Many greenhouse gas mitigation actions have double dividend potential and can provide ancillary benefits such as reduced local pollution. Myriad barriers however exist in the implementation of efficient energy and carbon mitigation strategies. Energy sector reforms, regional political dynamics and global co-operation in emission mitigation holds the key to lowering these barriers. The promise from co-operative technology transfer and cleaner investments, if realized, shall benefit sustainable national development and climate change. For this to happen, it is pertinent to evolve an energy strategy that harmonizes the needs of national development priorities with the goals of global climate change mitigation.

REFERENCES

Berger, C., Haurie, A., and Loulou, R. (1987), *Modelling Long Range Energy Technology Choices: The MARKAL Approach,* Report, GERAD, Montreal, Canada.

CMIE: Centre for Monitoring Indian Economy (1997), *India's Energy Sector*, Bombay.

——— (1999), *Energy,* March-April 1999, Bombay.

Edmonds, J., and Reilly, J. (1983), 'A long-term energy-economic model of carbon dioxide release from fossil fuel use', *Energy Economics*, April: 74-88.

Fisher-Vanden, K.A., Shukla, P.R., Edmonds, J.A., Kim, S.H. and Pitcher, H.M. (1997), 'Carbon taxes and India', *Energy Economics*, 19: 289-325.

Fishbone, L.G., and Abilock, H. (1981), 'MARKAL, A linear programming model for energy systems analysis: Technical description of the BNL version', *Energy Research*, 5, pp. 353-7.

Grubler, A., Nakicenovic, N., and Schafer, A. (1993), *Dynamics of Transport and Energy Systems—History of Development and a Scenario for Future*, International Institute for Applied Systems Analysis, Austria.

Hourcade, J.C. (1993), 'Modelling long run scenarios—Methodology lessons from a perspective study on a low CO_2 intensity country', *Energy Policy,* 21 (3), pp. 309-25.

IPCC (1996), *Climate Change 1995: Economic and Social Dimensions of Climate Change*, Bruce, J.P., Lee, H. and Haites, E. (eds.), Cambridge University Press, Cambridge, U.K.

Johansson, T.B., Kelly, H., Reddy, A.K.N. and Williams, R.H. (1993a), 'Renewable Fuels and Electricity for a Growing World Economy—Defining and Achieving the Potential', in *Renewable Energy—Sources of Fuels and Electricity,* Johansson, T.B., Kelly, H., Reddy, A.K.N. and Williams, R.H. (eds.), Island Press, Washington, D.C., U.S.A.

——— (1993b), 'A Renewable Intensive Global Energy Scenario', in *Renewable Energy—Sources of Fuels and Electricity,* Johansson, T.B., Kelly, H., Reddy, A.K.N. and Williams, R.H. (eds.), Island Press, Washington, D.C., U.S.A.

Kainuma, M., Matsuoka, Y., and Morita, T. (1997), 'The AIM Model and Simulations', *AIM Interim Paper*, National Institute for Environmental Studies, Tsukuba, Japan.

Loulou, R., Shukla, P.R., and Kanudia, A. (1997), *Energy and Environment Strategies for a Sustainable Future: Analysis with the Indian MARKAL Model*, Allied Publishers, New Delhi.

Manne, A.S. and Wene, C.O. (1992), *MARKAL-MACRO: A Linked Model for Energy-Economy Analysis*, BNL-47161, Brookhaven National Laboratory, Upton, New York.

Morita, T., Kainuma, M., Harasawa, H., Kai, K., Kun, L.D. and Matsuoka, Y. (1994), 'Asian-Pacific Integrated Model for Evaluating Policy Options to Reduce Greenhouse Gas Emissions and Global Warming Impacts', *AIM Interim Paper*, National Institute for Environmental Studies, Tsukuba, Japan.

——— (1996), 'A Guide to the AIM/ENDUSE Model—Technology Selection Program with Linear', *AIM Interim Paper*, National Institute for Environmental Studies, Tsukuba, Japan.

Shukla, P.R. (1993), 'Energy Conservation and Emission Control Policies in India for Industrial and Transport Sectors', Invited Paper for Workshop on *Strategies for Energy Conservation in Industries and Transport*, University of Twente, The Netherlands, October.

——— (1996), 'The Modelling of Policy Options for Greenhouse Gas Mitigation in India', *AMBIO*, XXV (4), pp. 240-8.

——— (1997a), *Energy Strategies and Greenhouse Gas Mitigation: Models and Policy Analysis for India*, Allied Publishers, New Delhi.

——— (1997b), 'Penetration of Renewable Energy Technologies in India: Assessment of Future Trajectories and Macro Policies', in *Renewable and Rural Energy Policy Perspective in Developing Countries*, Venkat Ramana, P. (ed.), Tata Energy Research Institute, New Delhi.

——— (1997c), 'Biomass Energy in India: Policies and Prospects', Proceedings of Workshop on *Biomass Energy: Key Issues and Priority Needs*, International Energy Agency (IEA), Paris, 3-5 February.

——— (1997d), 'Socio-Economic Dynamics of Developing Countries: Some Ignored Dimensions in Integrated Assessment', in *Climate Change and Integrated Assessment Models (IAMs)—Bridging the Gaps: Proceedings of the IPCC Asia-Pacific Workshop on Integrated Assessment Models*, Tokyo, 10-12 March.

——— (1997e), 'Energy for Sustainable Development: A Social Engineering Perspective', *The Social Engineer*, Vol. 6, No. 2.

Shukla, P.R. and Kanudia, A. (1996), *The Indian MARKAL: Innovations, Extensions and Policy Analysis*, Technical Paper, G-96-14, GERAD, Montreal, Canada, April.

Shukla, P.R., and Pandey, R. (1997), 'Energy and Emissions Projections for Indian Industries using AIM/ENDUSE Model', in *Energy and Emissions Studies using AIM Model*, Morita, T., Matsuoka, Y. and Kainuma, M. (eds.), Springer-Verlag, forthcoming.

——— (1999), *Climate Change Mitigation: Shaping the Indian Strategy*, Shukla, P.R. (ed.), Allied Publishers, New Delhi, 1999.

UNDP (1998), *Human Development Report 1998*, Oxford University Press, Delhi.

UNFCCC (1992), *United Nations Framework Convention on Climate Change—Articles*, United Nations, New York.

——— (1997), *Kyoto Protocol to the United Nations Framework Convention on Climate Change*, United Nations, New York.

The Role of Electricity in India's Agriculture

GILBERT ETIENNE

There is no other country where electricity plays such a major role in agriculture as in India, a fact which has important economic and political implications. While electricity has stimulated the Green Revolution and the overall process of agriculture, it has now become a negative factor of growth, due to poor supply of power. It is one factor, among others, which contributes to the slowing down of agricultural growth, at a time when agriculture still accounts for nearly 30 per cent of GDP and employs about 60 per cent of the active population.

The political implications are no less serious. The 30 per cent of total consumption (utilities) devoted to agriculture is heavily subsidized, if not free in certain states. The badly needed reforms, involving price increases, are therefore hindered by powerful farmers' lobbies in a number of states and at the centre.

IRRIGATION THROUGH ELECTRICITY

In 1931, the government of the United Provinces (now Uttar Pradesh, U.P.) started a scheme of public tube-wells in the western part of the province. Remarkably conducted by Sir William Stampe, it relied on electricity which had just become available. It included 1,500 state tube-wells irrigating 8,00,000 ha. A few years later some similar tube-wells were introduced in Punjab.

In those days, electricity was exceedingly rare in villages, so these experiments could not have much impact. With the advent of the first five year plan 1951-6, large scale rural electrification began to spread so that by the 1960s, from Punjab to western U.P. included, electric lines had become widespread. Similar progress happened in the south, in Maharashtra and Gujarat, while in eastern India the movement remained very slow until today.

Before the Green Revolution started in 1965-7, farmers of north-western India were already anxious to get their own tube-wells for a number of reasons. The supply of water from canals was, in a number of places, not secure. Then there were wide areas which fell outside the command areas of the canals, forcing farmers to rely on dug wells operated with a Persian wheel and bullocks. A tube-well offered several advantages: Water could be pumped at a greater depth. The pump and the engine increased and quickened the supply of water. Finally, electrical motors were more convenient and cheaper than oil engines, both in terms of investment, operation and maintenance.

Another factor that boosted the progress of tube-wells was the consolidation of holdings, a tedious and complex set of tasks which spread from Punjab to Benares between the early 1950s and mid-1970s. The progress of private tube-wells (often 5 HP irrigating 3-5 ha) was also stimulated by the poor operations of the state tube-wells which, in a number of districts, have now been discontinued.

While tube-wells were being introduced, the green revolution occurred. The new high yield varieties of wheat responded well to chemical fertilizers but required more water than traditional seeds, 5 to 6 waterings in northern India versus 3 to 4 for traditional varieties of wheat.

These interdependent factors were helped in north-western India by fine agricultural castes, particularly Sikh and Hindu Jats and by the overall level of development already reached in the British days.

Not only did the tube-wells enable farmers to double their yields of wheat in one or two years time, but later came further increases: Traditional irrigated wheat from 1,200-1,300 kg/ha, to 3,000-4,000. In the *kharif*, coarse grains were replaced by rice in Punjab and Haryana, giving a high yield of 3,000-3,500 kg/ha of clean rice versus 1,300 kg/ha of good traditional irrigated rice. Rice is appearing now in western U.P.

Gradually, tube-wells spread to eastern U.P. districts, for long renowned for their acute poverty. Though less spectacular than in the western districts, progress has nevertheless been significant in terms of agricultural production, better wages and more opportunities for landless labourers and small farmers.

Private tube-wells also expanded in Rajasthan, but on a lower scale because of physical constraints. Unlike the alluvial soils of the Indus-Ganges basin, subsoils here are often rocky with groundwater both limited and at much greater depth. The plains of Gujarat have also seen a faster growth.

In peninsular India, the traditional open wells using a pair of bullocks to pull water in a bucket (*mot*) were replaced by pumpsets from the 1960s onwards wherever groundwater was not too deep or scarce. Yet, because of soil and water constraints, the bulk of the crops have remained rainfed.

Another type of electrified irrigation, though not so common, involves low lift pumps taking water out of a river or a tank. It is used in various parts of peninsular India.

In the canal irrigated areas along the Coromandel coast, in Andhra and Tamil Nadu, small tube-wells called filter points have been introduced as a complement to the canals or in order to irrigate crops in the dry season when the canals are closed. (Unlike the north, the canals here are not perennial. They open in June/July with the arrival of the monsoon and are closed in January/February.) On the whole, tube-wells in such areas play only a minor role.

Finally come the wide plains of eastern India, in Bihar, West Bengal, Assam and Orissa, where agricultural growth has been sluggish. The enormous potential for irrigation both groundwater and surface water through tube-wells and canals respectively, has only been partially tapped even fifty years after independence.

The case of Bihar is particularly striking. Tube-wells are far from common. The existing ones usually rely on diesel for lack of electricity. In West Bengal, one comes across some state and private tube-wells, but there again the untapped potential remains very large. As a result, rainfed clean rice yields only around 1,000-1,200 kg/ha, which could treble with irrigation, new seeds, and chemical fertilizers, as it does elsewhere in the state, in limited areas.

THE SUPPLY OF ELECTRICITY AND MINOR IRRIGATION

At present, the total irrigated area in India amounts to 78 million ha. While 28 million ha depend on canals, the largest part, about 50 million, classified as minor irrigation, depend on 12 million electric pumps and 5-6 million oil engines. It is worth adding that, since independence, the largest increase in the irrigated area comes from tube-wells and pumpsets on open wells.

In most states located in peninsular India, irrigated land ranges between 15 and 30 per cent. While Andhra and Tamil Nadu deltas irrigated mostly by canals enjoy a rate of irrigation of around 80-90 per cent in the interior districts, it falls to approximately 20 per cent.

TABLE 1: 1992-3 PERCENTAGE OF IRRIGATED LAND OUT OF CULTIVATED AREA

Punjab	95
Haryana	76
Uttar Pradesh	62 (western U.P. being above the average)
Assam	15
Bihar plains	35
Orissa	26
West Bengal	22

Source: *Agriculture at a Glance*, New Delhi, Ministry of Agriculture, 1996.

At the all India level, the share of electricity consumed by agriculture (mostly engines for irrigation) went up from 3.9 per cent in 1950-1 to 32.5 per cent in 1994-5 (utilities only), a feature probably unique in Asia. However, considerable differences appear statewise, a normal consequence of the uneven progress of minor irrigation. For the agricultural champions, Punjab and Haryana, that supply the largest share of cereals procured by the government as bufferstocks, it amounts to 44 and 50 per cent of the electricity consumed respectively. Then come Andhra at 44 per cent, U.P. at 38 per cent, and Gujarat at 38 per cent. In the laggard states of eastern India, it falls to 15 per cent in Bihar, 2.6 per cent in Assam, 5.7 per cent in Orissa and 7.2 per cent in West Bengal.

Then comes the level of efficiency of the State Electricity Boards (SEB). Though no details on losses in transmission and distribution are available statewise, one indication is supplied by the plant load factor. The average for SEB amounts to 58 per cent. The best states are Rajasthan, Andhra and Tamil Nadu (74 to 78 per cent), followed by Karnataka, Gujarat and Maharashtra (64 to 67 per cent). In U.P., Haryana and Punjab, it comes down to 43 to 55 per cent. The worst performances are to be found in Bihar at 17.4 per cent, the lowest in India, and in Orissa at 21.1 per cent.

THE ELECTRIC SYSTEM IN RURAL AREAS

No doubt it has been a colossal task to electrify about 5,00,000 villages out of 5,80,000 spread over 3 million sq. km in the past fifty years. Although many households still do not enjoy electricity for lack of money, countless lines criss-cross the country. It would have been impossible to set a system working in a perfectly smooth manner.

The efficiency level of the State Electricity Boards is reflected in rural areas in the form of power cuts or irregular supply. Even the granaries of India, Punjab and Haryana are not spared. Fortunately, in the past years, good monsoons have partly compensated the shortage of power for rice cultivation. As one knows, rice requires much more water than wheat.

In Maharashtra, Andhra and Rajasthan, I did not register major complaints,[1] except here and there some power cuts. Elsewhere, after being a major growth factor, the lack of electricity brings all kinds of hardships to the farmers. Power failures due to breakdown of old equipment, as in Bulandshahr city (western U.P.), where some of it has not been replaced since 1930 when electricity first reached the district headquarters! Transformers often break down, leading to power cuts lasting a few weeks. If it happens in the hot season, it can ruin or at least badly damage crops like sugarcane. In Bihar, power cuts in addition to the limited spread of rural electrification worsen the situation further.

In certain areas as in U.P., electricity has been rationed in a planned manner. It is available for eight hours daily in the day or at night, which enables farmers to irrigate their fields, but frequently this schedule is not respected. While in Bihar even such a plan is non-existent.

Low voltage is another factor farmers have to contend with as it can cause damage to the electric motor of the tube-wells.

Other troubles occur when, taking advantage of a shortcut engineered with the connivance of SEB employees, people cut wires and sell them. I recorded a case in Bihar in the late 1960s. In Bulandshahr in 1992, on two occasions 2 km of electric wire were stolen. The replacement took 10 days in August and 25 days in December. The latter theft paticularly had adverse consequences, since it delayed wheat sowing and thus lowered yields.

Farmers are not only victims, they are also responsible for theft of electricity through illegal connections. Then comes the question of meters. In Tamil Nadu, where the level of administration is still relatively efficient, meters are used. In U.P., following frequent tempering of meters, the SEB introduced a flat rate, which has to be paid even when there is no electricity!

In Tamil Nadu, I recorded a number of complaints on power breakdowns, which seriously affected paddy nurseries irrigated by pumps before the release of canal water.

As alluded earlier, the future granaries of India lie in the eastern plains, since advanced areas cannot supply India forever with surplus grain, in view of the already fairly high yields. In the east, electricity could be a major factor of growth in view of the enormous potential for tube-wells. It would also be advantageous to introduce consolidation of holdings. With the lack of electricity, farmers reluctantly rely on diesel engines, which are more costly to buy and use than electric pumps.

What is distressing is that all these shortcomings have been known for at least fifteen years, and yet remedies are slow to come. In 1987-8 for instance, the central government launched a crash programme to promote private tube-wells supported by loans to the farmers. The state governments in eastern India were not even able to make full use of the money allotted to them.

It would also be appropriate to further expand the use of electric private tube-wells in the canal irrigated deltas in Andhra and Tamil Nadu as a complement to canals, especially when they are closed, because the relatively high yields of crop reached so far tend to level off due to inadequate supply of water. It would be of course even more urgent to improve and restore the canals which are badly maintained.

A faster rural electrification would present additional advantages in reducing the consumption of diesel oil and kerosene. Although 85 per cent of villages are electrified, the growth rate of households electrified is around 30 per cent, going up to 77 per cent in Punjab and down to 6 per cent in Bihar. Kerosene is widely used for cooking and lighting, and diesel oil for 5 to 6 million pumps all over the country.

Progress in rural electrification would help reduce the growing oil deficit in the country.[2]

Based on average tariffs the gross subsidy on account of sale of electricity to agriculture and domestic sector amounted to Rs. 153 billion and Rs. 39 billion respectively for 1996-7. The surplus generated by sales to other sectors amounted to only Rs. 67 billion. Then come total commercial losses of Rs. 105 billion.

The rates are particularly low in Andhra, Karnataka and Madhya Pradesh. In Tamil Nadu, power supply to agriculture has been totally free for a number of years. The same step has been taken by the new Akali Dal government which came into power in Punjab in February 1997, in order to fulfil its electoral manifesto, a measure typical of the lack of responsibility of some politicians.

TABLE 2: THE COST OF ELECTRICITY AND THE REFORMS
(average tariffs vary according to different uses)

1994-5	*Sales %*	*paise per kWh*
Domestic	15.7	92.1
Commercial	4.5	228.7
Agriculture	32.5	19.4
Industry	34.1	221.4
Railway traction	4.9	254.3
Outside state	8.3	109.7

Source: *Economic Survey*, 1996-7, p. 162.

Since 1997, the central government tried to improve the situation through the *Electricity Regulation Commissions Ordinance*, which aims at independent regulation of electricity pricing and radical overhaul of SEB. 'Some state level leaders have raised a hue and cry that the ordinance and the bill (to be adopted by the Parliament) are anti-farmers.'[3]

In spite of the negative attitude taken by several states, others are trying to reform their SEBs through various means. So far the most advanced state is Orissa. But many foreigners, when referring to that state forget or ignore that in view of the very limited consumption of electricity in agriculture, any reform leading to increased agricultural tariffs is relatively easy to introduce, since farmers are least concerned. Gujarat, Rajsthan, Andhra and Haryana are also envisaging reforms. The last two have set up their *Regulatory Commission* but, especially in Haryana where the farmers' lobby is not only powerful but also involves a large number of consumers of electricity, agitation had already started in 1997 and it seems that it contributed to the fall of the Bansi Lal government. A strong opposition has appeared in Andhra from SEB employees.

POLITICS AND ECONOMICS

As B. Ganguli pointed out: 'The SEBs can cut down losses, but the problem cannot be solved if farm tariffs are permanently set far below costs.'[4] To sum up, short-sighted politicians kill two birds with one shot: They not only endanger the future of agriculture but of the whole economy as well, particularly industry, and foreign trade.

One factor that could help find a solution would be a massive countrywide information campaign, explaining these issues, because it seems that even among leading politicians, the awareness of such problems is limited.

A widespread and regular supply of electricity to agriculture will have an enormous economic and social value. It would also generate more employment among the landless labourers and petty farmers. Electric pump owners would, under these conditions, soon realize that they too stand to gain even at a higher electric energy tariff from the electricity that is regularly available.

The reduction of SEBs' losses would improve the overall supply of electricity to industries and city dwellers. Even in New Delhi, power cuts have increased over the the past few years, affecting not only the poor but also the rich—sweating without aircondition in 40 °Celsius! While in Bangalore, new industries are reluctant to come because of power shortage.

One must however point out a ticklish problem. In order to improve the operations of SEBs, electricity tariffs in the agricultural sector will have to be increased, but there will be a time lag between tariff revision and improving supply of electricity, which will not be so palatable to farmers.

Finally, the whole issue is not just confined to prices. Improvement of SEBs could be achieved by: Strong discipline among the employees, firm and direct supervision by senior officers who not unfrequently prefer to sit quietly in their comfortable offices instead of touring districts and listening to farmers. In my early enquiries in western U.P., old farmers remembered how Sir William Stampe would personally check if engines were properly greased.

A massive campaign against corruption, power theft and other malpractices would be no less fruitful and immensely popular. Over more than thirty years, whenever I discuss about these malpractices with farmers in northern India, I get the same reply: '*Koi nahin sunta*!' (Nobody listens to us).

It is hard for town dwellers to realize how these malpractices affect rural life. No doubt these already were there during the Raj, but malpractices have increased enormously because of many more opportunities for *bakshish*, be it for electricity, agricultural loans, even programmes supposed to help the poor, etc.

All these negative aspects of electricity supply to the farmers does not mean that agriculture will stop progressing. One should not underestimate the ability of the Indians 'to muddle through' as they say. Farmers manage to partly reduce the damage by using oil engines, or if they can afford, by installing a second electric pump in order to irrigate all their fields during the limited availability of power. Here and there some improvements in SEB may occur. Water saving devices like drip irrigation or sprinkler for orchards are progressing in Maharashtra, Rajasthan, Punjab and Haryana.

Then, the weather has so far partly mitigated the shortage of power. If northern India enjoys good winter rains, the use of tube-wells is reduced for wheat alone. The same happens when the monsoon is generous. However, since 1987, the last disastrous year, the monsoon has been, with a few exceptions, rather favourable. But, under really bad monsoons, especially repeated, the consequence of the shortage of electricity in tube-wells areas would become worse. As for rainfed crops, they would of course suffer more.

CONCLUSION

A clear conclusion can be confined to the following points:

A fast agricultural growth appears doubtful in the next few years, not only because of power shortage, but also because of other weaknesses: in research, extension services, insufficient seeds renewal, inadequate use of chemical fertilizers or pesticides....

More hazy is the impact of farmers' lobbies which may try to check electricity reforms. In the states, situations vary a great deal, both at the government and the farmers' levels. Relying on more autonomy since 1991, some of the states are pushing their own reforms like Gujarat, Maharashtra, Andhra, and Rajasthan. Others are too weak to do much, such as U.P. or even worse Bihar.

Then comes the weight of the farmers' lobbies which, as alluded earlier, varies a great deal. It is particularly powerful in the Ganges basin and in the irrigated deltas of the east coast, that is why the outcome of the SEB reforms in those regions is of particular importance.

When appoaching the economy from the angle of electricity and agricultural development, one reaches similar conclusions as when one tackles other fields: Transport and foreign trade, electricity and industrialization, or the reform of the public sector, or the fiscal deficit. Development will proceed further, but in spite of improving economic performances in 1999/2000, sustained acceleration of growth up to 7-8 per cent looks quite uncertain in the immediate future.

NOTES

1. I conducted repeated enquiries in districts of U.P., Bihar, Orissa, Andhra, Tamil Nadu, Maharashtra and Rajasthan. See my *Rural Change in South Asia, India, Pakistan, Bangladesh*, New Delhi, Vikas, 1995.
2. *Economic Times*, 5 February 1997.
3. *Economic Times*, 16 June 1998.
4. *Business India*, 18-31 May 1998.

Energy Infrastructures in India: Assessing Power Sector Needs

S.K.N. NAIR

INTRODUCTION

Beginning with a brief introduction to the basic features of India's energy consumption patterns, this article will proceed to outline the share of the power sector in energy consumption and supply and then deal with the special characteristics of the power infrastructure, taking up the following aspects for detailed examination:

- Method of estimating demand
- Trends of capacity expansion and forecasts
- Main problems facing the power infrastructure
- Some basic long term aims

INCREASING SHARE OF COMMERCIAL ENERGY

There has been a significant change in the pattern of energy supplies with the share of commercial fuels increasing from 26 per cent in 1950-1 to about 60 per cent in 1994-5. The overall indigenous production of commercial energy in India increased from 112.4 million tons of oil equivalent (mtoe) in 1984-5 to 183 mtoe in 1994-5.

Total commercial energy supplies (after taking into account the changes in stocks) in India increased from 121.5 mtoe in 1984-5 to 223.2 mtoe in 1994-5. Coal production increased from an estimated 72.3 mtoe in 1984-5 to 126.4 mtoe in 1994-5. The net availability of commercial energy for final consumption increased from 85.8 mtoe in 1984-5 to 148.6 mtoe in 1994-5.

Economic developments—as also trends like increase in urbanization from 19.9 per cent in 1971 to 25.1 per cent in 1991—result in both qualitative and quantitative changes in the use of energy. The share of commercial forms of energy has increased steadily over the years, even though non-commercial energy sources continue to contribute significantly in meeting the energy needs, especially in the households of rural areas where energy is used mainly for cooking.

The final commercial energy consumption in India has grown at a rate of about 5.5 per cent per annum during the last five years. In terms of per capita consumption, commercial energy use is of the order of 248 kilograms of oil equivalent (kgoe), which is quite low, being only about nine per cent of that of Korea and just three per cent of the per capita consumption in the US.

The supply and sales/consumption data for various forms of commercial energy are relatively well documented. In terms of calorific content, direct use of coal (i.e. excluding coal used for thermal power generation) still accounts for nearly 50 per cent of the total commercial energy consumption, and petroleum products nearly 40 per cent. India possesses large reserves of coal, which is the country's dominant fuel. India is also a net importer of energy; the crude oil and petroleum product imports in 1994-5 was 41.7 mtoe, about twice that of 1984-5 (20.1 mtoe).

Although coal is the most important source of energy in terms of share of final energy consumption, its share has been decreasing. Notable features of final energy consumption are the following:

(a) A shift from coal to natural gas and electricity in the industrial sector;
(b) a shift from coal to diesel oil in rail transport; and
(c) rapid electrification in the household sector.

Owing to persistent shortages of coal and power supplies during the past decade, the consumption of petroleum products increased more rapidly than anticipated. Another reason is that oil can be imported relatively easily to help overcome energy shortages in the short-term. In fact, diesel oils are largely used to mitigate the effects of power shortages whereas fuel oils may be used in industrial boilers when coal is scarce.

India's Planning Commission has estimated the long-term trends in the growth rates of commercial energy requirements and shares of different user segments as shown in Table 1.

The industrial sector continues to be the largest consumer of commercial energy (although its share will decline). The transport sector is likely to register the second largest increase in the demand on the energy resources in future after the household sector. The percentage share of agriculture in the total energy demand is likely to fall. Higher growth rate in the case of the household sector is

TABLE 1: ESTIMATE OF CHANGES IN SECTOR-WISE SHARE IN COMMERCIAL ENERGY REQUIREMENTS

Sectors	*1986*	*2009*	*Growth rate (% per annum)*
Agriculture	8.7	4.9	3.8
Industry	55.3	47.2	5.6
Transport	22.0	24.2	6.9
Household	12.6	21.3	8.8
Others	1.4	1.7	7.1
All sectors	100.0	100.0	6.3

Source: Planning Commission, 1991. Sectoral energy demand in India, New Delhi: Government of India.

mainly on account of the replacement of non-commercial energy by commercial energy where continued urbanization tends to enhance both the availability and cost advantages of commercial over non-commercial energy for domestic use, and, hence encourage substitution.

IMPACT OF POWER SECTOR ON ENERGY DEMAND

Power sector has depended, so far, almost exclusively on indigenously available energy sources. Power generation uses up, quantitatively, about 67 per cent of the country's coal production. Reckoned in terms of the total availability of indigenous *commercial* energy sources of all types, the share consumed for power generation has been steadily increasing. It is calculated that between 1984-5 and 1994-5, this share (in terms of million ton oil equivalent) increased from 36.6 per cent to 50.8 per cent (Table 2).

Power sector also imposes significant losses of energy sources in

TABLE 2: AVAILABILITY AND CONSUMPTION PERCENTAGE OF COMMERCIAL ENERGY

Description	*1984-5*	*1994-5*
Availability (mtoe)	112.4	182.6
Consumed for Power Generation (mtoe)	41.2	92.8
Percentage to total	36.6 %	50.8 %
[includes petroleum products (mtoe)	2.8	2.6]

the conversion process itself and through auxiliary consumption and transmission. (The last mentioned category is especially high in India.) In 1994-5, the share of such losses accounted for some 38.8 per cent of total energy resources available indigenously.

Primary nuclear generation increased from 0.25 mtoe in 1980-1 to 0.5 mtoe in 1994-5. Primary hydro electricity generation also increased from 3.9 mtoe to about 7 mtoe during the same period.

METHOD OF ESTIMATION OF ELECTRICITY DEMAND

The periodic Electric Power Survey exercises carried out by the Central Electricity Authority adopt the 'partial end-use' method for the short-term forecasts and 'econometric modelling' for the long-term. The last survey was carried out in 1995 and a fresh one has just commenced.

The end-use method, adopted for projecting the power demand over short and medium time-spans in the fifteenth EPS Report, makes it possible to estimate the effects of policy decisions that may have impact on any sector(s). It relies on current estimates of the quantity of electricity end-use and the number of end-users.

FORECAST UP TO 2001-2

The exercise is quite detailed. The short- and medium-term forecast covering up to year 2002 has been made on detailed basis for each of the following eight categories of consumption:

1. Domestic
2. Commercial and miscellaneous
3. Public lighting
4. Public water works
5. Irrigation and de-watering
6. Industrial
7. Railway traction
8. Bulk supply to non-industrial consumers

For the first two categories, past growth trends are studied to forecast the number of consumers and energy consumption per consumer. (Typically, the annual rate of growth of domestic consumers could be about 6 per cent and of average consumption per consumer about four per cent). In states where power shortages were experienced in recent past, the growth rate for the forecast is based on long-term series analysis of growth in number of consumers.

In the irrigation segment, the model incorporates the number of pump-sets, average capacity of pump-set and average consumption per year per kW of connected load. The programme for electrifying pump-sets for the period of forecast is taken into account. In regard to average capacity of pump-set, trends could point either to a marginal decline or marginal increase. Average consumption per pump-set, however, typically reveals a rising trend, owing largely to extensive irrigation practices and growing of multiple crops. Average increase in hours of usage could be as much as 50 hours on a base of about 2000 hours.

Power requirement for the industrial sector is estimated under three categories:

1. L.T. Industries
2. H.T. Industries with demand of less than 1 MW
3. H.T. Industries with demand of 1 MW or above

The consumption by the first two categories is projected on the basis of past trends and expected growth patterns for the future. In the third category, consumption of each industrial unit is estimated separately, incorporating production forecasts and expansion plans.

LONG-TERM FORECAST

The econometric modelling used for long-term load forecast (up to 2012-13) links the consumption of electricity to economic variables. The basic methodology used for the study was single equation regression models to forecast electricity demand. Firstly, estimation of regression equation for individual sectors and individual regions by using time series data on electricity consumption and on explanatory variables was estimated. The regression models in most cases in the above study use one independent variable only. The regression equations are either linear or log linear. After having estimated the 'best fit' regression by using various criteria, the next step is to make projections of the explanatory variables for the forecast period. Target growth rates for sectoral and aggregate state GDP were assumed. Once the projections for the explanatory variables are made, the forecast for regional and sectoral electricity consumption follow.

The next step is to estimate the requirement for installed capacity to meet the expected energy and load demands. This is done by allowing for the loss of plant availability on scheduled maintenance, unplanned partial and total shut downs, auxiliary consumption and 'spinning reserve'. Differing norms are adopted for thermal, hydro, etc., units and between coal based and gas based units in thermal. Units of capacity less than 200 MW are given a somewhat lower availability rating as compared to units upwards of this size.

REQUIRED: DOUBLING OF INSTALLED CAPACITY IN TEN YEARS

The relatively high rates of growth registered by the national economy between 1992 and 1997 have pushed up the demand for electricity about two percentage points above the year-on-year forecasts of the fifteenth Power Survey. However, preliminary figures for 1997-8, a year in which rate of growth—both aggregate and the industry and agriculture segments—declined, shows a sharp slow-down in electricity demand, to below the levels projected in the survey.

The long-term forecasts are based on a compounded annual growth rate of about 6.4 per cent. On the evidence of last five years, actual demand will exceed this projection if the rate of growth of GDP of 6.5 per cent and above is reached again and sustained.

Estimates of physical infrastructure needs of the power sector have the installed generating capacity as the starting point. Independent estimates of the needed capacity additions have placed the 'minimum' requirements over ten years ending 2005-6 at about 84,000 MW. This is termed the 'minimum' being conditional on realizing several targets of loss reduction and end-use efficiencies, which in turn, are dependent on a number of organizational reforms and improvements.

CAPACITY ADDITION IN THE PAST

Over the last two decades, India's power sector effectively doubled its installed capacity twice over, but with significant changes in the capacity mix (Table 3).

Levels of public investment. Two main strategies have contributed to the high rates of growth registered by the sector: High levels of public investment and a successful form of institutional intervention involving the setting up of central undertakings for implementing and operating large thermal, hydel and nuclear power plants.

TABLE 3: CAPACITY EXPANSION: PAST TRENDS

(generating capacity: MW)

	Total	*Thermal*	*Hydro*	*Gas*	*Nuclear*
1976-7	21,468	11,668	9,025	135	640
	(54.4)	(42.0)	(0.6)	(3.0)	
1984-5	42,584	26,488	14,460	541	1,095
		(62.0)	(34.0)	(1.4)	(2.6)
1995-6	83,288	53,819	20,976	6,268	2,225
		(64.6)	(25.2)	(7.5)	(2.7)

Note: Figures in brackets indicate percentage shares.

Barring a slight drop to 16.7 per cent over the Sixth Plan period (1980-5), power sector accounted for a steady 18 to 19 per cent share of total national plan investment from the mid-1960s up to 1992. The sector share dropped sharply to 14.3 per cent in the Eighth Plan (1992-7).

SUCCESSFUL STRATEGIES

The central power sector public sector undertakings (PSUs) that were set up since the mid-1970s received adequate funding support through the plans and at least one of them, the National Thermal Power Corporation (NTPC), has reached a level of self-sustaining growth. This overall strategy of institutional intervention has been a major factor in the peak growth rates recorded in the 1980s. Central PSUs together account for close to 28 per cent of the installed generating capacity in the country currently and nearly one-third of the energy generation. Gross generation of electricity averaged an annual growth rate of 9.4 per cent in the decade of 1980s, but slowed down to 7.5 per cent per annum in the 1990s.

Growth of the distribution network was slower, and is calculated at 6.3 per cent per annum in the 1980s. However, in the case of grid management also, two specific initiatives—one early and the other recent—were of decisive impact. The first was the conceptual change in power planning introduced in 1964, by setting up the regional electricity boards (REBs). The REBs were entrusted with the task of ensuring and facilitating the integrated operation of the regional grids. However, the regional grids are not an unqualified success; breach of grid discipline is reportedly common and efficient concepts of power pooling and 'merit order' operation remain to be evolved even today.

The second and more recent intervention was the setting up, in 1989, of the Power Grid Corporation of India ('Power Grid') entrusted with the task of construction, operation and maintenance of trunk transmission lines and associated facilities (later including load dispatching stations) and also for managing commercial aspects of transmission of energy from the central government owned power stations and inter-regional energy exchanges. Power Grid has emerged as a key player in the plans to implement inter-regional links for power transfers and for the eventual link-up of a national grid.

LIMITATIONS OF STRATEGY

Over the long term, the signal success in terms of additions to capacity must not be overlooked. At the same time, the plan-based strategy failed to keep pace with growth of demand, leading to widespread shortages. The strategy also contributed to a host of problems, among them:

- Growing inefficiencies of state level utilities
- Excessive reliance on thermal, especially coal-based generation, with adverse implications for the system as well as the environment
- Relative neglect of investments in transmission and distribution, and
- High level of 'politicization' of the sector, especially of retail pricing.

The basic challenge facing the sector is to keep up the past trends of growth, but to do so by harnessing large volumes of private investment and also correcting the imbalances in energy sources. In order to accomplish this, the several weaknesses and structural faults of the sector need to be overcome.

While the generation segment of the sector, especially the part of it under central government ownership, and bulk transmission are in fair shape and have registered near-robust rates of growth, the distribution segment, under the control of the state governments is an area of sickness. This dichotomy is attributed principally to pricing anomalies; however, the problems go much deeper.

Significantly, the regulatory regime of the sector over this period was also marked by sharp contrasts. Both bulk generation pricing and tariff for bulk transmission were closely regulated through statute as well as in implementation. On the other hand, the regulatory regime applicable to retail distribution—both pricing and standards of service—escaped any form of intervention for decades, until the on-going efforts at power sector reform in certain states and the recent central ordinance on autonomous regulatory commissions.

STRUCTURE OF POWER SECTOR

Assessment of the power infrastructure needs have to take the prevailing organizational structure of the sector into account. Some seven years into the process of economic reforms, India's power sector is still predominantly state-owned. Some 65 per cent of the installed generating capacity and virtually all of the sub-transmission and distribution systems are owned and operated by the state electricity boards (SEBs), controlled by the state governments. Private distributor licensees are operating in three major metropolises (and in a small part of the national capital region). As noted, some 28 per cent of the country's generating capacity is with public sector undertakings owned by central government, fully or in partnership with state governments.

Other important players in the power scenario include the central undertaking co-ordinating the rural electrification programme (Rural Electrification Corporation—REC) and the dedicated centrally controlled financing agency of the sector—Power Finance Corporation (PFC).

CONSUMPTION PATTERNS

The present usage profile (share of total sales) by the different user categories (1996-7) is presented in Table 4.

Consumption by the 'domestic' segment has almost doubled its per cent share of total since 1965-6. More significantly, while the growth rates of the agriculture segment are tapering, that of the 'domestic' segment will continue at existing rate for several years.

TABLE 4: USAGE PROFILE

Share of Total Sales			
Industry	35.5 %	Agriculture	29.2 %
Domestic	17.6 %	Commercial	4.6 %
Railway Traction	2.3 %	Others	10.8 %

Source: *Annual Report on Working of SEBs*, Planning Commission, 1997.

The Fifteenth 'Power Survey' (1995) forecasts that the share of this segment in total sales will increase to 23.5 per cent over next five years.

High rates of growth characterize also the electricity consumption for railway transport, which, though accounting for only 2.3 per cent of the total consumption, has increased from 372 mkWh in 1970-1 to 5,995 mkWh in 1996-7—an annual growth of 11.3 per cent.

Industry, while still accounting for the highest percentage share of total electricity consumption, has dropped markedly from a peak of 70.6 per cent in 1965-6 to only 35.5 per cent 1996-7.

Much of the increase in household consumption would occur with urban consumers who would want to use up more electricity. This would make its effect felt on expectations of quality of supply, promoting, in turn, the willingness to bear higher rates for improved supply standards.

This should be a key factor in guiding the entry of private agencies into the distribution segment. The 'domestic' category should be in a position, increasingly so as its share in sales increases, to support a degree of cross-subsidization within the segment itself, and to facilitate a 'lifeline' rate designed for the urban poor, based on the household load compared to their income.

PRICING

As is well known, pricing inefficiencies comprise of heavily subsidized prices, fixed without relation to accepted economic principles of 'cost of service' or 'marginal costing'. The level of subsidies extended in most states to the agricultural and domestic consumer segments have pushed average tariffs well below average costs and they remain so some seven years into the process of economic reform.

As evidenced by the following table, the gap between cost and average realization in fact widened from a 17 per cent per unit shortfall between the average tariff and the cost of generation and distribution in 1992-3 to 21 per cent in 1996-7.

The distortions in electricity pricing, especially the under-pricing of supply to large consumer segments continue to cause economy-wide efficiency losses; under-pricing of energy—not only power—has led to efficiency losses which have been increasing over successive Plans.

Industrial consumers in several Indian states now bear charges

TABLE 5: RATIO OF REVENUE TO COST

	1992-3	*1996-7*
Average cost /kWh (paise)	128.2	186.2
Average revenue/kWh (paise)	105.4	147.0
Ratio of revenue to cost (per cent)	82.2	78.9

Source: *Annual Report on Working of SEBs*, Planning Commission, 1997.

per kwh that are among the highest in this category, anywhere. Despite this level of cross-subsidy through tariffs, all-India commercial losses of SEBs increased from Rs. 45 billion in 1992-3 to an estimated Rs 100 billion in 1996-7.

Pricing innovations. Recent initiatives by a few SEBs to introduce 'Time-of-day' tariffs are confined, at present to bulk industrial consumers. Advances in technology should soon be facilitating this form of pricing to the urban domestic consumer as well. Demand management through pricing strategies has been a neglected area; efficient pricing, in combination with measures to promote use of energy efficient equipment has the potential to secure overall reduction in demand of up to 8.21 per cent over fifteen years.[1]

LOCATION OF ENERGY SOURCES

Primary sources of energy are unevenly distributed. Bulk of the country's proven coal resources are located in contiguous areas spread over Bihar, Madhya Pradesh, West Bengal, Orissa, Maharashtra and Andhra Pradesh. Of these, the first four together hold some 85 per cent of the total reserves, Bihar alone accounting for 46 per cent.

Lignite reserves occur in fewer states; Tamil Nadu accounts for over 86 per cent of the country's total, followed, way behind, by Rajasthan (6 per cent).

Natural gas is an option increasingly drawn for power generation. Proven reserves of this fuel lie mainly offshore (62 per cent); onshore reserves are concentrated in Assam (24 per cent) and Gujarat (14 per cent). The natural distribution of recoverable reserves of crude closely mirror that of natural gas.

India has assured uranium resources of 34,000 tons, of which 15,000 tons are economically exploitable. Renewable energy sources are also expected to play an important role in solving the energy problems in scattered hilly areas where the extension of the grid system is considered comparatively uneconomical. The total small hydro (up to 15 MW capacity) and wind energy potential in the country is estimated at 10,000 MW and 20,000 MW, respectively.

Hydro-electric potential. Only some 22 per cent of the total potential for hydro-electricity in the country has been tapped so far, including projects under implementation. It is assessed by CEA that all-India hydro-electric potential (at 60 per cent load factor) totals 84,044 MW, as against which developed potential adds up to only 12,475 MW. Projects totalling 5,879 MW are under implementation.

Region-wise, the estimated potential and the percentage share of projects developed and under development (as of 31.3.1996) are as given in Table 6.

Projects to come up in future will be concentrated mainly in the two border states of Arunachal and Himachal Pradesh—together accounting for close to 60 per cent of the total exploitable potential in the country—and also the northern parts of Uttar Pradesh. Efficient exploitation of this potential is important both for the power sector itself and for realizing objectives of balanced regional development.

PER CAPITA CONSUMPTION

Per capita consumption of electricity in India registered an annual growth rate percentage of 6.7 from 178 kWh in 1985-6 to 319 kWh in 1994-5. However, there are substantial variations in different regions of the country.

Inter-state variations are even higher. While Punjab has per capita electricity consumption of 786 kWh, states in the north-east have per capita consumption of 60-70 kWh per annum. Per capita

TABLE 6: REGION-WISE PROJECT DEVELOPED AND UNDER DEVELOPMENT (HYDRO ELECTRICITY)

Region	*Potential (MW)*	*Exploited (%)*
Northern	30,155	21.0
Western	5,679	59.1
Southern	10,763	59.5
Eastern	5,590	29.2
North-Eastern	31,857	2.0
All India	84,044	21.8

Source: *TERI Energy Data Directory and Yearbook, 1997-8.*

TABLE 7: PER CAPITA ELECTRICITY CONSUMPTION BY REGION

Year	*Northern*	*Western*	*Southern*	*Eastern*	*N.-Eastern*	*All India*
1985-6	173	259	186	115	50	178
1986-7	192	275	202	119	50	191
1987-8	202	297	205	125	62	201
1988-9	217	314	229	135	63	217
1989-90	241	334	249	129	76	236
1990-1	249	367	272	150	89	253
1991-2	265	391	286	156	88	268
1992-3	282	406	312	162	93	283
1993-4	286	437	335	174	94	299
1994-5	303	465	368	179	102	319

Source: *Annual Report on Working of SEBs*, Planning Commission, 1997.

consumption in the western region is nearly 4.6 times higher than that of the north-east. Because of the low base, however, the rate of growth of per capita consumption in north-east is the highest, while this is the lowest in the eastern region. While the compound average growth rates of the northern and western regions are close to the national average, that of the southern region has been higher at 7.9 per annum during this period (as shown in Table 7).

ABSENCE OF MARKET FORCES

Not overlooking geographical and other peculiarities influencing this pattern, these distortions are, in some part, the effect of over-centralization of a sector where very little play of market forces has been allowed so far. In a continental-size economy the choice of fuel mix in different regions can be different given the resource endowment of the region, trade possibilities and the trading costs.

RURAL ELECTRIFICATION

The rural electrification programme (REP) which was introduced in a few states in the First Five Year Plan (1952-7) itself was designed to provide electricity as a social amenity to rural areas. The programme was progressively expanded to cover all states. It gained special importance after the severe drought in the mid-sixties when the programme enhanced access to electricity for rural areas for operating irrigation pump-sets to use available groundwater. It was further strengthened by the formation of the Rural Electrification

Corporation (REC) in 1969 which now provides some 90 per cent of the funds for rural electrification as concessional loans to the state electricity boards. As a result of these efforts, 84 per cent of Indian villages have been electrified (connected to the network) and over 11 million pump-sets energized. Apart from the pump-set energization, emphasis has also been placed on promotion of industrial load in villages by extending electricity connections for setting up low-tension (voltage) industries.

While the REP has been impressive in statistical terms of the number of villages electrified, *'electrification'* of a village means that at the minimum, just one connection has been provided in the village. According to the last census data of 1991, percentage of rural households with electric connections in the eight states that had achieved 100 per cent village electrification ranged from 37 per cent in Andhra Pradesh to 77 per cent in Punjab. It is estimated that on an all-India basis, while 84 per cent of villages have been electrified, only around 32 per cent of rural households actually have access to electricity.

The REP has other severe drawbacks as well, most notably the heavy financial losses incurred by the SEBs in providing electricity at low rates to the agriculture sector which is resulting in wasteful use both of electricity and of underground water. In addition, the programme has resulted in an increase in the transmission and distribution (T&D) losses, as the higher priority placed on building generation capacity combined with a lack of funds has meant that the extensions to the T&D network were sub-optimal.

PLANT UTILIZATION

The entry of central undertakings into power generation also denoted adoption of larger unit sizes, improved maintenance practices and better plant utilization. Average plant load factor of thermal power stations has been recording steady improvement. Over the five-year period 1991-2 to 1995-6, the all-India average rose from 55.3 per cent to 63 per cent. Improvements were registered both by centrally owned as well as by SEB owned plants, the former from 64.5 to 70.9 per cent and the latter from 50.6 to 58 per cent.

The standards attained are far below international performance levels. Large number of plants owned by SEBs and operating today are over twenty years old and of the designs of the 1960s. Progressive induction of new plants of latest design, *accompanied by the organizational upgrading of public owned utilities* should help to raise the performance levels further.

TRANSMISSION AND DISTRIBUTION (T&D)

India's T&D system comprises a 400 kV network as the main and bulk transmission system in each region; a 220 kV, 132 kV and 110 kV network as the main and support transmission systems in each state; a 66 kV, 33 kV and 22 kV network as sub-transmission system; an 11 kV network as primary distribution systems; and a 400 V (three phase) and 230 V network as local distribution systems.

While the predominant technology for electricity distribution and transmission has been alternating current (AC) technology, high voltage direct current (HVDC) technology has been introduced for back-to-back interconnection between the Northern and Western regional systems and also for the bulk transfer of power in the northern region.

Even though the T&D network expanded by about 6.3 per cent per annum during the 1980s, its growth has not kept pace with the capacity to supply power. There were instances when the generation levels of certain power stations, especially in the northern region, had to be curtailed because not all the required 400 kV lines could be commissioned in time to deliver the power generated.

Adding to an already over-burdened T&D system, T&D losses for Indian utilities in aggregate increased from 17.5 per cent in 1970-1 to 21.7 per cent in 1985-6, and then levelled off to about 22 per cent since 1990-1. As a result, for every mkWh of electricity demand about 1.265 mkWh must be generated.

'Technical' losses. The high T&D losses, attributable to technical reasons and reckoned at about two-third of the 22 per cent of energy loss, stem from:

- Plan investments that have assigned lower priority to T&D in relation to building generation capacity;
- the urgency to provide electricity for rural populations that results in long lines and low power factor without strengthening the back-up transmission and sub-transmission system;
- multiplicity of transformation stages causing high transformer losses;

- inadequate reactive compensation in the system; and
- an improper load distribution resulting in system overloading.

Higher transformation losses are attributable to the existence of many stages of transformation, viz., 132/66 kV, 66/33 kV, 33/11 kV, and finally 11/0.4 kV. Adoption of an inappropriate distribution technology, viz., low voltage distribution system which is suitable for countries with high load densities (like European countries) and not for a large country like India with loads thinly spread over wide areas, is another major factor. Technical experts are of the view that for India, high voltage distribution system is more appropriate which is the system adopted by the USA and Canada with load density conditions similar to that in India.

By undertaking suitable system improvement schemes based on computer studies it should be possible to bring down the 'technical' component of T&D losses in the distribution system to about 9 per cent. Attention to technical losses includes such measures as augmenting the network, installation of capacitors, 're-conductoring', and eliminating both under-loading and overloading of distribution transformers. Each system improvement scheme has to be essentially tailor-made in nature to meet the specific requirements of the system conditions of the particular city, town or village chosen for loss reduction programme.

In the end, reductions in T&D losses would mean more electricity delivered per unit kwh generated which would reduce the impact on the environment and lower the cost of electricity delivered. In recent years only some of the SEBs have taken up systematic studies for planning of their distribution systems using the available computer software, and other SEBs are expected to follow the same strategy for their distribution planning.

The feasibility of gradual switching over from the existing LT distribution system adopted in India to HT distribution system (which is the appropriate technology for Indian systems) also requires serious consideration, in order to bring down the losses on this account.

'Non-technical Losses'. Apart from technical losses, the incidence of non-technical losses is far too excessive. The reasons for this are mainly three: Electricity theft, faulty meters and un-metered supply. Reducing—if possible eliminating—the non-technical losses requires:

- Review of the *'flat-rate power policy'*, which encourages wastage of electricity and for which viable schemes still remain to be devised; possibly even if power is supplied on flat-rate basis, electricity meters could be provided for energy accounting purposes.
- A judicious mix of legislative support, increased customer awareness, improved billing and collection procedures, and reliable and high quality meters.

WEAK ORGANIZATIONS

The structure of SEBs was designed nearly fifty years ago, when the electricity sector was virtually non-existent in the country. The massive expansion that these organizations could bring about and the plan-linked mode of funding supported from state and central sources seem to have served to perpetuate organizational structures unsuited to commercial functioning and self-sustainable expansion. Three main shortcomings require note:

- Too close relationship with government.
- Neglect of management upgrading, institutionalized accessing of talent.
- Very inadequate accountability.

It is proposed here to elaborate the last-mentioned area, which needs to be addressed irrespective of whether the SEB is to be privatized or to remain under public ownership.

Accountability—the overlooked area. Managements of SEBs are accountable (through provisions in, or prescribed under, the statute) to government, the legislature, the auditing authority (for financial prudence of expenditure) and in a small degree to the consumer; in sum they do not add up to accountability to the owners' interests, which happen to be inadequately defined besides. The problem is partly generic to public enterprises and partly specific to the electricity sector, the retail distribution part of which is still not viewed as a commercial activity.

A change in ownership is perceived as the simplest solution, although this, in turn, dictates several other changes as well, including the facilitating requirements of corporatization and price reform. An added and compelling reason for ownership divestiture is the need to access funding for expansion and system upgrade.

Measures to introduce accountability while retaining public ownership are not to be ruled out; especially so by those states that do not favour forms of restructuring involving privatization. But this would involve a total recast of prevailing patterns in several areas and would include:

- Changes in relationship with government.
- Internal structural changes.
- Externally imposed regulation.
- Changes aimed towards a competitive environment for the industry.

Accountability to the government of the day has for long been confused with accountability to the owners of the public enterprise. A degree of distancing from the government is, in fact, a necessary condition for the management to be accountable in terms of performance to the owning public. Transparent forms of selection of top management and fixed tenures are among the first steps required. Autonomous regulatory systems are also crucial, especially for protecting the users' interests.

Essential internal structural changes would involve the demarcation of cost and profit centres and bringing transparency to inter-segment transactions (generation: :transmission and transmission: :distribution). More professional inputs into the commercial, financial and HRD functions would also be required.

Entry of private players into the generation segment, together with measures to promote 'trading' both within and across state boundaries will provide the minimum conditions for a competitive environment. Corporatization, especially with divestiture of part shareholdings to the public and to employees are other measures that could be considered.

INVESTMENT NEEDS

Macro level projections of additional capacity requirements point to the need to double the present installed generating capacity over a ten year period. Making full allowance for feasible improvements in levels of capacity utilization and end-use efficiencies, *The India Infrastructure Report* (1997) estimated the total investment need of the sector over ten years ending 2005 at US $140 billion. This would include the supporting transmission and distribution facilities;

renovation of existing under utilized plants would entail a further investment close to US $10 billion. Other assessments have broadly concurred with this estimate.

PLANT RENOVATION

As with 'green-field' power projects, inducting of private investment into plant renovation and repowering should be a priority objective. Real headway is yet to be made in this area.

A public funded renovation and modernization programme, aiming to improve the average PLF of 34 selected stations covered by the scheme, from 46 per cent to 53 per cent, was undertaken during the Seventh Plan. The programme is estimated to have succeeded in generating additional 10 bn.kWh per year.

Phase II of the programme, drawn up for the Eighth Plan proposes to cover 201 units of 46 thermal power stations, aggregating to a total capacity of 19,981 MW. The total cost is estimated at US $300 million. A further 211 units with aggregate capacity of 9,638 MW have been identified for renovation.

Power Finance Corporation which is extending credit at concessional rates to SEBs for this activity has recently invited global bids for pre-qualifying a panel of firms for extending consultancy services and for actually undertaking the R&M works. This is a sound approach and it is now up to the SEBs to plan and execute these schemes through the selected experienced agencies.

SCOPE FOR PRIVATE FINANCING

Studies undertaken in 1995 under the auspices of the US Agency for International Development had identified the levels of capacity expansion that can possibly be funded by all the agencies in a position to provide loans and guarantees for private power projects. These would include Indian financial institutions, SEBs and state governments, Power Grid, Indian corporates with requisite credit rating and the guarantee and lending support of the World Bank and export credit agencies. The maximum financing capability of all these sources put together was assessed at around US $2 billion per annum over the next five years.

The guarantee potential of SEBs was limited, in this study, to the receivables from the industrial sector that could be channelled through 'escrow' and similar arrangements to provide security for IPPs.

On this calculation, the additional capacity that could be put up through private financing over five years would be around 10,000 MW, or some one-fifth of the target addition for the Ninth Five Year Plan (1997-2002). It is also estimated that SEBs that go through restructuring and reform will be able to support larger private investments in generation. Optimistically, therefore, private capacity addition of up to 15,000 MW over a five year period could be feasible.

The IPP policy itself has been marked by serious delays in securing 'financial closure', caused by the financial weakness of the SEBs (the bulk power purchasers) and the unfamiliarity of most agencies concerned with the risk-sharing principles associated with 'non-recourse' financing.

LONG-TERM FUEL POLICY

The country is yet to develop a comprehensive long-term policy on fuels. The issues to be taken into account are several—regional balance in power development, long-term fuel import requirements, investments in matching port, storage terminal and transportation facilities, general location plan of plants of varying sizes, exploitation of renewable resources and environmental issues among them. Decisions on these issues should take into account the best expert advice that the country can muster.

On going efforts to induct private power units on significant scale should not obscure the fact that over 90 per cent of the electric power sector is still owned and operated by the central and state governments, who will continue to control or strongly influence several aspects of utility operations. The control of transmission and distribution will be retained by the respective state governments for the foreseeable future. Even if SEBs succeed in attracting investment in generation capacity promoted by private developers, the T&D system that has caused power bottlenecks in the past will likely limit delivery of the additional power to be generated by IPPs.

GRID MANAGEMENT AND TRADING

In order to expand the scope of electricity trade in the coming years, it would be necessary to devise a suitable tariff structure for inter-system energy exchanges which would be attractive to all participating systems and that would enable optimal operation of the regional systems. The necessary administrative structure at the regional and national level has already been created to promote effective integrated operation in the form of regional electricity boards and the Power Grid Corporation.

Current status of trading in power. The types of exchanges between systems currently taking place can be characterized as: (1) *emergency exchanges* during systems contingencies; (2) *firm exchanges* which are committed supply from a surplus state to a deficit state system; and (3) *inadvertent exchanges* which are unscheduled exchanges. Economy exchanges, which are based on consideration of incremental cost of energy of various power stations in the system, are not generally used in the Indian power system.

A factor standing in the way of inter-regional electricity trade is the difficulty in interconnecting the regions in AC mode, due to the fact that the operating grid frequencies of the different regional grids are somewhat different from each other. This is primarily because of power shortage conditions prevailing in the Indian power systems which forces them to operate their systems at frequencies below the standard frequency of 50 cycles per second (c/s). Since the extent of power deficit varies from region to region, the extent of frequency deviation (from the standard frequency of 50 c/s) is different for different regions. Under these conditions, the only way to interconnect the regions is to establish HVDC inter-ties with back-to-back DC stations at the interconnecting points.

Yet another factor limiting the extent of power exchanges is the lack of adequate load dispatching and communication facilities, without which it is difficult to operate a complex interconnected system. While a start has been made in establishing load dispatch stations at the regional level, matching facilities at the state level have yet to be set up. As regards communication facilities, Indian power systems are still largely dependent on primitive facilities like power line carrier communication (PLCC) and unreliable public telephone systems.

Another irritant in electricity trade in India has been the absence of standard commercial practices in regard to transactions involving the '*wheeling*' of power. In an integrated system, energy has sometimes to flow through the transmission network of a utility other than that of the donor/recipient system. This type of transaction involves two issues:

- The rate at which the utility whose transmission system is used for the benefit of the other utility is to be compensated; and
- determining of the incremental transmission losses payable to a wheeling utility.

In order to improve the prospects for electricity trade, apart from required technical measures, it will be necessary to formulate well defined commercial guidelines and a rational tariff structure to encourage the selling and buying of energy for mutual benefit.

Renewable sources—hydel power. The progressive decline in the share of hydro-electricity over successive plans has been identified as a problem needing correction.

In view of the location of exploitable potential in the border areas of north and north-east, there is need to transfer power to the load centres, necessitating massive investments in transmission lines (involving HVDC technology) by Power Grid Corporation or other government agencies. It will also be necessary to establish new institutional arrangements for bulk purchase and sale of power by a power trading company that would enter into contractual arrangements with generating companies as well as SEBs and bulk licensees.

So far hydroelectric schemes have been implemented through public investment, of either central or state governments. Regarding private generation projects, only 13 schemes (totalling 4,328 MW) have been sponsored of which only two—one each in Himachal Pradesh and Madhya Pradesh—have reached the stage of implementation. Private sector response has been poor probably owing to several special risks in the hydel projects. The joint venture route with government sponsorship is likely to be more successful; there are many prospective overseas investors who have expertise in hydro and are prepared to come to India on joint ownership basis.

CONCLUSION

India's electricity sector will have an increasing share of the commercial energy usage. However, the demands that the sector will make on the energy resources that the country can access will be conditioned by a number of options, and several uncertainties. The following is a tabulation of the sector specific issues that will determine the power infrastructure needs and the related uncertainties and constraints:

Main Issues	*Uncertainties/Constraints*
Levels of investments accessed	Organization upgrading, sector reforms
End-use efficiencies realized	Organization upgrading, incentives policy
Control of system losses	Organization upgrading, accessing investments
Facilitating inter-regional transfers	Institutional supports, accessing investments
Bringing market forces into play	Institutional supports, sector reforms
Optimized energy mix	Institutional supports, sector reforms

The speed with which existing organizations are upgraded and new institutions designed and positioned will have a determining influence.

Economy wide issues that will determine the long-term power infrastructure needs are, in the main:

- Rate of growth of GDP
- Country's foreign exchange earnings and capacity for financing of fuel imports
- Policies relative to the transportation sector, especially electrification of railway network and urban mass transit systems
- Thrust given to rural electrification and the technical solutions devised for the purpose.

NOTE

1. *Planning for the Indian Power Sector*, Canadian Energy Research Institute and Tata Energy Research Institute, 1995.

REFERENCES

Canadian Energy Research Institute and Tata Energy Research Institute, (1995), *Planning for the Indian Power Sector.*

Central Electricity Authority (1997), *Investment opportunities for Private Participation in Power Sector.*

——— (1994-5 and 1995-6), *Performance Review of Thermal Power Station.*

——— (1995), *All India Statistics: 1993-94 General Review*, Government of India.

——— (1995), *15th Electric Power Survey Report.*

——— (1996), *Investment Opportunity for Private Participation in Power Sector.*

——— (1997), *Fourth National Power Plan 1997-2012.*

Economic Survey (several years), Ministry of Finance.

Expert Group on the Commercialization of Infrastructure Projects (1997): *The India Infrastructure Report: Policy Imperatives for Growth and Welfare*, Vols. 1-3, NCAER.

International Energy Agency (1995-6), *Energy Statistics and Balances of Non-OECD Countries.*

Kohli (1997), *Choice for Efficient Private Provision of Infrastructure in East Asia*, World Bank.

Ministry of Non-Conventional Energy Sources (September 1994), *Background Note on Third Conference of Chief Ministers,* Government of India.

Ministry of Power (1997), *Improving the Health of Indian Power Sector,* Government of India.

——— (August 1998), *Policy on Hydro Power Development,* Government of India.

Mohan, R. et al. (1998), *Economic Issues Related to the Power Sector, Energy for Growth and Sustainability*, Indian National Academy of Engineers.

Planning Commission (1991), *Sectoral energy demand in India*, Government of India.

——— (1997), *Annual Report on Working of State Electricity Boards and Electricity Departments,* Government of India.

——— *Ninth Five Year Plan,* Vols. 1 & 2.

Rao et al. (1998), *The Economics of Electricity Supply in India.*

Sindhwani, J. (1996), *Re-modelling of distribution system,* Paper prepared for Haryana State Electricity Board.

TERI (1997), *TERI Energy Data Directory and Yearbook, 1997-8,* Tata Energy Research Institute, New Delhi.

US Agency for International Development (December 1995), *The Financing Capability of Indian Institutions to Provide Alternatives to Sovereign Guarantees.*

Infrastructure and Policy Constraints in Meeting India's Long-term Energy Demands

LEENA SRIVASTAVA

INTRODUCTION

Despite being endowed with large resources of coal, hydropower, and other renewable energy resources, India is faced with a high level of dependence on hydrocarbon energy and limited energy options for the future. Demand has at all times outstripped supply and the gap between the two has been constantly increasing. In trying to cope with perennial energy and capital shortages, the country has consistently made sub-optimal choices in the development of energy resources. This, accompanied by a pricing structure that does not ensure the generation of adequate internal resources—and in fact has resulted in mounting deficits, has forced the government to realize its own inability to be able to meet the investment requirements of this critical infrastructure sector. As such, the government is undertaking major reform programmes aimed at undoing the mistakes of the past. A major focus of the reform programmes is to invite the participation of the private sector largely by bringing tariffs in line with market considerations.

THE OVERALL ENERGY SCENARIO IN INDIA

India is relatively well endowed with both exhaustible and renewable energy resources. Coal is the major exhaustible energy resource of the country, and has a life expectancy of over 200 years. Table 1 presents the proven energy resources in India and the total world resources.

The indigenous production of commercial energy in India increased from 53 mtoe in 1972-3 to about 207 mtoe in 1997-8, registering an average rate of growth of about 5.6 per cent per annum (Table 2). Given the large resources of coal, it is obvious that

TABLE 1: PROVEN ENERGY RESOURCES IN INDIA AND THE WORLD

	Unit	*India*	*World*	*India in World (%)*
Coal	bmt	69.9	1031.6	6.8
Oil	bbbl	5.8	1016.9	0.6
Natural Gas	tcm	0.71	139.7	0.5

Source: *British Petroleum (BP) Statistical Review of World Energy*, 1997.

coal dominates the supply profile. However, while coal accounted for as much as 79 per cent of domestically produced energy in 1972-3, its share declined to 70 per cent in 1994-5. In direct contrast to this, the share of oil and gas increased from 16.3 per cent to 27 per cent in the same period.

India has a system of planned development wherein five-year plans are prepared, and financial outlays provided to the various sectors for fulfilling these plans. The energy sector has been a major beneficiary of total plan outlays and the share of this sector in the total has gone up from 15 per cent in the Third Five-Year Plan

TABLE 2: AVAILABILITY OF PRIMARY SOURCES OF ENERGY (*mtoe*)

	1972-3	1975-6	1980-1	1985-6	1990-1	1997-8
Coal						
Production	41.6	53.7	55.9	75.6	103.7	145.1
Net imports	0.25	0.23	0.68	0.89	2.4	7.0
Crude oil						
Production	7.3	8.4	10.5	30.2	33.0	33.8
Net imports	12.1	13.6	16.2	14.6	20.7	34.5
Natural gas						
Production	1.3	2.0	2.0	6.9	15.4	21.2
Net imports	–	–	–	–	–	–
Hydro power						
Production	2.3	2.8	3.9	4.3	6.0	6.3
Net imports	–	–	–	–	–	–
Nuclear power						
Production	0.09	0.22	0.25	0.42	0.52	0.9
Net imports	–	–	–	–	–	–
Total						
Production	52.7	67.3	72.6	117.5	158.7	207.2
Net imports	15.1	15.4	24.4	17.4	29.1	58.8*

Source: Compiled from energy balances in *TERI Energy Data Directory and Yearbook, 1990* and *1998-9*.

Note: *Incl. 20.2 mt of petroleum products.

period (1961-6) to nearly 27 per cent in the Eighth Five-Year Plan period which ended in March 1997. Of this, a major part of the allocation has been made towards power generation which still accounts for nearly 70 per cent of the total energy sector outlay.

As a result of the investments in the electricity sector, power generation capacity increased from about 10,000 MW in 1966 to a provisional estimate of 92,000 MW in 1994-5, an average annual rate of growth of 8.2 per cent. A large part of the capacity addition in the utilities has been in the form of thermal power as the gestation periods of thermal plants are significantly lower than that of hydro power plants. The share of thermal capacity in total utility capacity has gone up from about 50 per cent to nearly 70 per cent in 1994-5. On the consumption side, the share of agriculture and domestic sectors has increased significantly from about 8 per cent in 1966 to nearly 30 per cent in 1994-5 in the case of the former and from 9 per cent to 18 per cent in the case of the latter.

Coal production has increased at an annual growth rate of about 5.2 per cent over the last two decades increasing from a level of about 65 million tons in 1966 to 273 million tons in 1994-5. This magnitude of increase was possible largely due to a shift from underground mining of coal to the system of opencast mining—with the latter increasing its share from 20 per cent of overall coal production in 1966 to a little over 70 per cent in 1994-5. A major part of the coal consumption in the country is for electricity generation purposes. The share of the power sector in total coal consumption has increased from 18.5 per cent in 1970-1 to 60 per cent in 1994-5. However, at the same time as capacity additions, transmission and distribution losses have also increased substantially.

In the case of the hydrocarbons sector, India increased its hydrocarbon production after the discovery of the western offshore oilfields in 1976. However, due to the shortages that had been experienced in other energy sectors, the demand for hydrocarbons—petroleum products in particular—has increased substantially. The demand for middle distillates grew the fastest in the seventies and the eighties. Demand growth has been particularly high for gas oil (diesel) and for kerosene.

While India has an abundant supply of renewable energy it has not been able to exploit this energy efficiently. Biomass energy even today contributes to about 30 per cent of total energy consumed in the country. The Ministry of Non-conventional Energy Sources

TABLE 3: RENEWABLE ENERGY POTENTIAL IN INDIA

Sources/Technologies	*Approx. Potential/Availability (MW)*
Biomass	17,000
Small hydro	10,000
Wind energy	20,000
Ocean thermal	50,000
Sea wave power	20,000
Tidal power	9,000

Source: MNES, 1995-6.

(MNES) initiated a national programme on improved *chulhas* (stoves) in 1984-5 and sponsored the development of cookstoves with thermal efficiencies of between 20 per cent and 25 per cent (MNES, 1995-6). Unfortunately due to a host of problems relating to largely implementation and management, it has been estimated that this intervention has resulted in a saving of fuelwood of a mere 5 per cent (TERI estimates).

India also has an enormous renewable energy potential in the non-traditional areas (Table 3). If one combines with this the potential for bagasse based cogeneration of about 5,000 MW, renewable energy compares very well with the utility generating capacity of 81,164 MW in 1994-5 (Dadhich, 1996). However, this sector has received less than 1 per cent of the plan allocations for energy till the Seventh Plan and just a little more than that in the Eighth Plan and serious energy shortages continue.

These energy shortages combined with the increasing environmental pressures make renewable energy a very attractive option. There is thus an urgent need to improve the environment for an accelerated deployment of renewable energy.

EMERGING ENERGY SCENARIOS

A number of studies have been undertaken to estimate the energy demand in the country over the coming 15-20 years. The demand focus for conventional energy forms needs to be seen in the context of current energy situation wherein significant electricity shortages already exist in the country (Table 4).

It has been projected that electricity demand would grow at approximate 6.6 per cent per annum over the period 1997 up to the year 2012. Table 5 provides estimates of electricity demand in this

TABLE 4: ALL INDIA ENERGY AND PEAK POWER SHORTAGES

	1992-3	1996-7
Energy shortage (per cent)	8.3	11.4
Peak power shortage (per cent)	20.5	18.0

Source: *Fourth National Power Plan, 1997-2012*, CEA.

time period. These additions to the capacity need to be seen in the context of the fact that in the Eighth Plan period (1992-7) capacity additions that took place were a mere 3,500 MW per annum.

Nearly 70 per cent of electricity capacity in the country is based on coal resources. The high hydro scenario of the CEA expects the share of thermal electricity, even in 2011-12, to be in the range of 60-65 per cent. Indian coal is low in sulphur content but has a very high ash content varying between 30-40 per cent by weight. Thus, quite apart from the physical problems associated with the mining and transportation of coal is the huge problem of disposal of fly ash. Imported coal is likely to have a much higher sulphur content and would give rise to concerns relating to the acid rain phenomenon.

The working group on Coal for the ninth plan constituted by the Ministry of Coal, has assessed the coal demand to reach 835 mt in 2011-12. The anticipated level of production is significantly lower than the demand estimates (Table 6).

In the case of oil and gas, as brought out by Figure 1, the oil import dependence has been increasing in the last several years and it is expected that this will possibly continue. Oil demand is expected to increase to 155 million tons by the year 2006-7 whereas the current estimates place crude oil production in the range of 44 million tons (Table 7). Natural gas production is also fully committed uptil the year 2001-2 (Table 8). Several efforts are under way to explore the possibility of importing natural gas either in the form of liquified natural gas or as pipe natural gas both from the east coast as well as from the west coast of India.

TABLE 5: PLAN-WISE PROJECTIONS OF CAPACITY ADDITION

	Capacity Additions
1997-2002 (9th Plan)	49,530 - 52,820 MW
2002-7 (10th Plan)	45,682 - 45,730 MW
2007-12 (11th Plan)	55,593 - 57,572 MW

TABLE 6: COAL: PROJECTED DEMAND-SUPPLY STATUS

(in million tons)

	Level of Production	*Demand*
1996-7	289	332.7
2001-2	346	405
2006-7	473	653
2011-12	572	835

Source: Ministry of Coal, 1995.

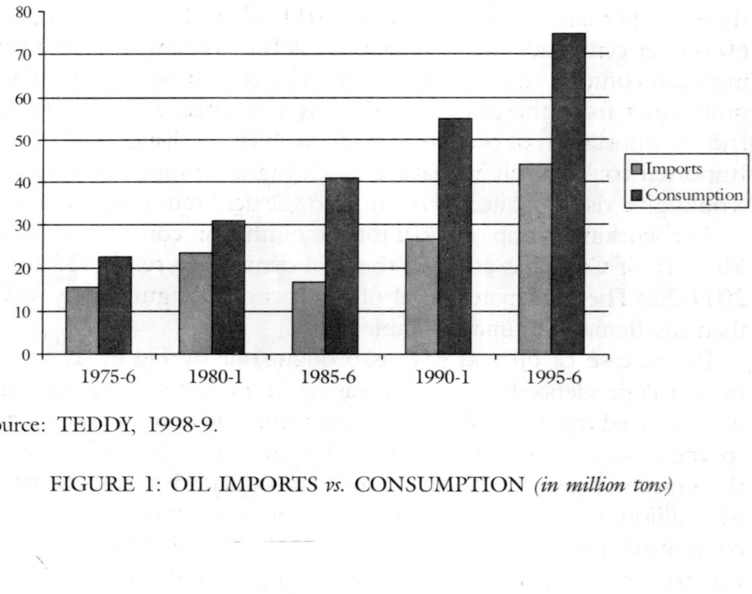

Source: TEDDY, 1998-9.

FIGURE 1: OIL IMPORTS *vs.* CONSUMPTION *(in million tons)*

TABLE 7: OIL OUTLOOK *(in million metric tons)*

	Oil Demand	*Refinery Capacity*	*Crude Production*
2001-2	112.8 (103)	(115.55)	44
2006-7	155.3 144.4	179.35 (161.45)	

Source: S.N. Mathur, CMD, IBP: Presentation on *Downstream petroleum industry: Past growth and future outlook*, at IOGC, December 1998.

TABLE 8: NATURAL GAS: PROJECTED DEMAND-SUPPLY STATUS
(in million cubic metres per day)

	Production	*Allocations*
1997-8	56.34	76.64
1998-9	58.22	79.90
1999-2000	58.39	82.68
2000-1	59.87	82.68
2001-2	64.10	82.68

Source: Draft Report of IX Plan.

CONSTRAINTS IN MEETING LONG-TERM ENERGY DEMAND

One of the major constraints in being able to meet the demand for energy in the future, both from a quantitative as well as a qualitative point of view, is the availability of investment resources. Using a thumb rule for investment requirements at US $1 million per MW, the investment requirement for power generation capacity additions alone works out to, on an average, a little over US $10 billion per year. Corresponding demand for transmission and distribution investments would take this requirement up to approximately US $16-17 billion per year. As against this, the Ministry of Power has provided for a plan outlay of US $2.5 billion for the year 1998-9. Obviously the gap between what is needed and what has been provided for is enormous and it needs to be questioned whether the private sector would be in a position to bridge this gap. Since the initiation of the reform process in 1991, several private investors have expressed an interest in setting up power plants in the country. However, against an initial interest amounting to a 1,00,000 MW of power, only 62,000 MW worth of projects are still alive of which a mere 15,000 MW are likely to be added by the year 2000.

In addition, another factor that needs to be kept in mind is the availability of fuels for power generation purposes. As mentioned earlier, coal is expected to contribute to nearly 65 per cent of the power generation in the country in 2011-12. The mega power policy recently announced by the government of India would further encourage the establishment of coal based power plants. It is unlikely that India will be able to produce the quantities of coal required for fuelling the power capacities envisaged. Import levels of coal are thus likely to increase substantially in the years to come.

Another major constraint that then emerges is that of port capacity.

The current total capacity of major ports is estimated to be 215 million tons and on the basis of the projected traffic, the requirements of port capacity is expected to increase to 315 million tons in 2000-1 and 540 million tons in 2006 (Government of India, 1997). Of the existing capacity nearly 56 per cent is already being utilized for the import of petroleum oil, lubricants and coal. Obviously, increases in the imports of these energy products would place a significant pressure on ports capacity.

Quite apart from the investment and import challenges, the challenges of internal movement of energy are also great. In the case of the power sector the transmission and distribution losses are officially reported to be in the range of 22-23 per cent. However, experience with those states that are going in for reforms reveals these losses, which include both technical and commercial losses, to be in the range of 40-50 per cent. The massive increases in generation capacity that are being envisaged would require the transmission and distribution network to be strengthened on various points so as to effectively move the power produced.

In the case of both coal and oil transport, there are already serious bottlenecks being faced by the railways in fulfilling their dual role as a commercial undertaking for freight movement and a public utility service for passenger movement. The railways have suffered significant revenue losses on account of subsidized passenger movement. In turn this has restricted the railways' ability to augment its capacity and improve services. Additionally, the budgetary support to this sector has also declined from 75 per cent of the Railways Plan in the Fifth Plan to 23 per cent in the Eighth Five Year Plan. As such, Indian Railways is also looking at innovative ways of attracting resources and has resorted to schemes like 'build-own-lease-transfer' and 'own your wagon' besides undertaking marketing of bonds.

INITIATIVES AND THREATS FOR MEETING ENERGY REQUIREMENTS

The Government of India, since 1991, has launched a major reform programme covering several sectors of the economy. This reform exercise was driven largely through: (i) a recognition of the existing and looming capacity and energy shortages; (ii) of the limitation of providing financial assistance to the infrastructure sectors through the budgetary process; (iii) the poor financial health of the concerned entities in particular the state electricity boards and the coal companies; and (iv) their consequent inability to generate internal resources for investment purposes. Unfortunately, the reform programmes in the energy sub sectors have not moved forward in a coordinated manner. As such, whereas the electricity sector has moved forward substantially in the last eight years, an exercise to define the restructuring required for the coal industry is just taking off. In the case of oil and gas sector, whereas the 'R' group (Strategic Planning Group on restructuring the oil sector) submitted its report in 1996, the reform is lagging behind the phased programme recommendation of this group. This clearly reveals the fact that whereas some attention has been given to the need for restructuring the energy sector so as to make it more attractive for private participation, however not all the linkages and influencing factors have been thought through. This lack of a clear goal oriented approach is apparent if one tracks the various policy developments that have taken place in the electricity sector. Box 1 provides highlights of some of these developments which are clearly quick reactions to immediate pressures.

Having said that, the incentives provided by India's Finance Minister in the presentation of the Union Budget for 1999-2000 should provide an impetus to transmission and distribution projects. The Finance Minister's recognition of the need to vertically disintegrate electricity supply services and the consequent provision of infrastructure status to transmission and distribution activities is a welcome step that will facilitate the restructuring efforts of various state electricity boards (SEBs). Transmission and distribution companies will now enjoy a five year tax holiday and a reduction of 25 per cent (30 per cent in case of companies) of profits in the subsequent five years.

BOX 1: POLICY DEVELOPMENTS IN THE POWER SECTOR

Since the start of the reform process in 1991, several policy pronouncements have been made by the government of India. Apart from providing counter-guarantees to the seven fast-track power projects, the GoI has been constantly reviewing progress in this sector and has, more recently, announced the following new initiatives:

- Counter guarantee to the pending fast track projects.
- Setting of CERC and SERC through enactment of the Electricity Regulatory Commission Act, July 1998.
- Revised policy guidelines for liquid fuel based power projects, July 1998.
- Hydro power development policy, August 1998.
- Revised mega power policy guidelines, November 1998.

In line with the policy announced by the Ministry of Power, mega power projects have been exempt from the nominal basic customs duty of 5 per cent applicable to other power generation activities.

A concession of 1 per cent on loans provided by the Power Finance Corporation to those states establishing regulatory commissions before 31 March 1999 prompted several states to meet the deadline. However, a number of state governments have opted to set up the state electricity regulatory commissions (SERCs) under the provisions (Section 17) of the Electricity Regulatory Commission Act 1998 which is a central government Act and therefore contains several loopholes. Given that electricity is a concurrent subject, it is desirable that SERCs should be set up through comprehensive state legislation. The current route adopted would give little powers to the SERCs' to meet the large challenges ahead.

Another major threat to the ongoing reform trend is the need for establishing capacities in the various infrastructure sectors urgently. This would undoubtedly compromise the optimal path that the country could have followed if it was not faced with such urgent new capacity needs. This would also have implications on the extent to which India is able to develop and exploit its own internal energy resources as against the extent to which it is tying itself to a path of higher import dependence. The sustainability of the latter path is highly questionable.

In sum, despite some of the initiatives the government has taken in recent time the country faces an uphill task in overcoming the existing and emerging infrastructure bottlenecks. It urgently needs to have a long-term vision for economic development as well as integrated energy and infrastructure policies.

REFERENCES

British Petroleum (1997), *British Petroleum (BP) Statistical Review of World Energy.*

Central Electricity Authority, *Fourth National Power Plan, 1997-2012.*

Confederation of Indian Industry (1998), Background paper: Debate on mega power projects—concept to reality, 16 December 1998.

Dadhich, P.K. (1996), Cogeneration: Policies, Potential and Technologies, p. 296.

Government of India (1997), Investment opportunities in infrastructure, p. 113.

——— (1997), *Economic Survey*, 1996-7.

——— (1997), Sub Group on Natural Gas—Ninth Five Year Plan, Draft Report of IX Plan.

Mathur, S.N. (1997), *Downstream petroleum industry: Past growth and future outlook*, IOGC, December 1998.

MNES (1996), *Annual Report 1995-6*, New Delhi: Ministry of Non-conventional Energy Sources.

McC (1995), *Annual Report 1995*, New Delhi: Ministry of Coal.

TERI (1990), *TERI Energy Data Directory and Yearbook, 1990*, Tata Energy Research Institute, New Delhi.

TERI (1998), *TERI Energy Data Directory and Yearbook, 1998-9*, Tata Energy Research Institute, New Delhi.

Long-term Carbon Emissions, Fossil Fuel Substitution and Greenhouse Gas Mitigation Strategies for India

SUJATA GUPTA

INTRODUCTION

Concentrations of greenhouse gases in the atmosphere are increasing steadily. This has led to an evaluation of energy scenarios for different regions and countries with a focus on strategies for reducing greenhouse gas emissions. Greenhouse gas (GHG) inventories for India indicate that the energy sector contributes 58 per cent of the three main GHGs (namely, carbon dioxide, methane, and nitrous oxide) (Figure 1). Of the emissions from the energy sector, carbon dioxide accounts for 90 per cent of the emissions. This paper addresses emissions of carbon dioxide from the energy sector and examines mitigation strategies for the same.

The main driving forces which determine energy demand are population, GDP and its sectoral composition and technology. Efficiency improvements and technological advancements will work

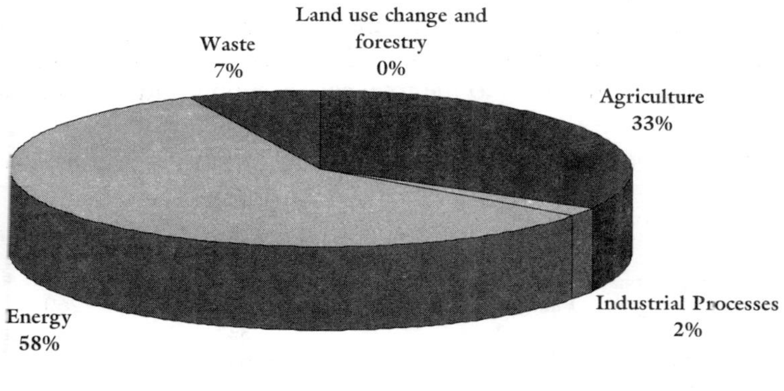

FIGURE 1: GHG INVENTORY BY SECTOR
(1990 CO_2 equivalent = 983.3 Tg)

towards decoupling growth rates for energy demand and economic development. If the share of non-carbon or low carbon fuels in the energy mix increases over time, then the growth in CO_2 emissions will be less than the growth in energy, and vice versa. This study projects an energy demand scenario for the Indian economy till the year 2050 using an energy sector dynamic optimization model.

The next section discusses the main features of the Indian economy relevant for projecting energy demand scenarios (energy resource endowment, per capita energy consumption). The third section discusses the model and the assumptions regarding the driving forces for energy demand. Section four presents energy demands and carbon emissions under different scenarios. The final section analyses the results and their implications.

ENERGY SCENARIO

An evaluation of energy reserves in India shows that coal is the most abundant source of energy (Table 1). The reserves-to-production ratio, which indicates the time over which proven reserves could be used at current extraction rates, is 260 years for coal, whereas it is 23 years for oil and 34 years for gas (Tata Energy Research Institute, 1997).

Primary energy can be classified as commercial energy and traditional energy. The term commercial energy is used for energy forms that are bought and sold, i.e. coal, oil, natural gas, hydro-electricity and nuclear power. Traditional energy sources are fuel wood, animal waste and crop or agricultural waste which are mostly non-traded forms of energy that are by-products of agricultural and allied activities. In India, traditional sources of primary energy are significant contributors to the total energy supply and are estimated

TABLE 1: PROVEN RESERVES OF PRIMARY ENERGY SOURCES, 1997

Energy	*Unit*	*Proven Reserves in India*	*Reserves to Production Ratio (years)*
Coal	Billion metric tons	72	260
Oil	Million tons	732	23
Natural gas	Billion cubic metres	660	34
Hydropower	Mega Watts	94,000	Renewable

to currently account for 40 to 55 per cent of total primary energy consumption (for example, Hall, 1991 and Government of India, 1991). Although traditional energy sources are important, data on their use are difficult to compile. Therefore, most energy analysis relates to commercial energy only.

Between 1985 and 1995, commercial energy consumption has increased at an average rate of 5.8 per cent per year (British Petroleum, 1996). Coal accounts for more than 55 per cent of commercial energy consumption. The share of natural gas has increased and that of oil has fluctuated around 30 per cent and seems to decline from 1989 onwards. The share of non-fossil commercial energy, that is hydro and nuclear power, is declining (TERI, 1997). Energy intensity in 1995 for India, the USA and Switzerland, in kilogramme of oil equivalent (kgoe) per US $1,000 of GNP while GNP in purchasing power parity terms are shown in Figure 2. It is important to note that India has an energy intensity lower than that of the USA in purchasing power parity terms.

Per capita commercial energy consumption was 248 kgoe for India and global average was 1433 kgoe in 1994 (World Bank, 1997). The average per capita income for India was US $340 in 1995 compared with the world average of US $4,880 (World Bank, 1997). The current levels of energy consumption and per capita

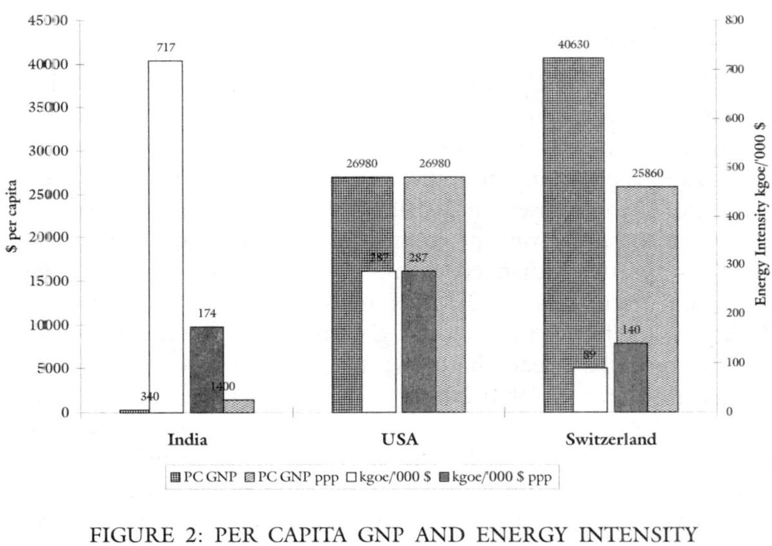

FIGURE 2: PER CAPITA GNP AND ENERGY INTENSITY

income in India are very low and with increases in per capita incomes it is expected that per capita energy consumption will increase. Beyond a certain level of per capita income, production techniques become efficient, but changes in lifestyle dominate the growth in commercial energy demand.

In future, commercial energy consumption is expected to increase due to the following reasons. Firstly, increasing per capita incomes will induce a switch on the fuel ladder where biomass and other traditional fuels (solid fuels) are replaced by commercial fuels (liquid and gaseous fuels) given the convenience of using these fuels. This shift is supported by higher per capita incomes improving the affordability of these fuels. Secondly, availability of non-commercial energy has reached a level of saturation, whereas energy demand continues to increase with an increase in population. Thirdly, increasing level of urbanization and incomes will change the composition and demand of fuels consumed due to the differences in the energy end-uses patterns in urban areas and due to a change in lifestyles. Data on ownership of energy consuming devices also support the increasing trend in energy use (Rao, 1994). Data collected by Rao also shows that the ownership of these devices is much higher in the urban households, thus indicating an increase in energy demand with an increase in the level of urbanization.

METHODOLOGY

Population and GDP growth are the major driving forces which determine energy demands in the economy. There are a number of estimates made by various government bodies and research organizations providing indications of energy demands for the short-term and in some cases till 2010. However, there do not exist any long-term comprehensive projections on end-use demands or energy demands for the Indian economy. In the absence of reliable and consistent estimates, TERI has made in-house projections to determine the trends in economic growth across various sectors and to determine the urban share in total population for India over a 60 year time frame (1990-2050).

The Indian economy has grown at a rate of over 5 per cent in the period 1990 to 1995. The process of liberalization will accelerate economic growth and it is expected that over the next decade or so the economy will grow at 7 per cent per annum. Population growth over the decade 1980 to 1990 was over 2 per cent, and has fallen below 2 per cent from 1990 to 1994 (Government of India, 1996). The rate of growth of population is expected to decline, however, given the large base over which this growth will take place, India would be the country with the largest population by the year 2040 (Bos et al., 1994) (Table 2).

GROWTH OF GDP

In this study, GDP has been disaggregated into four sectors—agriculture, industry, transport and other services and the growth for each sector is determined separately. For the industrial sector, growth of major energy intensive industries has been projected. Transport has been segregated from the traditional services sector; to examine the transport requirements in detail and to determine the impact of this energy intensive sector separately. (Details of the projections are available in Gupta and Girisha (1997).)

Sectoral value added contributions are projected and then aggregated to give total GDP. This is a point of departure from most other long-term forecasts, where GDP growth is predicted as a starting point and then sectoral contributions are determined. Logically, the weighted sectoral growths will determine the overall growth in the economy. Thus, growth rates are projected for the four sectors of the economy which then determine the economy's rate of growth.

The recent phenomenon of restructuring in the Indian economy, renders historical data an inappropriate indicator of future growth. Sectoral projections were made by expert groups for the year 2005 (*Infrastructure Committee Report*, 1996). These are used as the basis for determining growth rates beyond 2005. In all sectors, with the exception of agriculture, a gradual decline in the growth rates has been assumed after 2010.

In the case of agriculture, examination of the production data reveals that more than 50 per cent of the gross cropped area (GCA) is under five major crops (paddy, wheat, maize, pulses and sugar cane) which account for more than 80 per cent of the production. These five major crops are used as indicators of agricultural production as it is very difficult to compute growth rates for all the crops grown in highly heterogeneous and complex farming systems practiced in India.

Every plant species has an upper limit to biomass production and in this study one has equated this potential yield level to the highest yield values recorded anywhere in the world for a particular crop. This difference in the yield levels can be attributed to lower levels of fertilizer application, inefficient use of fertilizer, scarcity of and inefficient exploitation of water resources, lack of awareness about the use of farm machinery and implements, socio-economic constraints including poor purchasing capacity of farmers. The task of reducing this gap, though a difficult one, is not beyond the realms of feasibility. Enough work has been done to rectify these defects and various technologies have been evolved to improve the efficiency of inputs used in agriculture. It is assumed that in future these limitations would be eliminated through implementation of these technologies and yield levels will reach the potential levels. One has used the logistic function[1] to estimate the future yield levels for different crops. For any given time, production of a crop is the product of the average yield and the area under that crop. Land use statistics show that net area under cultivation has remained constant since 1970 indicating that the potential for expansion of crop lands is limited by other competing demands for land and many other factors including environmental costs and the cost of developing infrastructure in the remote areas. The Eighth Five Year Plan makes projections for the GCA till the year 2006-7. Based on these and past data, a rate of increase in the GCA is applied to determine the same in future. Again, there is a limit for the area which can be cultivated. In this study one has assumed that the limit for gross area under cultivation is twice the present net cultivated area. The problem of land degradation is increasingly becoming apparent and one assumes that this effect will be offset by reclamation of degraded land and the increased cropping intensity in healthy soils. Growth in output depends largely on the yields and on gross cropped area and is given by the following equation:

$$Output = Yield * Gross\ Cropped\ Area$$

The five crops studied here are the staple food and one assumes that these will continue to be the major crops. Since agricultural output accounts for 99 per cent of the primary sector output, agricultural production rates are assumed to be representative of growth in the primary sector. Growth in agricultural sector is 2.2 per cent over the period 1990-2050 which is higher than that of total population (1.1 per cent), therefore, the per capita availability of agricultural production will increase in future.

The growth rates for the four sectors, GDP, total population (Bos et al., 1994) and urban population are also shown in Table 2.

POPULATION

Total population, growth rates predicted by the World Bank have been used (Bos et al., 1994). The share of urban population was estimated using a logistic function and the maximum level of urbanization was set at 80 per cent. In addition to the data on past level of urbanization, projections for 2000, 2006 and 2010 made by the Standing Committee of Experts on Population Projections were included when projecting the share of urban population.

Per capita incomes in the country are expected to increase as a consequence of the rapid economic growth and the decline in population growth rates. Higher per capita incomes and the present low levels of energy consumption per capita will result in an increase in consumption levels in future. Efficiency improvements and technological advancements will work towards decoupling growth rates for energy demand and economic development.

MODEL

The MARKAL (MARket ALlocation) model, an energy sector dynamic optimization model incorporating supply, refining and conversion, distribution and consumption of energy is used. The

TABLE 2: POPULATION, GDP AND SECTORAL GROWTH RATES

(in per cent)

	Agriculture	*Industry*	*Transport*	*Services*	*GDP*	*Total Population*	*Urban Population*
1990-4	2.9	5.0	6.2	5.8	4.4	–	–
1995-2000	3.3	8.9	7.3	7.5	6.8	1.8	3.7
2000-10	2.7	8.9	7.3	7.5	6.8	1.4	2.7
2010-20	2.4	8.3	6.8	6.8	7.0	1.1	2.3
2020-30	2.0	7.0	6.5	6.5	6.3	0.9	2.0
2030-40	1.6	5.3	5.5	5.5	5.2	0.64	1.6
2040-50	1.2	4.5	5.0	5.0	4.6	0.6	1.5
1990-2050	2.2	6.9	6.3	6.3	6.0	1.1	2.4

model identifies the different energy end-uses and allows for technology/fuel mix substitution to meet the end-use demands. The objective function of the model is to minimize the cost of energy supply and use in the economy. This necessitates that all options, for the supply side as well as the demand side, are examined in an integrated dynamic framework.

The MARKAL model traces the flow of energy right from the extraction stages, through the conversion stages to the consumption stage. The demand for energy services, together with the efficiency of the device providing the energy service, determine the energy consumed by a particular sector. Supply of a fuel/energy source to a particular sector would in turn depend on the availability of a particular source of fuel/energy source and on competing demands by other sectors. Availability would depend on domestic extraction, imports/exports, conversion losses and the transmission and distribution losses in the transportation of energy to the end-users. A reference energy system (RES) tracks the flow of energy, its conversion, distribution and final use. A hypothetical RES is shown in Figure 3 illustrating the various stages of the energy chain.

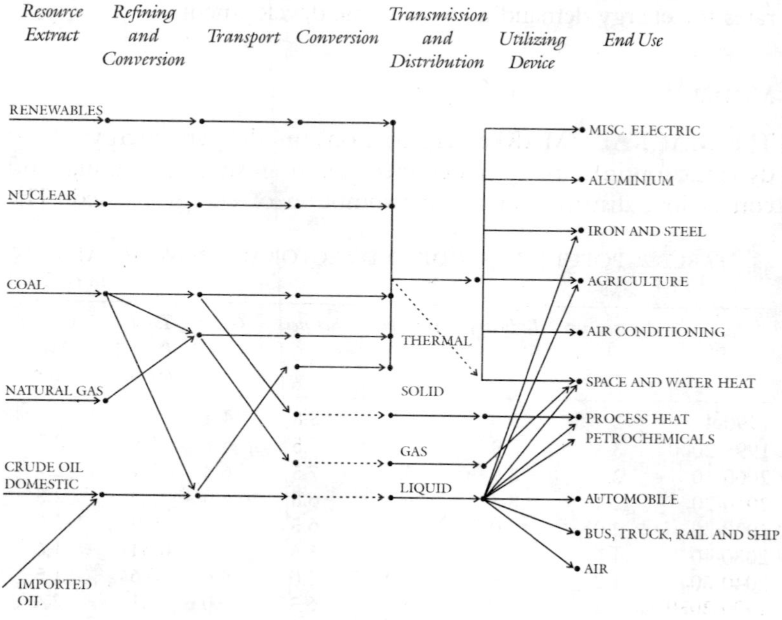

FIGURE 3: REFERENCE ENERGY SYSTEM

Sectoral outputs in the economy determine the demand for energy services which can be met by a range of devices. Their efficiency determine the energy requirement. A specific energy service can be provided by a number of demand devices, for example, cooking energy demand can be met by an LPG stove, a kerosene wick stove, a kerosene pressure stove, a traditional biomass based stove. Additional constraints are imposed in the system to reflect the availability of these fuel/device combinations. For example, a representative high income category urban household in India will not use a traditional biomass-based stove.

MARKAL solutions include details on the mix of primary energy fuels and technologies along with their investment and operating costs. Another benefit of using such an optimization framework is that the marginal costs of technologies, fuels and environmental constraints are available and therefore are able to provide a measure of the (un)desirability of a model component. The model can therefore provide a merit ranking or the relative attractiveness of each supply option and technology considered.

The model also produces solutions that provide guidelines for policy-makers for the development of the energy system to achieve their goals at least cost. It is therefore very useful in addressing the development of greenhouse gas and other emission inventories and in providing a merit ranking of technologies to help guide the setting of priorities for technology R&D.

The model determines the least cost options to meet a given level of useful energy demand. The energy costs as well as the costs of utilizing that energy are accounted for in arriving at the fuel technology choice. The model calculates the emissions of carbon dioxide associated with the least cost mix of energy. As one of the objectives of this study is to determine carbon emissions, imposing a constraint on the total level of carbon emissions in the model, gives the energy mix stricter or controlled conditions for the same. The difference in the system least costs for this carbon constrained scenario and the unconstrained scenario reflects the additional cost of abating carbon for the energy sector.

LIMITATIONS

One of the weaknesses of a system's model is that in its standard form it assumes a perfect market (including perfect knowledge) and common investment criteria and behaviour across all parts of the energy sector. Models tend to overestimate the rate and level of take up of energy efficiency options. These problems can, however, be reduced by constraining the model to limit the rate of penetration of energy efficiency options. For example, it is possible to constrain the rate of penetration of efficient refrigerators or improved cookstoves in the model based on non-economic considerations of the user group. The modelling approach also requires detailed projections of primary energy prices and energy demands in addition to technology data. Further, a modelling approach can involve only a limited analysis of market barriers and socio-economic factors and therefore does not yield sophisticated estimates of commercial potentials. Even though the model can serve as a very useful tool in analysing greenhouse gas abatement options, etc., it is important to bear in mind that results from any modelling exercise are directional only. These can at best provide indications of which technologies are more suitable than others, but cannot provide strictly quantitative judgments. There are a number of economic as well as external factors such as institutional barriers which are not completely captured during the modelling process. Therefore, it is important that the feasibility of implementation of any technological option be considered also in the light of such other restrictions and barriers.

The Indian MARKAL model has been set up for a 60 year time frame. With 1990 as the base year, the model extends till 2050 with 7 time periods of 10 years each. Demands in the Indian energy system have been considered across the 5 major end-use sectors which are residential, commercial, industrial, transport and agricultural sectors.

BASELINE

The most likely scenario identified has been the *baseline scenario.* Technological options considered in this scenario include those which are likely to be included in the normal course of economic growth and were/are not necessarily available in the past or currently. This scenario includes the autonomous energy efficiency improvements which are likely. Examples of new technologies (which do not exist today) that are included in the baseline are: efficient tractors, high efficiency refrigerators, efficient fans and air-conditioners, super critical boilers, etc. The baseline scenario is used as the basis for comparing other scenarios. In all scenarios, assumptions regarding the driving

TABLE 3: SCENARIO ASSUMPTIONS

	Base Year 1990	*2020*	*2050*
Population (million)	839	1,323	1,753
Urban population (%)	25.1	38.9	52.0
GDP (1980-1 billion Rs.)	2094	14,158	67,783
Agriculture GDP (%)	31.3	10.5	3.5
Industrial GDP (%)	28.7	45.1	48.0
Services GDP (%)	40.0	44.4	48.5
Per capita GNP (in 1990 US $)	350	1,500	5,422
Indigenous availability of fuels (million tons)			
Firewood	187	112	86
Crop residue	52	52	52
Dung (dry)	100	100	100
Coal	226	549	1,332
Oil	33	50	50

forces, that is, the GDP rate of growth, population growth, income class distribution and end-use demands are constant (Table 3). Average annual GDP growth is 6.6 per cent in 1990-2020, and 5.4 per cent in 2020-50. The economy grows at an average annual rate of 6 per cent over the period 1990-2050.

In the baseline a discount rate of 6 per cent has been used. Currently, real interest rates in the domestic market vary from 9 per cent to 15 per cent. It is likely that with complete capital convertibility, domestic interest rates will move towards international rates. The LIBOR is currently about 5.5-5.8 per cent and the perceived country risk for India varies between 0.4 per cent to 3 per cent (personal communications with local ADB office) LIBOR plus the minimum perceived country risk gives an indication of the minimum discount rate likely. A discount rate of 6 per cent has been used to represent the discount rate likely in the future.

RESULTS

The overall annual growth in centralized power generation capacity is 4.1 per cent in the first half of time period under consideration, that is, 1990 to 2020. Generating capacity is 70 GW in 1990. Projects planned and under implementation determine the upper bound on the power sector in terms of additional capacity for the year 2000. Beyond 2000 the system has fewer constraints and can

TABLE 4: CENTRALIZED ELECTRICITY CAPACITY—BASELINE SCENARIO (*GW*)

	1990	*2020*	*2050*	*1990-2050 Growth (%)*
Coal	43.0	55.9	51.7	0.3
Gas	2.6	164.7	642.7	9.6
Hydro and other renewables	23.0	37.0	80.0	2.1
Nuclear	1.6	2.0	–	–
Total	70.0	259.5	774.5	4.1

Note: Excludes captive capacity of industries.

use other (less expensive) types of capacity depending on the demand for electricity. By 2020 the total system capacity will be 259.5 GW with an annual growth rate of 4.5 per cent. In addition to this capacity, certain large industries have captive generation capacity to meet their electricity requirements. In the second half of the time period (2020-50), growth in generating capacity is lower at only 3.7 per cent, on account of a relatively slower rate of economic growth and the use of more efficient devices. The highest growth takes place in gas-based generating capacity in the combined cycle plants.

Generation for the first half and second half of the sixty years period grows at 6.4 per cent and 3.9 per cent respectively. The annual growth for the period 1990-2050 is 5.1 per cent. With the economy growing at 6 per cent this gives an electricity-GDP elasticity of 0.85.

The growth in generating capacity is much less than the historical trend. For 1980-90, growth averaged at 8 per cent. This can be explained by the optimization model (which may to an extent underestimate real demand), and over time there is an improvement in the average plant availability factor, the transmission and distribution efficiency and the efficiency of electricity using devices. The annual growth rate for electricity generation is higher than that of capacity as the improved availability of plants in future doesn't influence the rate of growth of generation.

Power generation in the baseline is dominated by coal till 2000, but its share declines considerably after 2000. From 55 per cent in 1990 the share of coal-based generation declines to 25 per cent in 2020 and to less than 10 per cent in 2050. The share of gas-based generation increases and in 2020 accounts for almost two-thirds of the total generation.

TABLE 5: ELECTRICITY GENERATION (*TWh*)—BASELINE

Type of Generation	*1990*	*2020*	*2050*
Coal	126.9	373.9	362.3
Gas	16.5	956.7	3,992.6
Hydro and other renewables	84.1	186.5	403.2
Nuclear	6.6	9.3	–
Total	234.1	1,526.5	4,758.1

PRIMARY ENERGY SUPPLY

Primary commercial energy supply in the economy increases from 6,834 PJ in 1990 to 35,238 PJ in 2020 and 98,822 PJ in 2050 (Table 6). The annual rate of growth decreases over time from 5.6 per cent for 1990-2020 to 3.5 per cent for 2020-50. Coal is the main energy source in 1990 but by 2050 oil dominates. The growth in oil demand outpaces domestic production, resulting in a higher percentage being met by imports. Indigenous reserves of gas are limited and in 2020, 6,415 PJ of natural gas will be imported, which is approximately 87 per cent of the gas used in the Indian economy in that year. By 2050, 26,609 PJ of gas will have to be imported (which is 95 per cent of the gas demand).

TABLE 6: PRIMARY ENERGY SUPPLY—BASELINE SCENARIO (*PJ*)

	1990	*2020*	*2050*
Coal	3,646	14,888	33,982
Indigenous	3,646	14,888	23,627
Imports	–	–	10,355
Oil	2,382	12,279	35,378
Indigenous	1,410	2137	2,137
Imports	972	10,142	33,241
Gas	480	7,365	28,009
Indigenous	480	950	1,400
Imports	–	6,415	26,609
Hydro*	302	672	1,453
Nuclear	24	34	0
Total commercial energy	6,834	35,238	98,822
Crop residue	763	763	763
Fuel wood	3,134	1,877	1,441
Animal waste	1,194	1,378	1,378
Total traditional energy	5,091	4,018	3,582

Note: *Energy in electricity generated.

TABLE 7: CO_2 EMISSIONS IN THE BASELINE (*Tg* CO_2)

	1990	*2020*	*2050*	*Annual Growth Rate 1990-2050 (%)*
Baseline	512	2,576	7,032	4.5
Coal	310	1,266	2,888	3.8
Oil	175	898	2,575	4.6
Gas	27	412	1,569	7.0

TABLE 8: BASELINE RESULTS

	1990	*2020*	*2050*
Commercial energy intensity (kgoe/thousand 1980 rupees)	75.7	58.2	34.1
Per capita commercial energy consumption (toe per capita)	0.19	0.62	1.32
Per capita carbon dioxide emissions (tons of CO_2 per year)	0.17	0.53	1.09
Per capita carbon dioxide emissions (tons of CO_2 per year)	0.61	1.95	4.01

Table 7 gives the CO_2 emissions for the baseline. Table 8 provides the energy intensity in the economy, the per capita energy consumption and the per capita CO_2 emissions. The data indicates that the carbon intensity of energy in the economy is decreasing.

SECTORAL ENERGY CONSUMPTION

Total final energy is defined as the energy consumed by the end-use sectors and includes electricity (both primary and secondary) and traditional energy sources (like fuel wood and crop residue). The share of traditional sources of energy declines over time, from 43 per cent in 1990 it reduces to 10 per cent in 2020 and is only 3.5 per cent in 2050 (Table 6).

Table 9 gives the sector-wise consumption of final energy. In 1990, the residential sector was the largest consumer of total final energy. The industrial sector accounts for the largest share of the commercial final energy consumption and this share increases over time. Beyond 1990, the share of industrial sector is the largest for both total as well as commercial final energy consumption. By 2050, the transport sector consumes the second largest proportion of energy.

There is a reduction in commercial energy intensities in all sectors over time (Table 10). In agriculture there is a marginal increase in

TABLE 9: SECTOR-WISE ENERGY CONSUMPTION—BASELINE SCENARIO (*PJ*)

	1990	*2020*	*2050*
Agriculture			
Diesel	224	231	194
Electricity	142	324	623
Biomass based decentralized electricity	–	39	166
Total	366	594	983
Industry			
Electricity	291	2,650	10,102
Coal	2,012	10,835	30,259
Natural gas	235	1,365	4,415
Oil	565	3,728	12,539
Total	3,103	18,578	57,315
Transport			
ATF	76	270	969
Diesel	638	3,229	7,907
Gasoline	124	870	1,938
Fuel oil	23	70	214
Electricity	10	65	95
Coal	77	–	–
Total	948	4,504	11,123
Services			
Coal	8	–	–
Electricity	90	408	1,437
LPG	22	131	3,818
Kerosene	19	736	803
Wood	701	1,216	581
Total	840	2,491	6,639
Residential sector			
Firewood	2,433	661	860
Electricity	124	1,008	2,060
Kerosene	241	1,199	2,505
LPG	202	250	435
Crop residue	763	584	–
Animal waste	1,193	1,378	1,378
Soft coke	24	–	–
Total	4,980	5,080	7,238

TABLE 10: COMMERCIAL ENERGY INTENSITY

(*TJ/million Rs.*)

Sector	*Base year (1990)*	*2020*	*2050*
Agriculture	0.56	0.40	0.41
Industry	5.10	2.91	1.76
Transport	8.49	5.37	2.54
Other services	1.18	0.46	0.23

energy intensity by 2050. Mechanization and larger share of high yielding varieties result in this increase.

ABATEMENT SCENARIOS FOR THE BASELINE

In these scenarios, baseline emissions of carbon are controlled at different levels. Cumulative carbon emissions over the period 1990 to 2050 are constrained to be lower by 5 per cent, 10 per cent, 15 per cent and 20 per cent. These are referred to as the:

5 per cent abatement scenario
10 per cent abatement scenario
15 per cent abatement scenario
20 per cent abatement scenario

The terms abatement scenario/case, reduction scenario/case and constrained scenario/case are used inter-changeably. In the baseline scenario, total carbon emissions over the period 1990 to 2050 are estimated to be 1,08,552 million tons of carbon (Table 11). In the 5 per cent abatement scenario, a constraint is imposed such that the total carbon emissions are 95 per cent of those in the baseline (that is, 1,03,124 million tons) over the 60 year (1990 to 2050) period. For the 10 per cent, 15 per cent and 20 per cent scenarios, the limit on carbon emissions is placed at 90 per cent, 85 per cent and 80 per cent, respectively.

TABLE 11: CO_2 EMISSIONS—BASELINE AND CARBON CONSTRAINED RUNS (*million tons of CO_2*)

	1990	*2020*	*2050*	*Total 1990-2050*	*Incremental Cost (billion Rs.)*
Baseline	512	2,576	7,032	1,08,552	–
5 per cent constraint on cumulative carbon emissions	512	2,440	6,723	1,03,124	122.2
10 per cent constraint on cumulative carbon emissions	512	2,340	6,239	97,697	871.7
15 per cent constraint on cumulative carbon emissions	512	2,128	6,096	92,269	2532.3
20 per cent constraint on cumulative carbon emissions	485	1,959	5,839	86,842	11649.2

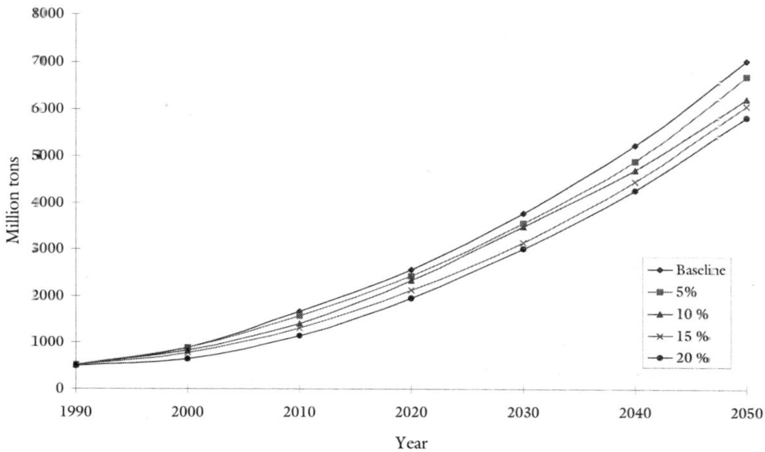

FIGURE 4: CARBON EMISSIONS TRAJECTORY

Table 11 gives the aggregate CO_2 emissions and emissions over time for the baseline and for the different carbon constrained runs. The last column gives the incremental cost for the total energy system for achieving the carbon constraint.

The carbon emissions profiles for these cases are shown in Figure 4. Most of the substantial reductions in each abatement scenario take place in the distant future. This is due to the discounting of costs which makes carbon reductions less expensive in the future. An analysis of the results reveals that carbon dioxide abatement is brought about primarily by fuel switching and to some extent by a shift to more expensive but more efficient technologies.

Table 12 gives the average costs for subsequent reductions of carbon dioxide. As expected additional abatement requirements are achieved at a higher average cost. Figure 5 plots the incremental cost as the level of carbon abatement increases.

TABLE 12: AVERAGE COST OF CARBON ABATEMENT

Cumulative CO_2 percentage Reduction over Baseline	*Cost (\$ per ton of CO_2)*
5 %	1.25
10 %	4.46
15 %	8.64
20 %	29.81

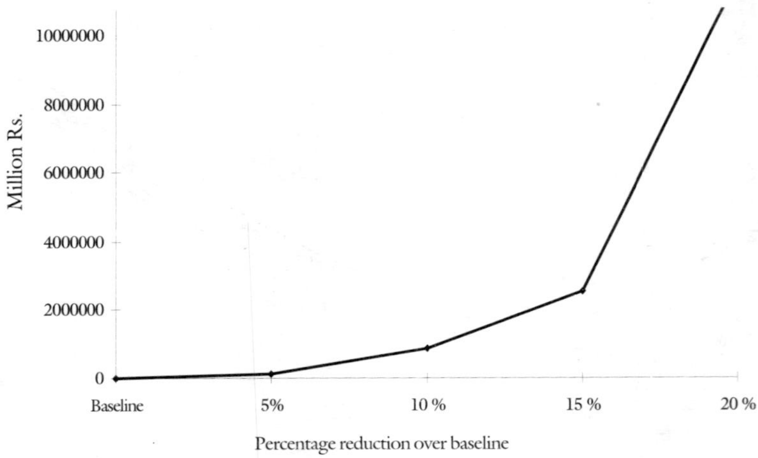

FIGURE 5: INCREMENTAL COST OF EMISSIONS REDUCTION

The costs presented here have to be interpreted with caution. The costs are on the lower side due to a number of factors. The costs are in 1990 prices and would have to be adjusted to arrive at costs in a more recent year prices. This adjustment is complicated by the rapid depreciation and deregulation experienced by the Indian rupee. The costs are in present value terms, arrived at using a discount rate of 6 per cent. Most abatement measures are undertaken during the later years as costs in later periods are discounted and there is more flexibility in choice of abatement options. The other cause for caution is the fact that these costs do not include all costs such as institutional costs, transactional costs, etc. This makes it necessary to review the options selected by the model in more detail with respect to incremental costs. The purpose of the model is to view most options possible for the energy sector in an integrated framework and prioritize these for the economy on the basis of cost minimization. For example, on the basis of an economic analysis, domestic natural gas will be an abatement option for both the transport sector and for power generation, but given the limited availability of natural gas, between the two, gas based power generation may be a better option. The model enables an inter sectoral ranking, on the basis of least cost. There may be other considerations, such as local environmental factors, which indicate a preference for or against a particular option. This necessitates a detailed assessment of each individual option identified by the model.

MITIGATION STRATEGY

One of the main carbon emission mitigation strategies suggested by the model is the substitution of fossil fuels, by renewable and nuclear sources of energy. Total primary energy production over the period 1990 to 2050 in all the scenarios is shown in Figures 6 and 7. Hydro power generation increases as the carbon constraints become more stringent. In the baseline, new nuclear power generating capacity is not indicated. In the carbon constrained scenario additional nuclear based power generation becomes an alternative to reduce carbon emissions. In the 5 per cent case there is significant increase in nuclear generation. There is a marginal increase over the 5 per cent case in the 10 per cent scenario, thereafter, nuclear generation stabilizes as it is constrained by the upper bound of 30,000 MW on nuclear capacity. There is no new renewable (wind and solar) based generation in the baseline, 5, 10 and 15 per cent abatement scenarios. In the 20 per cent scenario, new wind and solar based capacities are added.

In the abatement scenarios, total power generation increases marginally in 2020. In 2050, centralized electricity generation increases for the 5 per cent and the 10 per cent carbon constrained scenarios and then decreases for the 15 per cent and 20 per cent cases. The increase in generation is due to an increase in hydro and nuclear capacities. This extra production of electricity reduces fossil fuel based electricity generation and substitutes fossil energy by renewable electricity in some end-use. For the 15 and 20 per cent cases, as the nuclear and hydro potential is exploited to the full extent available, further reductions in carbon emissions are brought about by reduction in fossil fuel based power generation brought about by selection of high cost and higher efficiency devices.

In all cases, coal based generation decreases as the constraints on carbon emissions become stricter. In the 20 per cent reduction case, coal based capacity exists but is not utilized for generating power. Hydro based generation and nuclear generation increase in all cases (subject to the upper limit). With less stringent carbon constraints (5 per cent and 10 per cent cases) gas based generation declines in 2020, as this is substituted by nuclear and hydro power. In 2050, gas based generation increases with lower carbon constraints (5 per cent and 10 per cent scenarios) and then decreases (15 and 20 per cent scenarios). Within gas based generation the combined cycle generation increases while open cycle generation decreases with higher

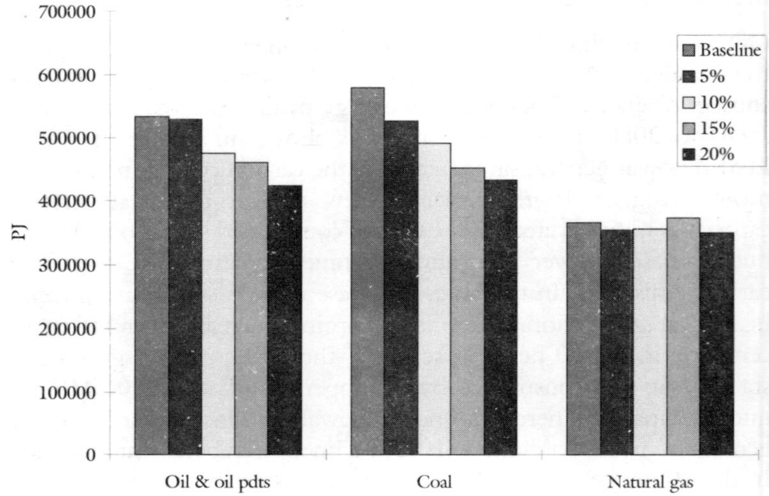

FIGURE 6: PRIMARY FOSSIL ENERGY (PJ) 1990-2050

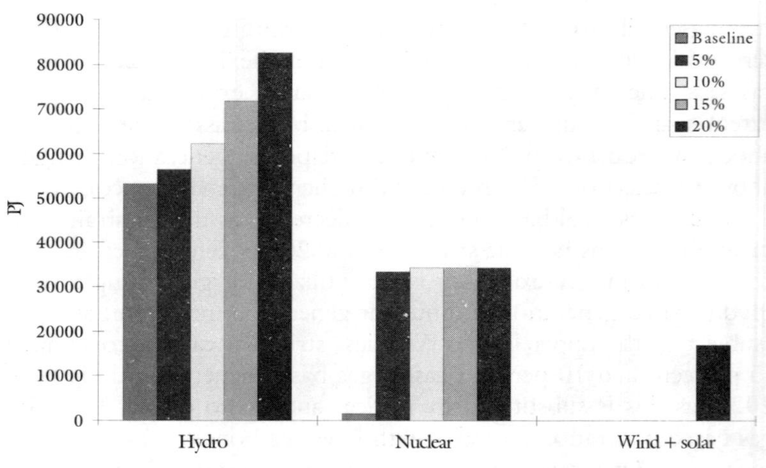

FIGURE 7: PRIMARY ELECTRICITY GENERATION 1990-2050

restrictions on carbon. This is due to the higher efficiency of combined cycle plants over open cycle gas generation. With carbon constraints of 10 per cent and more, high cost hydro (at Rs. 50 million per MW) is selected. As the constraints on carbon get tighter, the rate of induction of hydro capacity is faster, for example, with 20 per cent constraints on cumulative carbon emissions hydro capacity is 71 GW in 2020 compared with 47 GW (in 2020) in other lower (5 per cent, 10 per cent and 15 per cent) carbon constrained cases. At 20 per cent carbon constraint, additional wind based capacity and some centralized solar based power generation are chosen.

The trend for fossil fuels indicates a steady decline with increasing levels of carbon mitigation requirements. With the exception of the 15 per cent case, natural gas consumption doesn't increase with a reduction in coal and oil demands. This indicates that little fuel substitution takes place within fossil fuels. There is shift towards the use of gas in combined cycle plants rather than in open cycle plants. In the 15 per cent scenario, natural gas demand increases to compensate the decrease in the demand for coal and oil. In the 20 per cent case, natural gas demand falls as further reductions in coal and oil demand are not possible and carbon reductions are achieved by reducing natural gas consumption. Reduction in coal consumption is primarily due to the reduction of coal based thermal generation. Decrease in the consumption of oil is linked partly to lower coal based power generation and partly to improvements in the efficiency of utilization. Changes in natural gas demands are lower than those for oil and coal, thereby indicating improvements in efficiency of utilization. Imposition of carbon constraints reduces the import dependence of the economy as is evident from Figure 8.

The results indicate that:

- In the lower abatement scenarios the decline in fossil fuel demand is due to increase in hydro and nuclear power generation, that is, fossil fuel based power generation is replaced by non-fossil generation.
- In the more restrictive emissions scenarios, fossil fuels consumption declines partly due to more efficient utilization of energy and some additional wind and solar generation. In the 20 per cent abatement scenario, hydro and nuclear have both reached their maximum availability. In order to reduce CO_2 emissions further

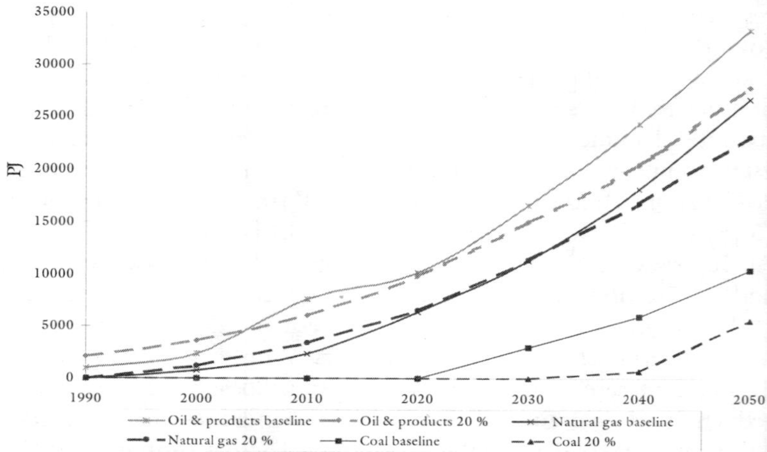

FIGURE 8: ENERGY IMPORTS—BASELINE AND 20 PER CENT ABATEMENT

the high cost solar option is included. This is one of the reasons for the very high incremental abatement cost in the 20 per cent case (Table 12).

CONCLUSION

The alternative paths to reduce emissions entail additional costs. Figure 5 and Table 11 show these incremental costs. The increase in the steepness or the gradient of the curve indicates that additional reductions in carbon savings are increasingly more expensive. It is difficult for developing economies to bear the burden of these additional costs given more urgent developmental priorities. A positive aspect of CO_2 abatement on the economy is the reduced dependence on imports.

The above analysis indicates the priority options for carbon dioxide abatement within the energy system. These results should be interpreted with caution as these represent the costs discounted to present value terms. The model, therefore, selects to control emissions of carbon dioxide towards the end of the analysis period. As yet, India does not have any commitments towards reduction of GHG emissions. There is no clarity on either the time frame in which such commitments might be applicable or the level to which these would be pegged. The abatement measures from the above analysis should be taken as indicative of measures that might be put in place once the country has some commitments.

A prerequisite to the successful implementation of abatement strategies, is a clear understanding of the processes, ability to monitor, determine impacts and future trends. This calls for substantial capacity building and research within the country, and requires technical and financial assistance and development of human capital.

NOTE

1. The logistic function of the form

$$Y_t = \frac{Y_{\max}}{(l + e^{a-bt})}$$

where Y_t is the level at time t, Y_{max} is the saturation point for the series and a and b are parameters which are determined econometrically.

REFERENCES

Bos, E., Vu, M., Massiah E. and Butalo, R. (1994), *World Population Projections Estimates and Projections with Related Demographic Statistics,* 1994-5 Edition, The World Bank, John Hopkins.

British Petroleum Company (1996), *BP Statistical Review of World Energy.*

Government of India (1991), *Sectoral Energy Demand in India*, Planning Commission, New Delhi.

——— (1996), *Economic Survey*, Economic Division 1995-6, Ministry of Finance, New Delhi.

Gupta, S. and Girisha, G.K. (1997), 'Economic Growth in India 1990–2050'.

Hall, D.O. (1991), 'Biomass energy'. *Energy Policy*, October, pp. 711-37.

Ministry of Finance (1996), *Expert Group on the Communication of Infrastructure Projects*, Vol. 2, Thomson Press, New Delhi.

Rao, S.L. (ed.) (1994), 'Consumer market demographics in India', National Council for Applied Economics Research, New Delhi.

TERI (1997), *TERI Energy Data Directory and Yearbook 1997-8*. Tata Energy Research Institute, New Delhi.

World Bank (1997), *World Development Report*, Washington.

Long-term Carbon Emission Targets Aiming Towards Convergence: A Comparative Investigation on Carbon Emission Path Options for Switzerland and India

OTHMAR SCHWANK
THOMAS VON STOKAR
NICOLE NORTH

BACKGROUND

This article is a contribution to the debate on the implications of the Kyoto Protocol for Annex I and non-Annex I parties and to the adequacy of their commitments within the UNFCCC framework. It summarizes results from an energy development related research project on 'Structural Transformation Processes towards a Sustainable Energy Development in India and Switzerland'. This research was funded by the Swiss National Science Foundation for a first phase and by the Swiss Agency for Development and Co-operation (SDC) for a second. The comparative research has been carried out since 1994 jointly by Indian research institutes (TERI and other Indian partners), INFRAS (a Swiss consulting group for policy analysis and implementation) and the International Academy of Environment in Geneva. The project has investigated carbon path options for Switzerland (being an Annex I party to the UNFCCC) comparatively with India (being a non-Annex I party) which would have to be adopted following the Kyoto Protocol commitment period 2008 to 2012 under the UNFCCC, if a long-term atmospheric stabilization of greenhouse gases (GHG) at a level to 'prevent dangerous anthropogenic interference with the global climate' were taken as a measuring rod to design action needed from 2002 onwards.

The UNFCCC Convention aims at a stabilization of CO_2 concentrations at a certain level so as to '*take precautionary measures to anticipate, prevent or minimize the causes of climate change and mitigate its adverse effects. Where there are threats of irreversible damage, lack of full scientific certainty should not be used as a reason for postponing such measures*' (Article 3.3 of the Convention, FCCC Secretariat, 1995).

The aim of the Protocol to be developed under the Convention shall achieve by 2100 and beyond a stabilization of the CO_2 concentration in the atmosphere below the 550 ppmv level, if the precautionary principle stipulated in the Convention is respected. The Second Assessment Report of IPCC (IPCC 1996) concludes that '*a range of carbon cycle models indicate that stabilization of atmospheric CO_2 concentrations at 450, 650, or 1000 ppmv could be achieved only if global anthropogenic CO_2 emissions drop to 1990 levels in approximately 40, 140, or 240 years respectively*'. The global emissions of carbon dioxide due to burning of fossil fuels in 1990 were approximately 6 GtC per annum. In per capita terms, emissions from OECD countries and countries with an economy in transition (Annex I countries) are much higher than those from developing countries (Table 1). While Annex I countries have to reduce their emissions, owing to industrial development and economic growth, the emissions from developing countries will increase on a per capita basis—an effect which is accelerated at the total emission level by population growth. China, and at a later date India, are likely to overtake the US as the largest emitting country worldwide.

TABLE 1: TOTAL ANNUAL AND PER CAPITA CARBON EMISSIONS (tC) DUE TO FOSSIL FUELS (1990)

Region	*Carbon Emissions (mtC)*	*Per Capita Carbon Emissions (tC)*
Global	5,700	1.1
Developed and transitional economies	3,500	2.9 (1.5-5.5)
United States	1,355	5.4
Japan	315	2.5
European Union	900	2.45
Switzerland	12	1.7
Developing countries	2,200	0.6 (0.1-2.0)
China	1,300	1.0
India	150	0.22

Source: IPCC, 1996.

LEADING IDEA

The aim of the Convention can be achieved following the principle of equity and of common but differentiated responsibilities only, if there is convergence of per capita emissions in the long run at a specified target or target corridor. This is the view shared by the authors with the Indian research partners. Such a corridor of sustainability could be set on basis of the IPCC *Second Assessment Report*, 1996. Accordingly, the long-term target respecting the precautionary principle should aim at a global warming below 0.1 degree per decade and a stabilization of CO_2 concentration in the atmosphere at 450 ppmv or at a level significantly below 550 ppmv. For targeting the 450 ppmv stabilization path, the year of maximum global carbon emissions is to be achieved around 2010 with a 'back to 1990 emission levels' by 2035-40. Considering population growth, a 500 ppmv path would set the 2040 global annual per capita emission average below 1 tC. This article does investigate the feasibility of a corridor set at a per capita CO_2 emission equivalent of 2 tCO_2 or less than 0.6 tC per year in 50-60 years time. A sustainable long-term level of world's CO_2 emission (sink capacity) past 2100 is estimated at about half of the 1990 emission level depending on the future population size (influence of land use).

The feasibility and implications of this transformation have been investigated taking Switzerland as a model case of a country in which any mitigation policies and measures do necessarily have to improve the efficiency of energy services. Switzerland consumes as of 1990 only marginal amounts of fossil fuel in the power sector, does largely import products of energy intensive industries and has, compared to other OECD countries, low per capita emissions (1.7 tC). The process of restructuring industry to high added value and low emission market segments leads to unaccounted carbon emission through imports of tradeable commodities such as steel, bulk chemicals, vehicles, etc., mainly from the European Union. Greenhouse gas (GHG) emission reduction targets will therefore have to be implemented by a policy mix strengthening the private sector's capacity to develop and market products of higher energy efficiency.

India will for different reasons in the future, have to take measures to control the growth of GHG emissions. India and Switzerland do in relation to other developing or developed countries share low carbon emission incremental departures for 1990 (Table 1). They however show significant disparities in per capita incomes: A GDP of US $33,000 per capita per year for Switzerland compares to US $260 for India. The investigation does refer to the range of carbon path options for India, which have been outlined by TERI within the framework of this joint project. It also assesses the time frame within which the transformation to much lower carbon intensities has to take place within a developed economy such as Switzerland.

Today, developed countries are, on a per capita basis, far away from globally sustainable production and consumption patterns. They must redirect their economies substantially to a path of reduced natural resource consumption per unit of economic output, i.e. by increasing the productivity in utilizing natural resources by a factor 2 to 4. Countries in the south shall initiate development strategies towards sustainable paths reducing their high growth rates of natural resource consumption through diffusion and application of advanced technologies of lower material flow intensity (Figure 1).

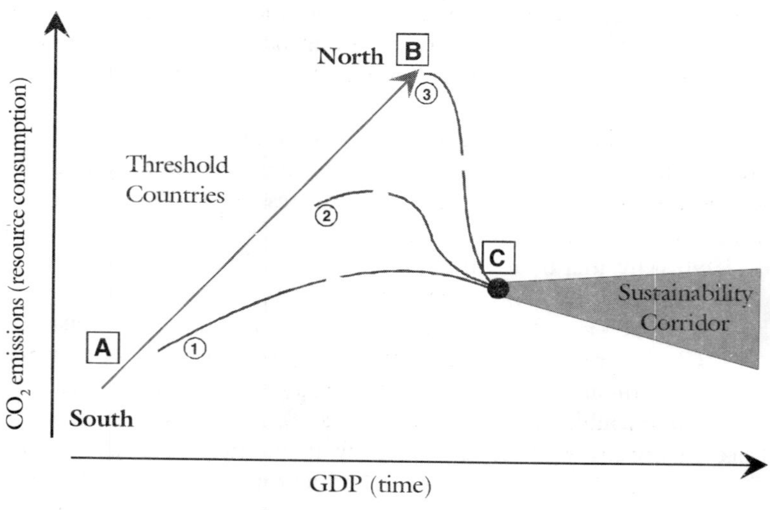

FIGURE 1: DEVELOPED COUNTRIES (3) ARE FARTHEST DOWN THE ROAD OF NOT SUSTAINABLE PRODUCTION AND CONSUMPTION, AND MUST REDIRECT THEIR ECONOMY MOST DRASTICALLY TOWARD A DEVELOPMENT PATH C. DEVELOPING COUNTRIES (1) MUST NOW START REDIRECTING THEIR TECHNOLOGIES AND ECONOMIES AS WELL

LONG-TERM CARBON EMISSION SCENARIOS

BASELINE PARAMETERS AND GOAL

For Switzerland, a sustainable energy scenario (SE) has been designed to cope with the convergence concept of carbon emissions (2 tCO_2 or 0.55 tC per year and capita in 2050). The carbon emission allocation to major sectors resulting from this scenario are highlighted and compared with the recently published climate policy of the Swiss federal government and other reference scenarios. The baseline parameters are summarized in Table 2.

TABLE 2: BASELINE ASSUMPTIONS FOR THE CARBON EMISSION SCENARIOS SWITZERLAND AND INDIA

Switzerland	
Baseline assumptions and CO_2 reduction target	• GDP growth rate within a 0.5-1.5%/a range, departing from US $33,000/cap/a in 1990. • 10% less CO_2 emissions until 2010 (reduction from 44 mt CO_2 (1990) to 39 mt CO_2 (2010). Kyoto Protocol demands 8% reduction. • Acceleration of emission reduction during the second commitment period up to 2020-30. • Approximately 2 tCO_2 emissions per capita and year (0.6 tC) in 2050 which corresponds to a global stabilization path of the carbon level in the atmosphere around 500 ppmv.
Additional constraint	Nuclear phase-out under liberalizing markets: • 2 power stations until 2010; total 700 MW, -23% • Additional 2 power stations until 2020; total 2,000 MW, -67% • The last power station until 2025; total 3,000 MW, -100%
Population	• 6.8 million in 1990 • 7.2 million in 2010 • 7.7 million in 2050
India	
Baseline assumptions	• GDP growth rate within a 5.0-6.0%/a range, departing from US $260/cap/a in 1990.
Population	• 839 million in 1990 • 1,323 million in 2020 • 1,753 million in 2050

For India, TERI has provided baseline long-term projections on carbon emissions for the purpose of sensitivity analysis. The question asked was: By when are the per capita emissions from India likely to move out of the convergence corridor range of 0.5-0.8 tC per year? Considering the low incremental departure of both countries, the principle of shared but differentiated responsibilities would suggest, that per capita emissions in a developed economy such as Switzerland would have reached or at least approached this corridor within this timespan.

THE SUSTAINABLE ENERGY SCENARIO SWITZERLAND (SE)

Method and Assumptions

The energy demand and carbon emission allocations have been investigated for 4 sectors (space heating for domestic and commercial buildings, transport, industrial processes and power sector) through a *bottom-up methodology.* Interim targets are set for 2010 (-10 per cent CO_2 emissions compared to 1990). The target for 2050 is an annual per capita CO_2 emission of 2 tons.

An additional constraint which is adopted as scenario assumption is the full *replacement of the nuclear power* generation capacity through fossil and renewable energies under conditions of liberalized power markets. There is a fairly wide consensus across Europe (based on experiences gained in the UK) that the share of nuclear power generation will drop in future since there is low interest among private investors to take over nuclear plants or to invest in new ones as long as the fuel for gas-combi power station is available at competitive prices. European governments may on the other hand decide to retain some nuclear power capacity to avoid the collapse of an industry sector still needed to train specialists for coping with the problem of safe disposal of the accumulated nuclear wastes.

The Sustainable Energy Scenario for Switzerland (SE) assumes the introduction of a *carbon tax.* According to Swiss Federal Council (1997) a carbon tax level of CHF60.-/tCO_2 is assumed to be introduced in 2004. The rates are significantly increased from 2010 onwards, leading in the SE scenario to prices in 2030 at a factor 3 above 1990 levels. This corresponds to an increase in energy prices of 4 per cent per year (also refer to the assumptions in the reference scenario in page 132). The *international harmonization* of the carbon tax rates is a prerequisite. A progressively increasing carbon tax is considered unfeasible as an isolated national policy. Coordination within Europe and within a second commitment period under the Kyoto Protocol is an important baseline assumption.

Further, the SE scenario assumes application of *best available technologies* (BAT) and assumes proactive policies for adopting such key technologies. Also *lifestyle changes* such as curbing the growth of heated/cooled building space and shifts from private to public transport are assumed.

Policies and Measures

In the *building sector* the SE scenario is based on statistical information and modelling available for the Canton Zurich (one-sixth of the population in Switzerland extrapolated to the total of Switzerland; Kriesi, 1994). The energy consumption of domestic and commercial buildings (fossil fuels) shall be reduced through technologies of higher efficiency by 50 per cent. 'Minergy' houses sourcing passive solar energy are an appropriate commercialization resulting from the 'zero-energy building technology'. Widespread application of such technologies—along with the renovation cycle of buildings—do contribute significantly to reduction of fossil fuel consumed in the sector.

There is evidence that in the building and *industrial processes sector* the use of fossil fuel can be reduced by a factor up to 10. In industrial processes fuel switching to wastes picks up. Application of best available technology has been assumed to be enforced through appropriate policies and measures.

In the *transport sector* there is a big gap between present demand trend and the requirements of a sustainable energy development path. On the other hand, the lifespan of the present fleet of vehicles, trucks and aircrafts is shorter than in the building sector. Accordingly, it was assumed that the long distance freight transportation across countries would largely shift to rail. As from 2030 onwards electric vehicles and vehicles powered by the low emitting fuel cell technology would largely replace the gasoline based fleet of today's cars through transition stages of highly fuel efficient vehicles.

Hydro shall remain the key pillar of the Swiss *power sector*, a target achieved through a refundable tax on non-renewable energies past 2000 also under liberalized market conditions. The 3,000 MW installed nuclear capacity is assumed to be phased out under a regime of liberalized power markets between 2008 and 2025. Nuclear generation is replaced by fossil cogeneration and renewables. No significant export surplus was assumed from 2030 onwards—or, if this surplus would still be economically advantageous, it would be covered by carbon trading (investments of Swiss power sector companies abroad).

Curbing CO_2 emissions is necessary within all sectors and the applications. In space heating, industrial processes and partly electricity reductions are more easy to achieve than in the transport sector, especially in air transport. As a result, higher reduction rates can be achieved in the former sectors.

Results by Sectors and Energy Sources

End energy consumption is reduced by 2 per cent in 2010 and 37 per cent in 2050 as compared to 1990. CO_2 emissions are reduced by 10 per cent in 2010 and by 65 per cent in 2050 (Table 3). Largest reduction in CO_2 emissions is achieved in the settlement/building sector (Figure 2). In 2050, the transport sector will still be the most important contributor to CO_2 emissions followed by the power sector (nuclear phase-out). Detailed results by sectors are indicated in the appendix in Tables 6 and 7.

In 2010, 25 per cent of the energy demand will be met by renewables, while in 2050 by 60 per cent respectively. 36 per cent of the reduction in 2050 compared to the 1990 level has to be achieved by efficiency increases, 33 per cent by renewables. *Fuel wood/biogas* and *solar energy* (but not photovoltaic) have the biggest potential.

The *natural gas* consumption is not reduced until 2050. It will be increasingly used for new applications in the power and transport sector. The same is true for *electricity. Coal* which is mostly used today in the cement production can be substituted through waste (wood, tires, solvents, etc.) or oil.

Through the substitution of *nuclear power* by cogeneration CO_2 emissions increase in the power sector by 1 mt until 2010 and by 4.5 mt in 2050. As a result, in 2050 one-third of total Swiss CO_2 emissions will be caused by the power sector which as of 1990 accounts for marginal emissions only (2 per cent of power generation is fossil fuel based only).

TABLE 3: SUSTAINABLE DEVELOPMENT OF CARBON EMISSIONS AND ENERGY CONSUMPTION BY ENERGY SOURCES UP TO 2050 IN SWITZERLAND

	1998/ 2000	*2010*	*Change 2010/ 2000*	*2030*	*Change 2030/ 2000*	*2050*	*Change 2050/ 2000*
CO_2 emissions							
Net Balance (Mio t/a)	42.1	37.5	-11%	22.5	-47%	13.0	-69%
Emissions total	44.5	39.9	-10%	24.9	-44%	15.4	-65%
End energy related emissions	43.5	39.1	-10%	24.3	44%	15.0	-66%
Total emissions per capita	6.5	5.7	-13%	3.4	49%	2.0	-69%
Primary energy consumption PJ	1,087	1,088	0	674	-38%	568	-48%
(a) Fossil	636	568	-11%	368	-42%	233	-63%
(b) Nuclear	271	209	-23%	0	-100%	0	-100%
(c) Renewable hydro	154	163	5%	167	9%	167	9%
(d) Other renewables	25	69	178%	138	500%	167	568%
End Energy consumption PJ	813	793	-2%	611	-25%	512	-37%
Fuel oil	262	222	-15%	92	-65%	20	-92%
Fuel	259	245	-6%	134	-48%	73	-72%
Gasoline	159	144	-10%	69	-56%	28	-82%
Diesel	52	48	-8%	27	-49%	15	-71%
Kerosene	48	53	11%	38	-20%	30	-37%
Natural Gas	70	72	3%	71	1%	70	0%
Coal	15	2	-87%	1	-95%	0	-100%
Electricity	167	187	12%	197	18%	215	29%
Hydro	111	117	5%	120	9%	120	9%
Nuclear	80	62	-23%	0	-100%	0	-100%
Cogeneration fossil fuels	4	15	247%	55	1,200%	62	1,335%
Cogeneration renewables	1	4	300%	22	2,100	33	3,200%
Net import balance	-30	-11	-63%	0	-100%	0	-100%
Other renewables	40	65	160%	116	191%	234	156%
Wood, biogas	24	28	15%	36	50%	42	73%
Waste heating	7	14	100%	30	300%	35	400%
Long distance heating	9	15	81%	25	200%	27	218%
Solar energy (direct/indirect/passive)	0.2	8	3,900%	25	12,400%	30	14,900%

SUSTAINABLE ENERGY SCENARIO SWITZERLAND

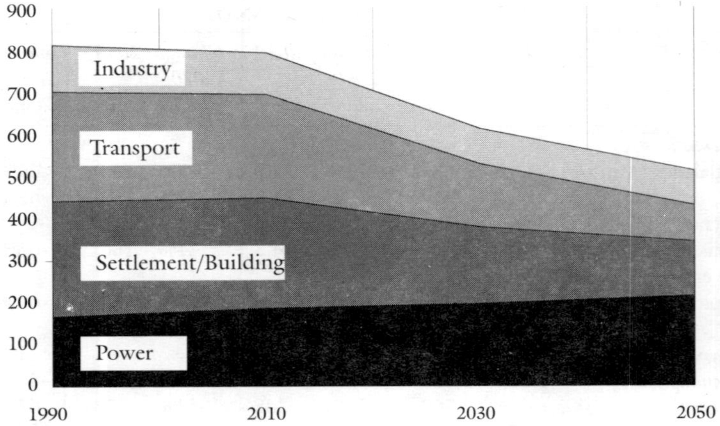

Energy consumption in PJ

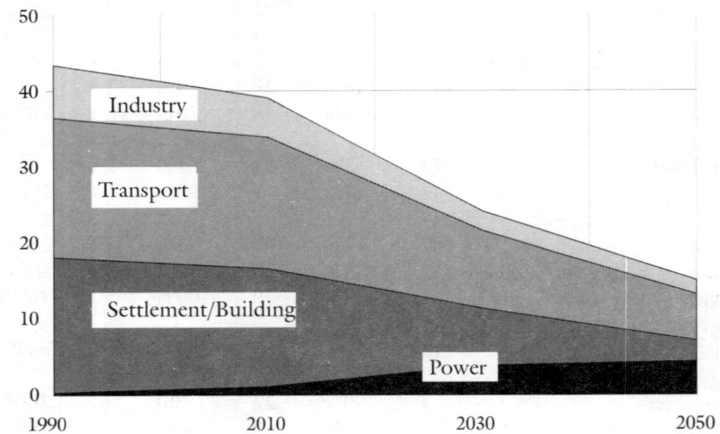

CO_2 emissions in Mio tCO_2

FIGURE 2: DEVELOPMENT OF TOTAL ENERGY CONSUMPTION AND CO_2 EMISSIONS IN SWITZERLAND FOR DIFFERENT SECTORS UP TO 2050

As the first step, 18 PJ generated by two smaller nuclear power stations are scheduled to be substituted by alternative fuels by 2010. 11 PJ shall be substituted by *fossil cogeneration*, 4 PJ by renewables. Generation of hydropower is expected to be gradually increased mainly through modernization of existing plants. Additionally, 20 PJ of power production could be saved through gradual reduction of export surplus. As Switzerland is today exporting approximately 30 PJ electricity, consumption can still be allowed to increase until 2010. By 2030, a total of 80 PJ of nuclear power generated in 2000 are assumed to be substituted.

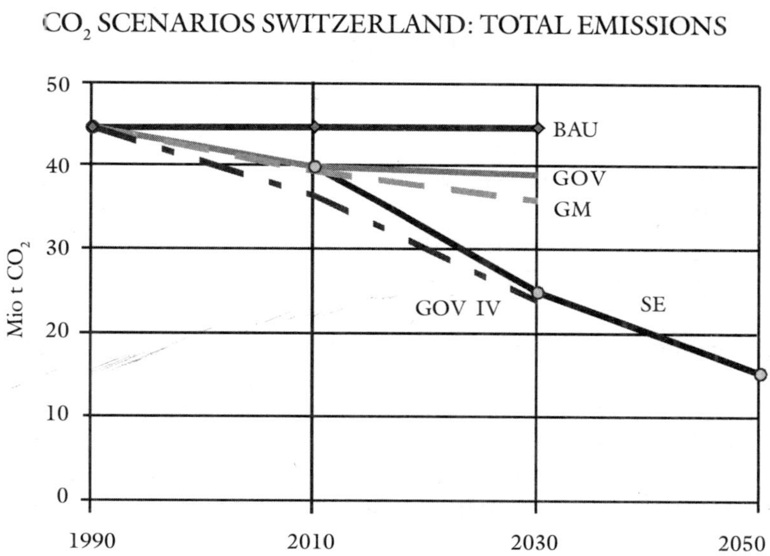

Notes: SE = Sustainable energy scenario based on the convergence corridor concept; BAU = Business-as-usual trend projection; GOV = Official climate policy of the Swiss government; GM = Scenario based on the solar and ecotax initiative by a green movement; GOV IV = Government scenario with stronger reduction targets aiming at sustainable energy consumption.

FIGURE 3: COMPARING DIFFERENT CO_2 EMISSION SCENARIOS FOR SWITZERLAND UP TO 2030

(in $mtCO_2$: 45 $mtCO_2$ is equivalent to 12 mtC (=1.7 tC/cap/a))

REFERENCE SCENARIOS SWITZERLAND

Reference scenarios to the investigated SE scenario as indicated in Figure 3 project CO_2 emissions up to 2030 only. The comparison with Kyoto Protocol based reference scenarios does reveal that by 2030 a significant gap between the emission paths in the order of 10 $mtCO_2$ was to accumulate unless early actions are launched past 2000 to reach a convergence corridor on a long-term basis.

Business-as-usual (BAU)

According to the BAU scenario, CO_2 emissions can be stabilized on the 1990 level up to 2030. This scenario is based on policies and measures adopted up to 1994. Nuclear phase-out is targeted two years later than in the SE scenario. BAU is the reference scenario for the implementation of the Kyoto Protocol.

Government (GOV)

The Swiss government scenario is based on the actual target of the Swiss Federal Council, i.e. -10 per cent CO_2 emissions in 2010. The measures to be introduced are defined in order to achieve this target:

- Energy law: Emission targets for equipment, vehicles and buildings, financial incentives, higher prices for water.
- Measures in the transport sector: Heavy freight vehicle charge, alpine transit charge, promotion of public transport.
- A gradual introduction of a carbon tax until 2010: Charge of 60 CHF per tCO_2 for fuels and transportation fuels (Scenario IIb, Variant 1) up to CHF 210 (US $140) for transportation fuels only which corresponds to an increase in the price of transportation fuel by CHF 0.5 (US $0.35) per litre (Scenario IIb, Variant 2).
- As the schedule for nuclear phase-out is not defined yet, CO_2 emission targets have not yet been proposed for the years past 2010.

As these measures will not be enforced before 2001-4 CO_2 emissions are reduced by 10 per cent until 2010, a 2 per cent margin above Kyoto requirements. By 2030 emissions under the GOV scenario are reduced to 39 mt which corresponds roughly to a stabilization of the 2010 level. Impacts on the national economy as a whole are considered as slightly positive and therefore politically acceptable.

The Swiss action plan for a sustainable development of the 'Conseil du developpement durable'[1]—elaborated under a mandate by the Swiss Federal Council—though recommends to stabilize CO_2 emissions until 2000 on the level of 1990 and to achieve a 20 per cent reduction up to 2010. This reduction shall be achieved by the introduction of an ecological tax in 2000. Further, the Conseil assumes that fuel efficiency of new cars will be increased by 50 per cent up to 2005 and that energy recovery contributes to conversion from fossil fuel to wastes in industrial processes (e.g. in cement production).

Green Movement, Solar and Ecotax Initiative (GM)

This scenario models the impact of the implementation of an initiative submitted to a referendum by a green movement of Swiss NGOs.[2] This initiative targets at a stabilization of fossil fuel consumption within 8 years and a reduction by 1 per cent every year during the following 25 years. Towards that end, it proposes to adopt an energy tax which raises the consumer price of energy by 30 per cent up to 2010 and by 100 per cent up to 2030. Additionally, CHF 0.05 (US $0.03)/kWh are levied from non-renewables in favour of promotion of solar energy and efficient energy use. This initiative is at present in the parliamentary process. The National Council has proposed to adopt the proposal of the Solar Initiative (CHF 0.05/kWh levied on non-renewables) in the framework of the energy legislation. The council of states has not endorsed this proposal, but the project of a refundable non-renewable energy tax is investigated further. Politically interesting from a climate policy viewpoint is the formation of a coalition between the alpine cantons who's stake is to defend the market position of hydropower, the renewable energy traces including agriculture and the green movement. A referendum in this matter is scheduled for 1998 or 1999.

Government IV (GOV IV)

Aim of this (Prognos, 1997) scenario is to study the feasibility of increased reduction targets aiming at long-term sustainability By 2030 60 per cent of the total CO_2 emissions are targeted to be reduced (households: 75 per cent; services: 70 per cent; industry: 45 per cent and transport: 55 per cent). In order to reach this target far-reaching measures in energy policy were to be implemented.

Such measures, assumed to be beyond empirical experience, include:

- An energy tax that increases the price of fossil energy sources and electricity in 2030 by a factor 3.
- Promotion of R&D in renewable energy sources through allocation of public and private funds.
- Implementation of new approaches such as tradable emission permits.

These measures shall be harmonized internationally. Further, the scenario assumes accelerated technological progress in key technologies such as improvements in building insulations, increased efficiency of heat pumps, market success of the fuel cell technology and the reduction of electricity production cost based on renewables. Changes in lifestyles have not be assumed.

The projections indicate that an overall CO_2 emission reduction of 46 per cent can be reached up to 2030 with the measures implemented. The target of 60 per cent reduction is assumed as unfeasible to be achieved by 2030.

INDIA

Baseline Scenario

For the Indian case study the Tata Energy Research Institute has provided baseline projection up to 2050 applying the macro-economic model MARKAL. In this model the demand perspectives as per business-as-usual technologies have been combined with a gradual energy efficiency improvement in the order of a few per cent per decade. The results for the different sectors are accordingly analysed for the 60 years time period under consideration. Though the model is developed for seven time-periods each of 10 years, results are presented for the initial year, that is 1990, the mid-year 2020 and the final year 2050 of the model.

The projection exercise (Table 4) shows that carbon emissions in India may rise from 150 mtC in 1990 to about 700-810 in 2020 with no explicit change in production technology and carbon efficiency. The extrapolation to 2050 has indicative character. A continuation of business-as-usual practices over such a long timespan is not reasonable to assume. The MARKAL based scenario indicates that with a GDP growth rate of 6.0 per cent over a period of 60 years will increase per capita income levels in the economy to US

TABLE 4: ENERGY SUPPLIES, PRIMARY ENERGY CONSUMPTION AND CARBON EMISSIONS IN BASELINE PROJECTIONS BASED ON A MARKAL MODEL WITH 6 PER CENT GDP GROWTH AND IN 20 PER CENT MITIGATION PROJECTIONS (TERI, 1997)

	1990	*2020*		*2050*	
Energy supplies	*Actuals*	*Baseline MARKAL*	*Mitigation 20%*	*Baseline MARKAL*	*Mitigation 20%*
Coal (PJ)	3,600	14,900	11,000	34,000	25,000
Oil and natural gas (PJ)	2,900	19,640	15,700	63,400	50,000
Renewables (PJ): fuel wood, hydropower, agric. waste	5,500	4,700	5,000	5,000	5,500
Total primary energy (PJ)	12,000	39,260	31,500	1,02,400	82,000
Carbon emissions total (mt)	150	701	560	1,910	1,520
Carbon emissions per capita (t)	0.2	0.53	0.43	1.09	0.87

$5,400 (in 1990 constant prices) in 2050. Per capita carbon emissions do reach 1.1 tC. These compare with per capita incomes of US $21,600 for the US (at per capita carbon emissions of 5.4 tC in 1990) or US $33,000 for Switzerland (1.7 tC per capita in 1990). This analysis reveals that under a high GDP growth scenario India would not exceed the per capita carbon emissions of the EU or Japan in 2050 and a significant disparity in income levels would still remain. The issues to be addressed under the Climate Convention are though of very fundamental nature, and beyond the reach where quantitative macro-economic models can provide answers.

GHG MITIGATION COST

Carbon constrained runs of the baseline scenario suggest that within a per unit abatement cost range of US $5-30/t$CO_2$ 10-20 per cent of the projected carbon emissions can be abated in India (TERI 1997). Enhanced penetration of high efficient and low-to-zero carbon technologies have significant impact on energy consumption and thus the carbon emissions, but need sufficient gestation period to show impact. Empirical and theoretical estimates of marginal abatement costs (MAC) vary widely according to source and model simulation based on different aggregation levels and assumptions about the economy of the energy system, the technological development and the inclusion or exclusion of the residential and transport sector. The MAC generally increase with the percentage

MARGINAL COST OF CO_2 EMISSION REDUCTIONS IN 2020

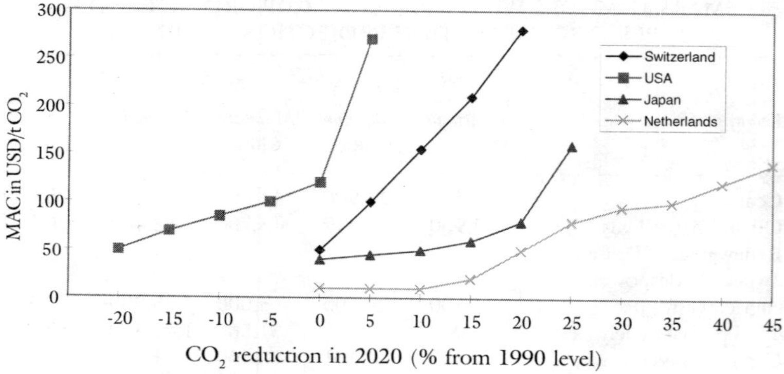

Source: Kram, 1993 in IPCC 1996.

FIGURE 4: MAC IN 2020 IN THE ETSAP STUDY

MARGINAL ABATEMENT COST FOR SWITZERLAND

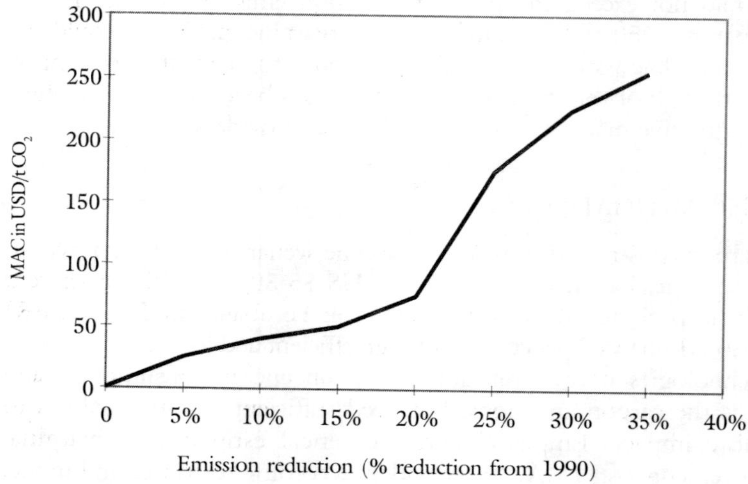

Source: Jepma, 1997.

FIGURE 5: EMPIRICAL RESULT FOR MAC IN SWITZERLAND

level of reduction, and they are high in industrialized and very low in developing countries. Some studies indicate that the MAC decrease with time for similar reduction targets from baseline simply because more technologies are available (UNEP, 1994). According to (Kram, 1993), Switzerland which together with Norway and Sweden now emits the least CO_2 per capita within the OECD will be among the countries measuring the highest cost to achieve a specific reduction in CO_2 emissions (Figure 4). Other estimations of MAC for Switzerland vary from US $25 t - 160/tCO_2$ (Jepma, 1997) projects MAC for Switzerland as indicated in Figure 5.

The MAC analyses presented in Figures 3 and 4 confirm that progressively increasing carbon taxation is needed to curb carbon emissions by 30 per cent and more below 1990 levels.

CONCLUSION

The target set for the sustainable energy scenario Switzerland (SE) appears to be very ambitious (to reduce CO_2 emissions by 10 per cent by 2010, 44 per cent by 2030, and 65 per cent by 2050). The period 2010-2030 will be crucial for implementation of any long-term stabilization target of the atmospheric carbon level below 550 ppmv. To achieve this, the emissions from burning of fossil fuels have to fall on a global scale from approximately 2030 onwards after reaching a maximum of around 10 billion tons of carbon. The sensitivity analysis conducted for India shows that from 2030 onwards per capita emissions of this developing economy depart from the sustainability corridor (Figure 6).

The timing of mitigation measures taken within Annex I economies is crucial for a number of considerations:

- To pass legislation for policies and measures and implement them across the country takes time in itself. The impact of policies and measures on the economy has to materialize within 5-10 years to reach a 2010 target. The reduction targets set for 2010 for Annex I economies in Kyoto are not adequate to achieve the turnaround towards convergence for an emission stabilization path below 550 ppmv. The principle of early action suggests that on basis of the Third Assessment Report submitted to the IPCC (2002) and in review of the adequacy of demonstrable progress under the Kyoto Protocol, further strengthening of the commitments for

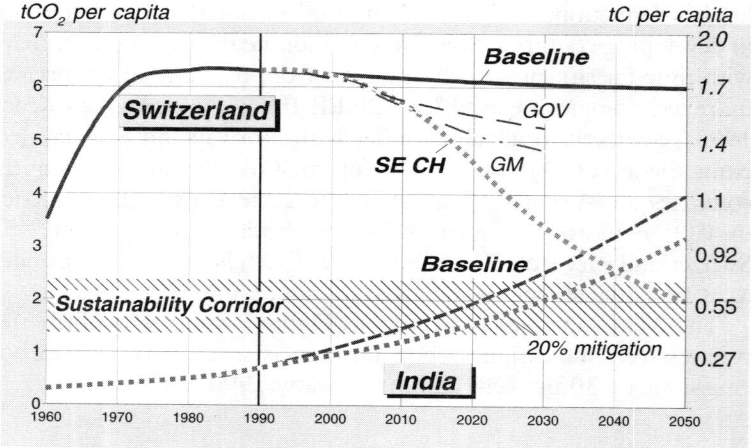

FIGURE 6: THE DIFFERENT SCENARIOS FOR INDIA AND SWITZERLAND INDICATE THAT THE TURNAROUND TOWARDS CONVERGENCE WILL NOT BE ACHIEVED UNLESS SUBSTANTIVE REDUCTION TARGETS ARE SET FOR 2010-30 FOR ANNEX I COUNTRIES

the period following the Kyoto Protocol shall be taken up 2005 at the latest.

- The principle of early action with respect to adoption of adequate policies and measures is of crucial importance for development of environmentally sound technologies as well as for the transfer of such technologies to developing countries and to countries with an economy in transition. The view that actions taken today are significantly more costly than actions taken later does underestimate the stimulating effects of an early flat reduction target on technology development. The future world is predetermined by present costing patterns of technologies to a lesser extent than suggested by top-down macroeconomic model analysis.
- If Annex I countries such as Switzerland with comparatively favourable starting conditions (hydropower, low aircondition demand, public transportation rail network already established) delay action for approaching sustainable emission levels by 2050, it will be difficult to convince large carbon emitting nations in the south such as India, or even more so China, to target for per capita emission stabilization and reduction past 2020. Unless an understanding for a global long-term atmospheric stabilization

level and convergence target of per capita emissions in between 0.5 tC to 0.75 tC per capita and year can not be reached for the second half of the next century, it will be difficult to stabilize the atmospheric carbon concentrations at such a level which prevents dangerous anthropogenic interference with the global climate system.

- It appears to be most essential to change the attitude and perceptions under which commitments are debated. A structural transformation process at global level inducing necessary changes in technology patterns and lifestyles warranted for safeguarding the Earth climate does need policies and measures based on early action in Annex I countries.

NOTES

1. The 'Conseil' has been mandated to define most important fields of action for a sustainable development in Switzerland and to make proposals on necessary implementation steps.
2. 'Energy-Environment Initiative' and 'Solar Initiative' combined.

APPENDIX

CO_2 EMISSION FACTORS FOR DIFFERENT ENERGY SOURCES

I. CO_2 EMISSION FACTORS

	Emission Factors	*Emission mt CO_2*						
	Mio t/PJ	*1990*	*2010*	*Change 2010/1990 (%)*	*2030*	*Change 2030/1990 (%)*	*2050*	*Change 2050/1990 (%)*
Total CO_2 emissions		44.52	39.95	-10	24.92	-44	15.38	-65
Fuel oil	0.07	19.39	16.43	-15	6.82	-65	1.48	-92
Fuel		18.52	17.49	-6	9.60	-48	5.21	-72
Gasoline	0.07	11.30	10.22	-10	4.93	-56	1.99	-82
Diesel	0.07	3.83	3.50	-8	1.96	-49	1.10	-71
Kerosene	0.07	3.39	3.76	11	2.71	-20	2.13	-37
Natural Gas	0.06	3.84	3.96	3	3.89	1	3.85	0
Coal	0.10	1.47	0.20	-87	0.07	-95	0.00	-100
Electricity		0.00	0.00		0.00		0.00	
Hydro		0.00	0.00		0.00		0.00	
Nuclear		0.00	0.00		0.00		0.00	
Cogeneration fossil fuels	0.07	0.31	1.07		3.94	1,173	4.44	1,335
Cogeneration renewables		0.00						
Rest (Conversion losses etc.)		1	0.8		0.6		0.4	

Note: Wood and biogas are considered to have a CO_2 emission factor of 0 because they are renewable. Energy production in waste incinerators is also considered CO_2 neutral because the waste would have to be burnt anyway.

CO_2 EMISSIONS IN MT CO_2 BY SECTORS IN SWITZERLAND

II. CO_2 EMISSION BY SECTORS

CO_2 emissions in mt/sectors	*1990*	*2010*	*Change 1990/2010 (%)*	*2030*	*Change 1990/2030 (%)*	*2050*	*Change 1990/2050 (%)*
Settlement/building	17.8	15.5	-13	7.4	-58	2.7	-85
Fuel oil	15.5	13.1		5.5		0.7	
Natural gas	2.3	2.4		1.9		1.9	
Transport	18.4	17.4	-6	10.3	-44	6.0	-68
Fuel	18.4	17.4		9.5		5.2	
Natural gas				0.8		0.8	
Industry	6.9	5.1	-26	2.6	-62	1.9	-72
Fuel oil	3.9	3.3		1.4		0.7	
Natural gas	1.5	1.6		1.2		1.2	
Coal	1.5	0.2		0.1			
Power cogeneration fossil fuel	0.3	1.1	247	3.9	1,173	4.4	1,335
Rest	1.0	0.8		0.6		0.4	
Total	44.4	39.9	-10	24.9	-44	15.4	-65

END ENERGY CONSUMPTION IN PJ BY SECTORS IN SWITZERLAND

III. END ENERGY CONSUMPTION BY SECTORS

	1998/ 2000	*2010*	*Change 2010/ 2000*	*2030*	*Change 2030/ 2000*	*2050*	*Change 2050/ 2000*
End energy consumption PJ							
Settlement/building	276	263	-5%	183	-34%	129	-53%
Fuel oil	210	178	-15%	74	65%	10	92%
Natural gas	42	43	3%	35	16%	25	16%
Other renewables							
Wood, biogas	18	21	15%	27	50%	32	73%
District heating	6	13	105%	23	253%	24	281%
Solar energy (direct/ indirect/passive)	0	8	3,900%	24	11,775%	29	14,150%
Transport	259	245	-6%	149	-43%	87	-66%
Fuel							
Gasoline	159	144	-10%	69	-56%	28	-82%
Diesel	52	48	-8%	27	-49%	15	-71%
Kerosene	48	53	11%	38	-20%	30	-37%
Natural gas	0	0	0%	14		14	
Industry							
Fuel oil	111	99	-11%	83	-25%	81	-27%
Natural gas	28	29	3%	21	24%	21	25%
Coal	15	2	-87%	1	-95%	0	100%
Other renewables							
Wood, biogas	6	7	15%	9	50%	11	73%
Waste heat recovery	7	14	100%	30	329%	35	400%
District heating	2	2	9%	3	18%	3	27%
Solar energy (direct/ indirect/passive)	0	0		1		2	
Power	167	187	12%	197	18%	215	29%
Hydro	111	117	5%	120	9%	120	9%
Nuclear	80	62	-23%	0	-100%	0	-100%
Cogeneration fossil fuel	4	15	247%	55	1,200%	62	1,335%
Cogeneration renewables	1	4	300%	22	2,100%	33	3,200%
Net import balance	-30	-11	-63%	0	-100%	0	-100%
Total	813	793	-2%	611	-25%	512	-37%

REFERENCES

Bahn, O. et al. (1996): *National and International Options for Switzerland to curb CO_2 Emissions*. A publication from the Paul Scherrer Institute, Zurich.

FCCC Secretariate (1995): FCCC/CP/L13. Framework Convention on Climate Change, Conference of Parties, Geneva.

INFRAS (1995): Quantitative Aspekte einer zukunftsfähigen Schweiz. Länderstudie der Kampagne 'Sustainable Europe' von Friends of the Earth, Schweizer Umwelt und Entwicklungsorganisationen, Zurich.

INFRAS, et al. (eds.) (1996): Structural Transformation Processes towards Sustainable Development in India and Switzerland. Priority Programme Environment of the Swiss National Science Foundation, Zurich.

IPCC (1996): *Second Assessment Report, Summary for Policy Makers*, Geneva.

——— (1996b): *Second Assessment Report, Economic and Social Dimension of Climate Change*, WG II, Cambridge University Press, Cambridge.

Jepma, J. (1997): National marginal abatement costs (manuscript).

Kram, T. (1993): *National Energy Options for Reducing CO_2 Emissions*, Vol. 1, Netherlands Energy Research Foundations (ECN), Amsterdam.

Kriesi, R. et al. (1994): Vision einer langfristigen Entwicklung des Energieverbrauchs in der Schweiz. Folgerungen für die Energieforschung, ATAL, Zurich.

Prognos, A.G. (1996): Energie und CO_2 Perspektiven 1990-2030, Szenarien I, IIa, IIb. Arbeitsbericht vom 15. März, Basel.

——— (1997): Ergänzungen zu den Energieperspektiven 1990-2030, Szenario IV: verschärfte und auf Nachhaltigkeit ausgerichtete CO_2-Reduktion, Synthesebericht vom 29. Mai, Basel.

Swiss Federal Council (March 1997): Botschaft zum Bundesgesetz zur Reduktion der CO_2 Emissionen (Bill to parliament on climate policy and carbon mitigation legislation), Berne.

TERI (1995): 'Institutionalizing Sustainable Energy Development in India', in: INFRAS, et al. (eds.) (1996): *Structural Transformation Processes towards Sustainable Development in India and Switzerland*. Priority Programme Environment of the Swiss National Science Foundation, Zurich, pp. 87-181.

——— (1997): The Energy Scenario for India—2050, Structural Transformation Processes, phase 2, draft, Delhi.

Climate Change and Allocation of GEF's Funds: Trying to Learn from the Indian Case

PIERRE AUDINET
EMMANUEL FAGES

This article aims at deriving some operational recommendations for the activities of the Global Environment Facility (GEF). One starts from a survey of the operations in India, based on a series of interviews. The institutional framework and the actors are presented, then a review of the project (existing and planned) is displayed. One will focus on the Facility's operational principals, and analyse the way official texts translate into practice—in particular through the project cycle. One will identify the difficulties encountered. The technological biases, GEF's insufficient budget and the actors' conflicting incentives are some of the reasons pointed out.

In a second step this will help one to propose some specific modifications for the Facility's operational methods. This is done along two directions: Project selection and project financing. As it concerns the first direction, the host countries' domestic market distortions and the project replication (i.e. market creation) issues are addressed. One will show that a better targeting of the selection criteria is needed to solve these and could suffice to do it. As far as financing is concerned, focus will be on the allocation principles and on the resource management issues. One will argue that the incremental cost principle, if administratively needed as an accounting benchmark for the GEF, is in practice not used. The consideration of the incidence of a particular project (a notion defined in the text) could prove more appropriate. Moreover, resources could be managed more effectively with respect to the Facility's objectives if more diversity in the use of financing instruments was introduced, and if the GEF could directly be backed by the strong financial markets.

I. GEF: THE EXPERIENCE IN INDIA

A. The Institutional Scene and the Projects

India has signed (June 1992) and ratified (November 1993) The United Nations Framework Convention on Climate Change (UNFCC). It is a non-Annex I country, i.e. submitted to greenhouse gases (GHG) inventory and inventory report obligations (Article 12.1), but not submitted to abatement constraints. This status makes it eligible to GEF's funds, whose role is to help support the costs of fulfilling the Convention obligations.

1. Actors

(A) IMPLEMENTING AGENCIES

Up to now, projects in India have been under the responsibility of two out of three GEF implementing agencies, the United Nations Development Programme (UNDP) and the World Bank. The Bank is in charge of large investment projects, between US $10 and 50 million; UNDP is in charge of smaller, under US $10 million projects, which mainly consist of technical assistance and feasibility studies.

The review of existing projects shows that GEF's projects have been included by each agency into its usual management and fund disbursement methods, creating no new logic on their own.

(B) COUNTERPART AGENCIES AND EXECUTING AGENCIES

GEF's secretariat requires that responsible domestic agencies be appointed by the host country for each project. For financial matters, this counterpart is generally the Department of Economic Affairs, Ministry of Finance, government of India. For operational matters, a country's focal point must be designated, to act as an interface with the GEF. In India the Ministry of Environment and Forests (MoEF) and the Ministry of Non-Conventional Energy Sources (MNES) are generally concerned. The Ministry of Power and the Ministry of Coal may also be associated. The projects are implemented by smaller, specialized actors called executing agencies.

One such important agency is the Indian Renewable Energy Development Agency (IREDA). Set up in 1987 by the Department of Non-Conventional Energy Sources (DNES, formerly MNES), this public organism is in charge of managing a revolving fund (ca. US $200 million) to promote renewable energies. It is funded by several multilateral agencies. GEF funds are part (35 per cent) of a US $42 million budget devoted to photovoltaïcs (PV).

(C) PRIVATE PARTIES

Today the main private entities in the GEF projects are financial intermediaries working with IREDA (Tata Finance Ltd., Birla Finance Ltd., Escort Finance Ltd.) or industrial firms such as independent power producers (IPPs), looking for additional funds.

NGOs and energy consultants are also involved in the projects. In India, the Tata Energy Research Institute (TERI) and Development Alternatives (DA) are first ranking. TERI acts as a consultant (with MoEF, IREDA and UNDP) at every stage of design, proposal and implementation. DA manages the GEF small grant programme in India (cf. Table 1).

Many research institutions are associated for R&D and technology transfer studies: National Environmental Research Institute (NERI); Indian Institute of Science (IISc); National Chemical Laboratory (NCL) are some of these.

2. *The Projects*

(A) IMPLEMENTATION STAGE

Today there are 7 projects being implemented in India. UNDP is in charge of 4 of them, for which GEF's budget is US $20 million. The World Bank is responsible for 3 of them, for which GEF will disburse US $100 million. India is the second beneficiary of GEF funding (after China, US $140 million), with 6.6 per cent of the GEF budget allocated since 1991.[1] Most of the projects to date were designed during the pilot phase (1991-4), and deal with climate change. Only one project has come to an end (ALGAS, cf. Table 1), while the majority have not started the operational phase yet. They appear in Table 1.

(B) HARD AND SOFT PIPELINE PROJECTS

The main feature for the coming years is the increasing share of biodiversity projects. UNDP seems to take a prominent role. The median size of projects under this implementing agency increases

TABLE 1: GEF'S PORTFOLIO IN INDIA (1997)

(projects in the implementation stage)

	Title	*Implementing Agency*	*Realm*	*Project Description*	*Length*	*GEF's part 10^6 US $ (% total)*
Projects being realized						
1.	Optimizing development of small hydel resources in hilly regions of India	UNDP (pilot phase)	Climate change	Setting up of 20 hydro demonstration projects (100-500 kW) + design of management methods + formulation of a national action plan	1995-9	7.5 (51.2)
2.	Development of high rate biomethanation processes as means of reducing GHG emissions	UNDP (pilot phase)	Climate change	Demonstration of the viability of garbage methanation through the setting up of 16 units (30-250m3/j et 30t/j) + formulation of a national action plan	1994-9	5.5 (55)
3.	Asia least-cost GHG abatement strategies - regional	UNDP	Climate change	GHG inventory in 13 countries	1995-7	0.45 (n.a.)
4.	Alternate energy project	Worl Bank (pilot phase)	Climate change	Revolving fund dedicated to loans to private projects on PV (Solar PV market development programme), solar thermal and wind power, to catalyse mass production)	1992-7 (last Bank disburse-ment planned for 1999)	26 (14) (computed after wind, solar thermal and PV loans only)
5.	Ecodevelopment	World Bank (pilot phase)	Bio-diversity	In 7 zones: protection of biodiversity + village ecodevelopment + education + monitoring	1996-2001	20 (41.7)

6. India: Solar thermal power	World Bank	Climate change	140 MW hybrid solar parabolic (35-40 MW)/ fossil energy power plant + technical support	1997-2002	49 (20)
7. Small grant programme	UNDP	Climate change/ Bio-diversity	Financing micro-projects ($5,000-25,000 per project; exists for 36 countries	Renewed every year	0.3 (n.a. in 1996) 0.6 (40 in 1997)
Projects being prepared					
8. Photovoltaic market transformation initiative (PVMTI)	World Bank/ IFC	Climate change	Continuation of the alternate energy project/ directed towards the private sector (goal: measure learning from alternate energy project)	5 years	30,00 (n.d.)*
9. Selected options for stabilizing GHG emissions for sustainable development	UNDP	Climate change	n.a.	2 years	1.5 (n.a.)
10. Management of coral reef ecosystem of the Andaman and Nicobar Islands	UNDP	Bio-diversity	n.a.	1 year	PDF-B: 0.35 Project: 5
11. Strengthening the management of India's Gulf of Mannar biosphere reserve	UNDP	Bio-diversity	n.a.	1 year	PDF-B: 0.19 Project: 7
12. Carbon emission reduction through biomass energy for rural India	UNDP	Climate change	n.a.	6 months	PDF-B: 0.20 Project: 11

Title	*Implementing Agency*	*Realm*	*Project Description*	*Length*	*GEF's part 10^6 US $ (% total)*
Planned projects					
13. Coal bed methane capture and utilization	UNDP	Climate change	n.a.	n.a.	9
14. National biodiversity action plan	UNDP	Bio-diversity	n.a.	n.a.	0.35 - 0.75
Envisaged projects					
15. Solar PV systems to supple-ment and augument power grid	UNDP	Climate change	n.a.	n.a.	PDF-A: 0.025
16. Fuel cells for the transport sector	UNDP	Climate change	n.a.	n.a.	PDF-A: 0.025
17. Renewable energy for rural development	UNDP	Climate	n.a.	n.a.	PDF-B: 0.17
18. Biomass power generation	UNDP	Climate change	n.a.	n.a.	PDF-A: 0.025

Notes: n.a.: not available.

*Project 8 is at world-level: US $30 million shared between India, Morocco and Kenya.

from US $5-7 million to US $7-11 million. As far as climate change is concerned, emphasis is laid on clean biomass use—but PV remains dominant. They appear in Table 2.

B. From Selection to Realization: Projects Practice and Problems

1. *The Modes of Project Management*

(A) OBJECTIVES AND CRITERIA

The idea in this section is not to repeat what the official, well known texts say (GEF, 1996b), but to draw a rapid picture of what one has found to be the leading concerns behind GEF's intervention.

(1) *Keeping a balance in the allocation of funds between geographical zones.* This criterion, if quite unsurprising, is not official. Thus it is not declared to the applicants. This translates into less transparency of decisions, and blurred signals to local agencies as far as the quality of projects is concerned.

(2) *Looking for leverage effect and know-how.* The GEF tries to associate private parties to the financing of coherent alternative projects (as opposed to 'end-of-the-pipe' solutions). The goal for the Facility is to add a minimum amount of funds that will help catalyse projects otherwise too risky or not competitive (GEF Council, 1996a).

The other idea is to promote projects with a high potential for replication, i.e. eliminate barriers to the adoption of clean technologies. The GEF will help reduce unit costs with the help of scale effects and building know-how. This method should be improved by the programmatic approach now defined by the Facility (GEF, 1996b).

(3) *Maximizing the marginal benefit from the project.* 'Cost-effectiveness' is required by GEF's administration (GEF, 1996b). But it is not very precisely defined. In practice it seems to translate into management control at the project selection level: The GEF ensures that methods are correct, and through 'cost-norms' that costs are maintained at decent levels.

(4) *Financing only not economically viable alternative projects.* There should not exist national economic benefits, other than improved local environment, to GEF's financed alternative project—in other words there should definitely be positive identifiable incremental costs to the project for the GEF to intervene (GEF Council, 1996b).

(B) THE PROJECT CYCLE

The title of this section is also that of the official document describing the procedures to prepare and submit a project (GEF, 1996c). However, in practice it is different.

(1) *The origin of the project and the correspondence with the host country needs.* The operational strategy insists on the fact that GEF's approach to project proposal and selection procedures rest on the 'country-driven' perspective. In India, this does not seem to be entirely the case. Indisputable is the fact that MNES is free to present projects according to its priorities. Most of the proposals today originate from the Indian government. But multilateral agencies are by no means neutral in the selection. It seems that UNDP directs the choices towards technical assistance and studies, its main expertise, and that the Bank primarily promotes certain types of investments, e.g. PV against biomass use, the latter being one of India's main potentials, though.

(2) *The calculation of incremental costs: Conventions as a remedy to uncertainties.* Despite the official method provided in the document Incremental Costs (GEF Council, 1996b), their evaluation in India is on a case to case basis. However, this does not imply detailed and costly analysis on each project. A non-official typology of baseline exits (according to size and nature of the project). Project officers use standard hypotheses common to each type of baseline. In the medium run, direction seems to be to use the best available technique in the host country to provide the reference.

This must be appreciated as a pragmatic, sensible response to the many uncertainties affecting the determination of a baseline project. However, the risk is to transform these conventions into norms and conceal substantial variations between projects due to differences in local situations, such as climatic conditions (implying different maintenance costs), nature of the combustible (e.g. grades of coal), or land costs.

(3) *Selection: The procedures are differentiated according to the project size.* For small projects (< US $10 million) selection is real. One half to two-thirds of the proposals appear to be rejected, even at an advanced stage. This is not the outcome of an open competition between the proposals, but GEF administration's case by case decision. As a result the submitting country does not shape its project with a view to make it more attractive than the others or to propose characteristics as good as possible.

For big projects, the situation is different: The GEF is one source of funds among others, and its contribution is much smaller than the Bank's, in particular. Decision level changes accordingly. Due to their size, proposals are not many and what one observes is more of a negotiation-revision process than a 'yes or no' decision. This generally takes long, in India, as it involves large administrations.

(4) *Realization.* This phrase started late, due to GEF's long setting up and to specific procedures not known to host countries. Since mid-1995 routine operations seem to be under way. As far as the bank and UNDP were concerned, the control of the investment phases was treated according to the usual procedures ('follow-up, monitoring and evaluation'), and the budget was taken to this end on the regular agency budget (not on GEF's). Local representatives are present on the spot. They send reports every trimester to the project managers in Delhi, who continuously follow the advancement. Bills are checked by executive agencies (e.g. IREDA). There exists in the GEF a monitoring and evaluation budget. A project completion review is carried out eventually.

2. *Difficulties*

Up to now, the GEF has not contributed to GHG emissions reduction in India, though this was its main mission in this country. It is difficult to say whether this plain fact remains a failure—though it could be a sign. In any case, one can identify some biases and structural weaknesses.

(A) THE NATURE OF THE GAME

(1) *Costly money, uncertain criteria.* In the beginning of GEF's operations in India, quality proposals were few. Multilateral agencies seized the opportunity to ensure their living and proposed technical

studies which did not lead, even with the help of the usual demonstration project, to emission abatement. Even now this type of operation is dominant, and will remain so for the years to come (cf. Table 2). Studies are obviously needed, as lack of information, inadequate training, and institutional gap are the main barriers to proper action being taken in the realm of climate change and diffusion of new technologies. But should they prevail?

Knowledge of the existence of GEF's funds and its procedures even if known, is not of much use as access remains long and complex, which implies a transaction cost many would be unwilling to endure. 'Time too long, funds too small: costly money' sums up the main grievances of the Facility from local actors.

Lack of transparency in the decision process plus top-down, conditionality-driven approach of the World Bank is the classic criticism, among others, of the Facility.

(2) *Biased choice of techniques*. GEF's official texts make replicability of projects one of the main conditions for their selection. But the present portfolio allows doubt on the achievement of this requirement. Technical studies cannot be repeated. Demonstration projects, generally small, are not sufficient to make displayed new technologies feasible and affordable. The bank's large projects are by nature difficult to reproduce, all the more so as GEF's funds represent a very limited fraction of the total costs.

Another concern is that GEF seems to focus on some technologies, even if they are not the best-fitted to local conditions. The example in India is PV. This technology has used a good deal of GEF's funds. But the analysis shows that the Facility does not act incremental there; either PV already stands as a profitable option in rural areas as compared to grid connection; or it cannot penetrate due to poor final users, unable to pay for any kind of unsubsidized commercial energy. Each case lies out of GEF's attributions.[2] Up to now, IREDA projects' review shows that GEF has contributed mainly to ease already viable applications. This could lead one to suspect that the Facility defends interests and goals other than those written in the texts. In particular, to repeat the GEF is not supposed to use the host country as a testing ground for new, yet to mature technologies. PV is a solid example where many actors, industrial ones first, are eager to see the market expand. Some high return potentials lie in the north, but the market is too narrow to enable producers to cash in on present costs levels. Cost reductions and corollary technology diffusion can be achieved by tapping the larger and easier south market potential through the setting up of large production capacities. Is GEF accumulating technological know-how for north's sake in this case?

(B) THE SMALL SIZE

(1) *The small budget, allied with conflicting objectives.* It is commonplace to state that GEF's limited budget cannot contribute to emissions reduction, however efficiently employed.[3] That is why the GEF relies on the 'leverage' effect. In a large country, like India, the question is particularly acute.

However constraining though, the limitation could certainly be managed. The existence of a problem seems to come from conflicting objectives within GEF's mission. On the one hand, the Facility is supposed to foster portfolio diversity in order to explore technological alternatives to prepare backstop techniques in case the hypothesis of a future dramatic change in climate conditions is suddenly confirmed. On the other hand it seeks to accumulate know-how and capacity building, provoke scale economies, which is possible only through the exploration of each technological option—a 'programmatic approach' which should induce 'programmatic effects'. With a small budget the GEF is torn between these two directions, to which is added the geographical balance concern—whereas scale economies can often be realized only through concentration of experience and capacities. The result is that the Facility does not devote enough money to either objective, and satisfactorily fulfils neither.

(2) *The small influence, disproportionate to large requirements.* India is receptive to fresh funds. It has, however, no abatement obligation from UNFCCC. As a consequence, it is not ready to accept stringent conditions linked to the allocation of project funds from the GEF. These conditions exist: In order to be able to correctly compute incremental costs, the GEF for example demands that energy subsidy systems be dismantled. The problem specific to such requirement is that it far exceeds the project level to reach the realm of macro-economic management. Even backed by the World Bank, it seems to be too large as compared to the economic stakes involved by the sole project for Indian authorities—let alone Indian pride and

reluctance to have conditions dictated on them. Conversely the GEF has no way to impose its commands. On the contrary, it is submitted to internal disbursement constraints, and as a result has to make do with India's way of managing the economy. This would cause no worry if the project did not suffer from the conflict. The Mathania project is a good example of the fact that it does: Project documents state that the application of market prices is a condition to its realization. Rajasthan state signed to obtain the project but with no intention at that time to modify the price system, as has became now clear. The private partners (here German KFW) find themselves in trouble, as the profitability of the project is not ensured. Delays could end up in the private parties stepping out.

II. TRYING TO IMPROVE

From the beginning, criticisms to the GEF were many, and in fact most of the observers' contribution to the Facility can said to have consisted in expressing distrust. Until recently, GEF's future appeared very uncertain. But the initial investment period seems to be over. GEF is launched, and, after the many suspicions and doubts endangering its existence, it now seems to be safe. More delays would certainly kill the GEF. The sensible attitude therefore is not to keep on questioning, even if still justified, but to make do with the available potential. One has to remember that if the GEF disappears, nothing else will come up to replace it. The efforts to set it up as it is were too large so one can expect to see them renewed in case of failure.

It is not proposed here to reform the GEF—nor does one claim to have the competence to do so. This is too heavy a task as compared to the possible benefits, especially at a time when the Facility's operations are taking off, with recipient countries getting to know its goals and proposals, when the donor governments express more confidence in the instrument—as could be seen at the GEF assembly in Delhi, April 1998.

One thus shall try to remain pragmatic. The previous remarks helped define some points where marginal action is possible, at low costs, with substantial benefits—a kind of 'no regret' policy for the GEF. These points concern the choice of projects, and project financing. One expects them to be applicable beyond the Indian example.

A. The Selection: Fitting the Project into the Host Country Context

1. *Domestic Economic Policy and Conditionality Temptation*

(A) THE GEF STAND: NOT SOLIDLY GROUNDED

A considerable part of GEF's intervention in the realm of climate change is unsurprisingly directed towards energy sector. In most developing countries, prices (and supply) are state-regulated in this sector. As previously evoked, the GEF and most of the other donors blame this situation as a source of waste and mismanagement. They try to impose the liberalization and particularly the dismantling of administered price mechanisms as a pre-condition to aid. Arguments seem logical: Giving funds, and thus allowing the situation to continue, would make the Facility appear as accepting and even supporting practices it rejects (GEF Council, 1996c). Moreover, GEF's principle of incremental cost financing cannot be worked out in a distorted context. The GEF thus asks for an 'environmentally reasonable baseline' (GEF Council, 1996b).

Host countries oppose these points. GEF's intervention should not mix with broad domestic economic policy options. If the GEF exists to protect the global environment, it cannot ask the host countries to make most of the effort towards this objective. GEF's principle is incremental, i.e. it wants to finance what host countries *would not have financed* without this intervention, representing specific environmental care. Thus it cannot demand from the recipient countries to do what they would not have done without this intervention.

Both are right and it is difficult to completely subscribe to one or the other's position. One remark, though, GEF is indeed hindered by the existing systems. But its demand is of a political nature,[4] and its theoretical rhetoric lacks grounds. The GEF cannot logically ask for an environmentally reasonable baseline to be implemented prior to its action. Once the baseline is environmentally reasonable, the GEF has no reason to intervene any more. It exists only to make things environmentally reasonable. It is also suggested that baseline is not that reasonable in the north, so GEF is hardly credible trying to impose this to (at least per capita) less polluting countries. Beyond the logical debate, however, the most important is that this requirement is not necessary.

(B) A WAY OUT THROUGH A PROPER TARGETING OF THE SELECTED PROJECTS

The real and practical problem to be considered is the sorry fact that GEF's alternative projects are not viable in the host country's economic context. Though there may be a solution to that, at GEF's level. Here one can use the combination of GEF's small size and willingness and ability to pay by certain segments of the host country's population.

The idea is a compromise: To allow market pricing for the project's specific output—but not to try to intervene at the country's level. There is an indisputable willingness and ability to pay from two categories: The well-off, and the professional users for whom access to an improved quality and reliable service would be highly beneficial— for example middle level farmers in rural areas that need regular electricity supply for water pumping purposes. But these consumers will pay more only when assured they will actually get improved service by the extra payment. Today, the problem is as follows: These segments know their additional contribution will not translate into better-being. Money is absorbed through inefficiency and corruption at every level, or the service is actually tapped by fare dodgers—for example those who pilfer power, causing overload as well as power and financial deficit to the supply company. So the rich users prefer to keep paying less—the subsidized rate—for the bad service. In practice, they hijack most of the subsidy thanks to higher per capita consumption. To make profit from those who have the ability to pay, the solution might be to ensure exclusivity of market-priced product (e.g. power) for them. This seems debatable at first sight, as the GEF is not here to make profit from the rich. However, everybody could benefit from such a scheme: First, the GEF is not big enough to create a two-tier system, which is good luck; second the existing utilities, presently mainly trusted by the rich, would be made available for the poor. This way the larger contribution of the rich is of use to everybody, making this a positive (as opposed to regressive) policy.

Achieving this requires certain conditions. First, the final users must be clearly identifiable—to ensure payment ability and the possibility of exclusivity. This in turn is feasible if the group is geographically well delimited and homogeneous. If one takes the example of power supply to farmers it is possible to set up an off-grid plant with specific voltage to supply the pumps. In case of domestic users, in Delhi for instance there exists clear area segregation. The districts closely correspond to different revenue levels, the well-off being grouped in selected, well-known colonies.[5] There again it is possible to supply them with at least base load from a specific source. Secondly, it has to be technically feasible that the group enjoys effective exclusivity with the improved service. This is not always easy, and represents a limit to the proposal. Alternatively, it sets a condition to GEF's intervention: Work on projects where exclusivity is possible. Lastly, capacity trusting should be avoided: The beneficiaries of the new service should not cumulate it with the previous one. In the case of power supply, ensuring this should be possible as supply equipment (cables) is relatively out of the influence and control of the user, and double wiring in a house is not so easy to install.

All this would not be achievable if GEF had to act on a big scale: Neither exclusivity nor undistorted pricing would be feasible then. But what usually is a drawback is exploited here as an advantage. As it does not modify the overall situation, GEF is almost neutral. It can sneak into niches without changing the overall scene—and in this way will not attract opposition. It can be used to improve the situation punctually—which is the best it can achieve anyway. This should make the project acceptable for the donors and attractive for the recipient.

2. For an Effective Replication of the Projects

(A) THE CONDITION TO REPLICATION

In the texts, the GEF implicitly defines the conditions for a project to be replicable. It should lose its incremental cost—then it becomes commercially viable. As one knows, GEF's mission is to reduce transaction costs, trigger scale effects and learning, and also influence domestic regulations that might help a technology to reach profitability (for example through more stringent environmental norms). This however is not enough. If then the project becomes replicable, it does not mean actually replicated. A technique is picked up if it is the most competitive option available, a word that for developing countries often means cheapest. In other words, the condition of success for the GEF is to bring the project to the competitiveness threshold, which is lower than the zero incremental cost. So an answer to the question of the numerous technical studies is to focus on those studies that evaluate cost reduction potentials according to the volume of equipment produced or the number of units installed. Such studies are rare today. They could help giving elements on which technologies could concentrate for a dynamic cost-effectiveness.

(B) CONSEQUENCES ON GEF'S OPERATIONS

The previous lines meet the fundamental diversity versus programme dilemma. One has no real solutions here but the significance of the scale economies phenomenon, central to GEF's technology strategy is emphasized. For a given budget size, the context in which one reflects, more projects mean smaller projects on an average. One clearly distinguishes between learning, which accumulates with the number of projects, and scale economies, for which the influence of the increasing number of projects (i.e. of the correlated decreasing size) is ambiguous. Scale effects can be expected at two levels: Technology production process; project setting and operation. Four cases are possible:

- If there are no scale economies at any level, only small, but similar projects are to be picked up, so that learning is maximized and scale diseconomies minimized. Technology diversity is to be fostered;
- If there are scale economies only for production, equipment should be built in a centralized way, but projects should be many and scattered. As compared to the previous case, efficiency *a priori* commands less technological diversity—less programmes;
- If there are scale economies in the project's investment and operation, technological diversity will be encouraged but where the learning and size-related cost reduction of projects is concerned, it is hard to say what the bottom line will be;
- If there are scale economies both in technology production and at the project level, it is again difficult to tell *ex-ante*, without further studies, which effect—learning or size—will dominate, and which is the optimal size for a project. One can however say that technology diversity will not be looked for following a strict cost-related criterion.

Given these elements and with a concern to remain realistic, one suspects the 'right' choice will (or should?) move around four or five technology options,[6] implemented through a good number of small or medium-sized projects to benefit from learning, foster know-how and give a chance to own replication by host countries. One would add that concentrating on mature low-incremental cost technologies, plus on projects which can be repeated with minimum changes (i.e. additional costs) could help.

B. The Financing: Making it Transparent, Adding Possibilities

1. *A Need to Clarfy the Rationale*

(A) IS INCREMENTAL COST APPROPRIATE?

Available literature on the subject informs one that the incremental cost concept has large advantages and drawbacks. The idea here is to inquire into the practical handiness of the concept, in other words, to see how it is used by executing agencies, at the project level. The answer to this seems to be an interesting criterion to decide on its value.

At the beginning of GEF, incremental cost was a rigid concept embodied in the 'Type I/Type II' perspective. The GEF did not want to finance no-regret, negative incremental costs projects. As a result it was ignoring the best, cheapest reduction options, under the reason that these options should have been picked up by the host countries, following the nice economic logic. This was rather absurd, all the more so as the GEF was professing the cost-effectiveness principle; the sharp dichotomy was smoothened even before the end of the pilot phase. The transition was eased by the discovery of hidden, 'transaction' cost, up to then missed in the analysis. They explained why apparently economically viable GHG reducing options had been left untapped: Information imperfections, risk, funds and credit rationing or institutional gap could help understand the paradox. The good thing with the transaction costs was that they allowed to retain the incremental cost concept at the root of the GEF—avoiding a back-to-square-one situation. Incremental costs that had seemed negative were turned positive by closer examination.

If practical, this approach gives way to almost anything. Transaction cost is a vast and moving notion. Even without suspecting dishonesty on the part of applicants, one easily realizes that finding positive incremental costs is a matter of interpretation in the projects' proposals. There must appear something called incremental costs, that will be the basis for funds transfer—so lets find them. Every actor is satisfied with the process: GEF's administrators which must be able to justify their disbursement, and the host country that makes its project eligible. Procedural, re-tape logic turns the economic rationale into rhetoric, and spoils its grounds.

Another reason why incremental costs are difficult to rely upon in day to day operations is the reality of GEF's position and significance for the projects considered. When the investment starts, the GEF is a mere (soft credit line in the middle of a much larger, often complex financing scheme. A GEF's project exists only in Washington. From the square 'project documents' to money use on the field, the Facility's logic gets diluted, and the incremental costs disappear. The concept is not used, because it is not applicable, by the executing agents as at their level the GEF finances renewable energy. This confusion is impossible to avoid, as GEF's dollars are associated with other funds which do not pursue the same objectives.

It is fair that the term incremental cost is used as an accounting principle, but it is unrealistic to expect it to perform as a selection criterion. A clearer signal is needed for host countries.

(B) FITTING TO LOCAL DEVELOPMENTAL GOALS AND NEEDS: THE INCIDENCE PERSPECTIVE

This signal could partly result from a narrowing of the scope of eligible projects and programmes in a direction such that host countries are ensured that the country-driven perspective is a reality—which would eventually make them more confident with the instrument.

For this one proposes to use the incidence perspective. Though difficult to identify from the yet limited experience on GEF's projects, the incidence question has been widely debated (Pearce and Barrett, 1993). It concerns the distribution of positive and negative local impacts from a project: Who do they accrue to? As far as positive impacts, i.e. gross benefits are concerned, the nature of GEF's projects tells one that they should be the same from the alternative project as from the baseline, as the same service is to be achieved by the cleaner project.[7] But the costs have no reason to be the same, neither supported by the same actors; jobs balance or nuisance could be different.[8] This is incidence. As experience already shows, it is not easy to forecast, nor is it to control. It has a big influence on the success of the project, though. To remedy the problem, it has been suggested to carry out a 'social impact appraisal' in each case. One deems it to be difficult.

Instead one would recommend to play safe and restrain the GEF to zero-incidence projects. This means additional as opposed to substitutive projects, a distinction that appears in the document 'Financing of GEF's Projects' (GEF Council, 1996a). Projects are additional if new funds or funds dedicated to other activities than GHG emitting ones are used to GEF's objectives; they are substitutive if existing, GHG-related funds are redirected towards the GEF. Additional projects are set up where nothing exists or is planned—they replace nothing. Their baseline is fictitious, to this extent that it is reconstructed for the GEF to identify its level of contribution ('what would have been done if...'). One's recommendation may appear questionable, as it comes to excluding all the 'dirty' projects which are going to emit and could have been avoided. Once again, however, one finds it realistic given the small size of the GEF; its mission is not to substantially abate emissions[9]—in which it cannot succeed—but, through the abatement it achieves, to modify the future emission pathways by including technological change.

On the whole, one thinks there is a clear trade-off to strike between the satisfaction of focusing on 'real baseline' abatement and host countries' reinforced involvement.

2. *Enlarging the Financing Tools and Channels*

(A) USING VARIOUS INSTRUMENTS

What one has to say here is rather common, still it deserves to be repeated. The GEF should enlarge its resource base as much as possible. First, this means perfectly manage the existing funds. (Soft) loans should be used where possible instead of gifts, especially for commercial activities where the market barrier originates from a lack of funds for initial investment. Once the business is on, the GEF can be refunded out of the profits. When risk is involved, the GEF can guarantee losses: Acting to a limited extent like an insurance would save from disbursing funds systematically.

Adequate phasing of disbursement with the project financing needs should be ensured: Delays in completion mean waste, but so does an initial flow of capital which cannot be readily absorbed.[10]

This phasing could for example be done through the creation of 'trust funds' receiving the entire budget at the beginning and managing it in the name of the GEF.

(B) APPEARING ON THE GLOBAL FINANCIAL MARKET

Finally one can suggest that the GEF can directly come into international capital markets, where it would lend, and borrow through the issue of bonds, like any public entity can do. From what one knows, this has not been done yet. Why not enlarge the role of the Facility to an environmental bank? This would at least be an attempt at providing it with the means proportionate to its mission.

CONCLUSION

This conclusion aims to draw an operational, project-oriented picture from the various remarks made in the text. One thinks they build a coherent set.

The first point, that comes as a product from the observation of the Indian scene, is that more emphasis should now be laid on emission abating projects than on technical studies. Remaining studies should be focused on the evaluation of costs reduction potentials for each technology, thus serve as a direct input to the selection of investment projects.

The GEF does not have to work with macro-ranging conditionalities, as it harms more than it helps. GEF's projects could however be market-priced and tap local pockets of willingness and ability to pay, provided the users of the new exclusive service make the existing capacities available for the needy and keep on contributing to the public facilities. The possibility of enforcing this will provide a criterion to be checked in selection procedure.

Replication of GEF's project by the host country is a must. This concern could lead to the achievement of numerous small projects—but the answer will ultimately depend on the technology production and project's operations characteristics, in particular the expected scale effects. Technologies selected should be mature but unconventional for host countries.

The incidence of GEF's intervention on local populations could usefully become a criterion for project selection. Recognizing this will encourage host country co-operation and trust in the scheme.

To a sense, it would lead to focus on additional,[11] as opposed to substitutive projects. Incremental cost remains as an accounting principle.

Applying these recommendations, at first sight while reducing the range and diversity of GEF's projects, would have some large positive side-effects. They provide GEF's administration with precise decision elements, and host countries with a clearer signal of the Facility's priorities, which happen to be beneficial for them. They might also expedite the selection to disbursement process. Summing up, one would say, this method of action comes to use developmental means to an environmental goal.

NOTES

1. For the period 1995-8, GEF had a budget amounting to US $2 billion. In February 1998, the new envelope for 1998-2001 has been revised upward to US $2.75 billion.
2. Whatever cost reductions, PV power plus appliances is bound to remain too expensive for the rural poor without exogenous, development-driven purchasing power increase for this segment.
3. It has been estimated that even used in most cost-efficient options, GEF's money could abate at most one month world emissions on a three year budget period.
4. One may say that some industrial interests are pushing hard behind GEF's front-window?
5. All the more so that these colonies suffer less from power cuts....
6. Because the (political) requirement of technology diversity is written in GEF's principles and a minimum number of programmes is needed to abide by the precaution principle.
7. The typical example is that of a power plant, whose users will be the same whatever the fuel source.
8. Here the example is that of the imported PV as opposed to the coalmine, or the small hydro option versus the big dam project....
9. Still its mission is to abate emissions.
10. This may happen when the project has long gestation period, or when there are recurrent costs.
11. In other words, with no real or planned baseline.

REFERENCES

Ahuja, D. (1993), *Incremental Cost of Actions to Mitigate the Risk of Climate Change,* Communication, Workshop for GEF Participants on the topic of incremental costs, 21 September, Washington, DC.

Brandon, C. and Hommann, K. (1995), *The cost of inaction: Valuing the economy-wide cost of environmental degradation in India,* Asia Environment Division, World Bank, Washington, DC.

Chen, X. (1997), 'The "Dieselization" of the Indian Economy', *Geopolitics of Energy,* 19/1, pp. 9-12.

CMIE (1996), *India's Energy Sector*, Centre for Monitoring Indian Economy, Mumbai.

CSE (1991), *Global Warming in an Unequal World: A case of environmental colonialism*, Centre for Science and Environment, New Delhi.

——— (1997), *Dying wisdom, State of India's Environment: A Citizen's Report*, Centre for Science and Environment, New Delhi.

FFEM (1996), *Rapport du CST au titre de l'exercice 1995*, Fonds Française pour l'Environment Mondial, Paris.

GEF Council (1996a), *Financing GEF Projects*, Global Environment Facility, Washington, DC.

——— (1996b), *Incremental Costs*, Global Environment Facility, Washington, DC.

——— (1996c), *GEF Strategy for Engaging the Private Sector*, Global Environment Facility, Washington, DC.

——— (1996d), *Work Program Proposed for Council Approval*, Global Environment Facility, Washington, DC.

——— (1996e), *Casting the Net Widely: A Project to Enable Country-Driven Project Development*, Project for Review, Global Environment Facility, Washington, DC.

——— (1996f), *India: Solar Thermal Power*, Project for Review, Global Environment Facility, Washington, DC.

——— (1996g), *Renewable Energy and Energy Efficiency Fund*, Project for Review, Global Environment Facility, Washington, DC.

GEF (1996a), *India, Ecodevelopment Project*, Project Document, The World Bank, Washington, DC.

——— (1996b), *Operational Strategy,* Global Environment Facility, Washington, DC.

——— (1996c), *The Project Cycle,* Global Environment Facility, Washington, DC.

——— (1994), *India, Optimizing Development of Small Hydel Resources in the Hilly Regions*, United Nations Development Program, Washington, DC.

——— (1994a), *India, Development of High-Rate Biomethanation Process as Means of Reducing Greenhouse Gas Emissions*, United Nations Development Program, Washington, DC.

——— (1992), *India, Alternate Energy Project*, Project Document, The World Bank, Washington, DC.

Menanteau, P. (1996), *Note de travail sur le FEM*, Working Paper, IEPE, Grenoble.

Ministry of Finance (1997), *Economic Survey 1996-7*, Government of India, New Delhi.

Mintzer, M.I. (1993), *Implementing the FCCC. Incremental Costs and the Role of the GEF*, Working Paper no. 4, Global Environment Facility, Washington, DC.

MNES (1997), *Annual Report 1996-7*, Ministry of Non-Conventional Energy Resources, government of India, New Delhi.

Pearce, D., Barrett, S. (1993), *Incremental Cost and Biodiversity Conservation*, Communication Workshop for GEF Participants on the topic of incremental costs, 21 September, Washington, DC.

Shukla (1994), *Global Greenhouse Gas Policy and the Developing Countries: Problems with Abatement Approach and Incremental Cost*, Working Paper, Indian Institute of Management, Ahmedabad.

TERI (1996), *Tata Energy Directory and Yearbook, 1996-7*, Tata Energy Research Institute, New Delhi.

Venkata Ramana, P. (ed.) (1997), *Rural and renewable energy: Perspectives from developing countries*, Tata Energy Research Institute, New Delhi.

Venkata Ramana, P., Kozloff, K. (1995), *Renewable Energy Development in India, Analysis of the US Policy Experience*, Tata Energy Research Institute, New Delhi.

Venkata Ramana, P., Srinivas, S.N. (eds.) (1997), *Biomass Energy System*, Proceedings of the International Conference, 26-7 February 1997, TERI, New Delhi.

Coal and Energy for the Twenty-first Century in India

JOHN J. GALE

INTRODUCTION

India is the second most populous country in the world, with a population estimated at 954 million in mid-1996. The population growth rate has been around 2 per cent per annum since the 1980s. This growth rate represents an incremental population increase of 15 million per year. India could become the most populous country on the earth by 2030, with its population predicted to stabilize at around 1.5 billion. Economically India is making steady progress although it has under performed compared to some of its neighbours. In the 1980s the economy grew at an average rate of 5.5 per cent. However growth could not be sustained and the economy overheated leading to a liquidity crisis in 1991. This crisis lead to a process of economic reform and greater deregulation and liberalization of the economy. Over the next five years the economy grew at 6 to 7 per cent per annum but growth again slowed in the latter half of 1996. GDP at market prices stood at US $330 million in 1996. GDP per capita is only US $346, one of the lowest in the world.

Growth in economic activity has been accompanied by a substantial increase in energy consumption coupled with growing use of commercial fuels. Commercial energy consumption has doubled since 1985, from 184 mtce/y to 350 mtce/y in 1995. An average growth rate of 5.6 per cent per annum. It is projected that India's growing economy will drive energy demand growth at 4.6 per cent annually until 2010. Trends in energy consumption have been strongly influenced by the growth in population. One of the major growth areas in India's commercial energy demand has occurred in the industrial sector. Industry now accounts for approximately half of India's commercial energy consumption. India has a high energy demand in industries such as iron and steel, cement, fertilizers and chemical feedstocks. However growth in the industrial sector fell back in 1996 due to an infrastructure problem; namely a lack of electricity. Demand for electricity has also grown in sectors such as agriculture. For instance, irrigation accounts for 27 per cent of India's electricity consumption.

Electricity is vital for India's economic development. However, the country currently faces a power shortage of around 11.5 per cent and a peaking shortage of 18 per cent. With demand increasing at about 10 per cent per year power shortages will increasingly jeopardize future economic growth. The current energy scene in India is dominated by the use of coal. Coal now accounts for over 50 per cent of the primary energy demand and over 70 per cent of the electricity generated is produced in coal fired plant. India has large reserves of coal and lignite compared to other fossil fuels and alternative energy sources, and mining output has steadily grown over recent years to meet increased demand. It is therefore reasonable to expect that indigenous supplies of coal and lignite are likely to remain the dominant fuel resource for future development of the Indian economy in the next century.

This article explores the prospects for coal in India in the twenty-first century and highlights potential issues such as the environmental impact of increased coal use. This latter issue represents a significant challenge, how to reconcile increased energy consumption and economic growth with protection of the global climate. One way of reducing the impact of increased coal burn is to introduce more efficient clean coal burning technology.

ENERGY RESOURCES

India's energy resources are summarized in Table 1.

FOSSIL FUEL RESOURCES

As can be seen from Table 1, India's most abundant energy resource is coal. The estimated reserves quoted in the table represent around

TABLE 1: SUMMARY OF INDIAN ENERGY RESOURCES

Fuel	*Resource*	*Mtce*
Coal	69,947 mt	47,240
Oil	600 mt (4,300 mbbl)	880
Natural gas	686 x 10^9 m^3 (24,226 bn.f^3)	1080
Uranium	13,030 t	190
Hydro	600 tWh/y	74 (per year)

7 per cent of the total world coal reserves. At current extraction rates these reserves would take more than 200 years to become depleted. Estimates of total coal resources are as high as 200 Gt.

Compared to coal, India has only modest oil and gas reserves. Oil reserves are currently estimated at 600 mt with an estimated 17 year exhaustion time at current utilization rates. Two-thirds of oil production comes from the offshore Bombay High oilfield.

To date, India has been effectively self-sufficient in natural gas. Reserves are estimated at 700 billion m^3, which is mostly located offshore in the Bombay High gasfields. Gas production in 1996 was 20.4 billion m^3. At current consumption rates these reserves are sufficient to last for around 33 years.

Coal bed methane offers an interesting prospect as a new energy resource. Coal bed methane resources have not been estimated accurately but could be as high as one trillion m^3. Estimates of possible production rates vary from 5 to 11 billion m^3 per year. However, as yet there are no commercial extraction projects.

NUCLEAR POWER

Ten nuclear reactors are operational in India and a further eight are under development. The total installed capacity is around 2,225 mWe. Indian government sources have indicated that indigenous resources of uranium are sufficient to support around 8,000 mWe of nuclear capacity. There have been considerable problems with the development of the nuclear industry in India and it is not expected that the full potential will ever be achieved. One major issue has been a lack of foreign investment and assistance due to political fall out from India's nuclear tests in 1974. The most recent nuclear tests will obviously not be beneficial to further nulear power developments in India.

RENEWABLE ENERGY

The resource potential for large-scale hydroelectric power has been estimated at 600 tWh/y. Of the total potential about 20 per cent has, or is, being developed. Current installed capacity is 21 GWe with a further 24 GWe under construction or planned. Currently, the large hydroelectric schemes represent about 25 per cent of the total electricity generating capacity but in fact only supply about 3.3 per cent of India's primary energy supply. The greatest potential for further development of large hydroelectric projects is in the north and north-east of the country, especially in the lower hills of the Himalayan region. There is also interest in the development of small-scale hydro schemes for the provision of electricity in more isolated areas. Resource estimates are around 5,000 mWe, however progress in developing this resource is slow, principally due to the large capital investment requirements. The total installed capacity of small scale hydro schemes to date is 121 mWe with a further 234 mWe under construction.

The use of other renewable energy resources is being actively encouraged by the Indian government. Government projections are for 3,000 mWe of additional power from renewable resources. These resources include: Crop residues such as rice husk and bagasse, wind energy, solar power and geothermal energy. It is, however, recognized that the total amount of power that can be generated by these resources is small compared to fossil fuels. The renewable resource can however provide a significant contribution to satisfying energy demand in rural and remote regions.

CURRENT ENERGY SITUATION

Coal is currently the major commercial primary energy source in India. Coal accounts for 56 per cent of the commercial energy mix. (see Figure 1). This proportion has remained unchanged since the mid-1970s.

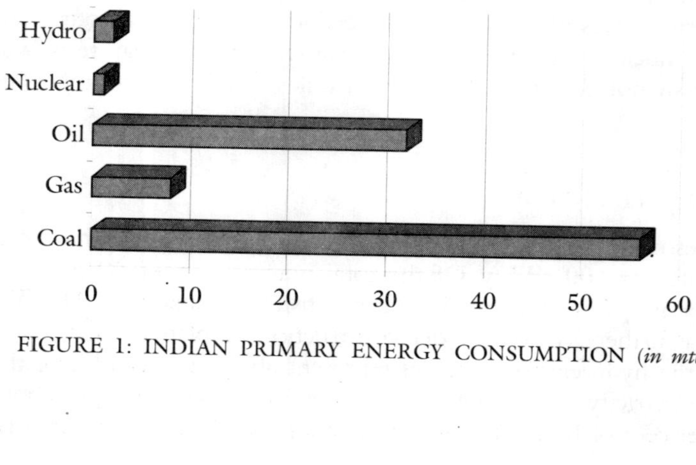

FIGURE 1: INDIAN PRIMARY ENERGY CONSUMPTION (*in mtce*)

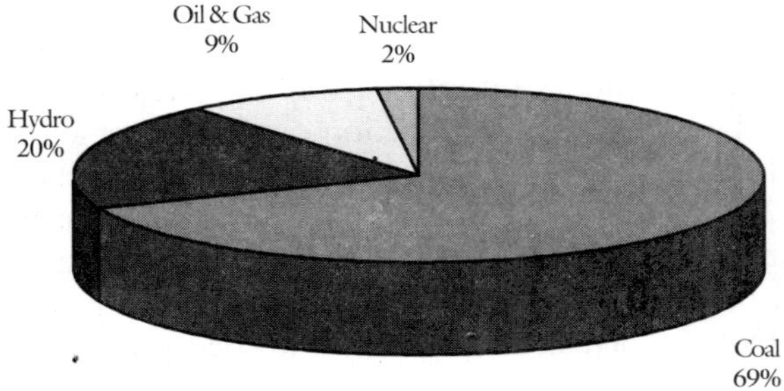

FIGURE 2: POWER GENERATION FUEL MIX, 1995

The major market for coal is in the power generation sector where coal fired power plant comprise 64 per cent of the total generating capacity and 69 per cent of electricity output. Oil and gas fired plants provide about 8 per cent, hydro 20 per cent and nuclear 2 per cent. The market share for the fuels discussed are illustrated in Figure 2.

As discussed India is currently experiencing a major infrastructure problem; namely it cannot generate sufficient electricity to meet its demand. With demand increasing at about 10 per cent per year, the gap between supply and demand can only widen which has the potential to jeopardize future economic growth. To meet increasing electricity demand the Eighth Five Year Plan (1992-7) projected the need for an additional 48 GW of power generation capacity. However, annual installed additional capacity barely reached 30 GW due to financial constraints. Most of the new capacity coming on stream is based on coal fired plant. It is projected that an annual increase of 10-12 GW is needed over the next ten years to meet projected demand. It is recognized that the Indian government has insufficient resources to meet the full growth requirements and that a climate for private sector investment in the power sector is required. India has therefore embarked on a programme of encouraging private sector power station development. Development of independent power projects (IPPs) has been slow to date, but is now expected to increase due to the relaxation of government restrictions. IPPs will, however, not make a significant impact on power generation capacity before 2002.

Oil now accounts for 32 per cent of India's primary energy supply. Growth in the transport sector has largely been responsible for increased oil use. India's oil refining capacity cannot meet current demand and indigenous oil production can only meet about half the demand. India is therefore becoming increasingly dependent on oil imports. The need for oil imports is placing a heavy burden on foreign exchange. Almost half of India's trade deficit is due to imports of oil and petroleum products. Natural gas use has grown steadily and in 1996, the demand marginally exceeded production for the first time. Increased domestic demand can only be met by imports which will increase the foreign exchange burden.

India's nuclear power industry is not expected to make a significant contribution to future power generating capacity requirements. The existing nuclear power plants have a poor reliability record and low load factors (40 per cent) compared to western plants (75-80 per cent). The principal reasons for the poor performance of the nuclear industry in India are:

- Lack of foreign investment and assistance due to political factors.
- Grid instability which causes frequent plant outages and long plant restoration times.

The problems associated with grid instability are not limited to the nuclear industry alone. All industrial production sectors such as steel, cement and fertilizers have major problems. Each time there is a fluctuation in the frequency of the electricity supply (due to undersupply of the grid) production plant shut downs occur. Some production facilities can take as long as five days to reinstate full production capacity. Some fertilizer plant in the south of India have indicated that up to 3 months operational production can be lost in one year. This degree of lost production can seriously undermine the profitability of companies. In many industrial sectors such as cement and fertilizers there is now considerable interest in the installation of cogeneration plants. These cogeneration plants can provide both process steam and sufficient electricity to meet internal demand, in this way production companies can become self sufficient in energy. The big issue preventing an expansion of cogeneration plant in India is again capital investment requirements, with most companies state-owned, this would place a large burden on the Indian Treasury.

ENERGY TRENDS

Growth in economic activity in India has been accompanied by a substantial increase in energy consumption. Commercial energy consumption has doubled since 1985 on average by 5.6 per year, from 184 mtce/y to 375 mtce/y today. Growth in commercial energy demand has been fairly constant over the last decade. Table 2 lists primary energy consumption figures for commercial fuels used in India from 1990 to 1996.

Growth in the use of fossil fuel has mirrored that in commercial energy as a whole, nuclear and hydro power have suffered capacity constraints. As stated earlier, one of the major growth, in India's commercial energy demand has been in the industrial sector in industries such as iron and steel, cement, fertilizers and chemical feedstocks. However, growth in the industrial sector fell back in 1996 due to an infrastructure problem namely a lack of electricity. As discussed earlier the shortage of electricity is seriously undermining the profitability of Indian industry and is effectively hindering industrial growth.

It is projected that India's growing economy will drive energy demand growth at 4.6 per cent annually until 2010. Also, the current gap between energy production and consumption will widen. In 1995 total indigenous energy production was 8,245 PJ (281 mtce) whilst consumption totalled 10,101 PJ (345 mtce), with net imports accounting for 21 per cent of the total. By 2010, energy output is expected to reach 14,500 to 17,500 PJ (500-600 mtce) but demand could be as high as 20,500 to 23,500 PJ (700-800 mtce). This means that energy imports will have to rise by 300 per cent from current levels.

The future fuel mix is expected to remain similar to the current fuel mix at least until 2010. On the production side the output of

TABLE 2: PRIMARY ENERGY CONSUMPTION IN INDIA BY FUEL

Fuel	*Primary Energy Consumption (mtce)*						*% Change*
	1992	*1993*	*1994*	*1995*	*1996*	*1997*	
Coal	167	172	177	187	200	212	7
Gas	20	21	22	25	28	31	10
Oil	89	90	96	104	112	121	8
Nuclear	2	2	2	3	3	4	5
Hydro	9	9	10	9	9	8	-8
Total	287	294	307	329	352	376	7

coal and gas will increase in line with demand apart from oil production which will begin to decline after 2005.

FUTURE COAL DEMAND

Projections for future coal demand in India are given in Table 3 based on industry sector requirements. The figures in brackets represent percentage demand changes.

As can be seen, coal demand in the electricity sector is projected to double by 2010. Steel manufacture and cement production will also increase coal demand but to a lesser degree. Demand for coking coal will be double that of steam coal in the steel sector. Only a fifth of India's coal has coking properties. Demand from the steel industry has outstripped supply, which has meant that import of coking coal has been necessary to meet demand. Coal is also the dominant fuel used in the cement sector. The coal industry has however failed to keep pace with the cement industry and production has been maintained by switching to lower quality coals, substituting lignite for hard coal and by using imports. Since the demand for coal in cement manufacture will double by 2010, the gap between domestic supply and demand can be expected to widen.

Other industry sectors such as fertilizers have expanded their demand for coal. Coal demand in this sector has grown from 0 in 1970 to 4.3 mt/y in 1995. This sector in particular will continue to expand due to the need to increase fertilizer production to meet increased demand for food from an ever increasing population. Coal is increasingly being looked at as an energy resource to meet this growth in production because of the high comparative cost of alternative feedstocks such as oil and gas.

The increased use of coal in production industries such as cement

TABLE 3: COAL DEMAND FORECAST

Sector	*Estimated Coal Demand (mt)*			
	1996-7	*2001-2*	*2006-7*	*2009-10*
Power	215	285 (+6 %)	400 (+7 %)	500 (+8 %)
Steel	40	49 (4 %)	60 (+4 %)	68 (+4 %)
Cement	18	21 (+4 %)	30 (+7 %)	37 (+7 %)
Other	52	61 (+3 %)	75 (+4 %)	85 (+4 %)
Total	325	416 (+5 %)	565 (+6 %)	690 (+7 %)

and fertilizers largely goes against Western practice since the process is much less energy efficient compared to those that use oil or gas.

To meet the increased demand it will be necessary for indigenous coal production to increase significantly. However as noted earlier there is already a gap between supply and demand in certain industrial sectors which can only widen in the future. It has been predicted that government owned mining companies should be able to increase their output to produce around 530 mt by 2010, from their current output of 290 mt, this will require a year on year capacity increase of 20 mt. Assuming this projected increase in production can be met, it still leaves a supply gap of 160 mt. Significant government investment in the mining sector will be required to close this supply gap. Some private mining projects could come on stream but it is clear that imports will be needed to augment domestically produced coal.

ENVIRONMENTAL ISSUES

To meet its growing energy demand due to its increasing population and increased economic growth India needs to increase energy production. Coal will be the major energy source for this increased energy production. However, the increased use of coal in India will significantly increase emissions of global pollutants such as CO_2 at a time when the rest of the world is increasingly looking to reduce CO_2 emissions in order to alleviate the potentially devastating effects of global climate change.

To date, environmental issues relating to the extraction and utilization of coal have not had top priority in India, but this situation is beginning to change. Coal users are now coming under pressure to use coal more efficiently and cleanly. The main issues relating to coal use are gaseous emissions of particulates and SO_2 and NO_2, ash disposal. SO_2 and NO_2 and particulate emissions have more regional effects than that of CO_2 but can adversely affect the health of the population, which in turn can become an economic burden through increased health care requirements. Ash disposal requires large quantities of land and significant quantities of water. In this case, water resources are diverted from agricultural purposes and polluted such that they are not fit for future use. As coal consumption increases so will the environmental impact of coal use.

The average calorific value of coal used in Indian power stations has decreased from 22 GJ/t in 1970 to 15 GJ/t currently. As a result, unit consumption of coal per unit of power generated has increased and the efficiency of electrical power generation has decreased. The main reason for the reduction in quality is the increase in coal ash content from 30-35 per cent to 40-45 per cent. The increased coal ash content means greater ash discharged as fly ash per unit of electricity generated. It is now mandatory for all power stations to fit Electrostatic Precipitators to reduce particulate emissions. Large amounts of ash are currently disposed of in ash lagoons using wet disposal methods which require high levels of water use. Increased use of coal will lead to even greater ash disposal problems than at present.

The amount of ash produced can be reduced by coal washing. However there is a serious shortage of washery plant in India which means that greater tonnages of run of mine coal have to be transported which itself leads to infrastructure problems. The shortage of washery plant has meant that priority has been given to washing coking coals rather than power station coals. There are plans to construct more washeries to endeavour to reduce the coal ash content back to 30 per cent after 2000. Again significant investment by the government is required. Private sector coal washeries are also planned.

Ash utilization in India is low, only about 5 per cent of the ash generated from power station is used in brick and concrete manufacture. Increased utilization of ash would have direct environmental benefits.

Currently there are no emission standards for SO_2 and NO_2. Ground level concentrations are set by minimum stack height requirements. These stack heights are 200 metres for plants with a capacity of 200-500 mWe and 275 metres for plants greater than 500 mWe. Indian coals are typically low in sulphur so there is less of a need to introduce flue gas desulphurization equipment. Low NO_2 burners are being fitted at new power stations because these represent a low cost investment to reduce emissions. It is not yet mandatory to fit low NO_2 burners on existing plant, but this may come in a few years.

THE ROLE FOR CLEAN COAL TECHNOLOGY

In the Western hemisphere there has been considerable activity in the development of advanced clean coal technology for utility scale power generation applications. This technology has been designed to increase the efficiency of electrical generation and significantly reduce environmental pollution compared to conventional combustion technology. The benefits of this technology to India are:

- Reduced emissions of CO_2 per unit of electrical energy generated.
- Reduced production of ash per unit of electrical energy generated.
- Significantly reduced emissions of SO_2 and NO_2 per unit of electrical energy generated.

The standard technology for power generation from coal is pulverized fuel (pf) combustion. Modern Western hard coal fired pf plant can operate at electrical generation efficiencies of up to 38 per cent. However, a new generation of advanced pf plant, with local favourable conditions, have been demonstrated to attain 43 per cent efficiency and plant fitted with supercritical steam cycles have been predicted to attain efficiencies up to 45 per cent. In India with high ash and lignites, coals efficiencies as low as 28 to 30 per cent are quoted in practise on some of the older and smaller units. The more advanced coal fired systems under development include:

- Circulating fluidized bed combustion (CFBC).
- Pressurised fluidized bed combustion (PFBC).
- Integrated gasification combined cycles (IGCC).

The electrical efficiencies and emissions from these technologies compared to existing pf plant are compared in Tables 4 and 5.

These technologies have two main advantages over conventional pf technology namely: Higher electrical generation efficiencies and lower environmental impact. In the Indian context higher power station efficiencies mean reduced amounts of pollutants produced (in particular ash and CO_2) per unit of electricity generated.

In a circulating fluidized bed combustor (CFBC) the fuel is burnt in the combustor along with limestone for sulphur reduction. In a CFBC the gas velocity is such that a substantial part of the bed

TABLE 4: COMPARISON OF EFFICIENCIES OF ADVANCED COAL FIRED PLANT

Technology	*Nominal Size, mWe*	*Efficiency, LHV*
Pf	200	38
CFBC	200	38
PFBC	200	41
IGCC	250	45

TABLE 5: ENVIRONMENTAL IMPACT DATA

Technology	*Nominial Size mWe*	*CO_2 kg/kWh*	*SO_2 Retention per cent*	*NO_2 mg/m^3*	*Particulates mg/m^3*
Pf	200	0.87	5	1,000-1,400	150
Pf+FGD	200	0.87	90	600-800	<50
CFBC	200	0.86	90	100-300	<30
PFBC	200	0.82	90	150-300	<30
IGCC	250	0.78	99	120-300	Negligible

material is entrained in the upward gas flow. The entrained hot solids then leave the combustor reactor and are captured in a high efficiency external cyclone and are then returned, often via heat exchangers, to the base of the combustor unit. Steam can be generated in the water well construction of the combustor and/or in external heat exchangers. Some designs also incorporate super heater panels in the combustor freeboard. The units are used for process steam generation or more typically for power generation in a steam cycle system (electrical efficiencies 39-41 per cent).

The pressurized fluidized bed combustors uses a bubbling fluidized bed operating at pressures up to 12 bar and 850 °C. Limestone is again used for in-situ sulphur retention. The exhaust gas from the boiler then passes to a gas turbine to generate electricity. Steam is raised in in-bed tubes and from the gas turbine exhaust. The steam is then used to generate electricity in a steam turbine. This type of cycle is called a combined cycle and has a higher overall efficiency than a conventional cycle like in a CFBC plant.

Integrated gasification combined cycle is one of the newer technology developments for power generation based on the application of gasification technology in integrated combined cycle systems. Gasification technology is a coal conversion technology which can be further subdivided into three generic types each with its own advantages and disadvantages.

- Entrained flow gasifiers
- Fixed bed gasifiers
- Fluidized bed systems

Each type differs in the characteristics of the zone where the gasification reaction takes place between the fuel and a restricted amount of air or oxygen, usually in the presence of steam.

In integrated gasification combined cycles (IGCC) coal is

converted to a fuel gas (mainly carbon monoxide and hydrogen) by reaction with oxygen or air and steam. The fuel gas is cleaned and burned in a gas turbine which generates power. Heat from the gas turbine exhaust and the gasification and gas cleaning plant is used to generate steam that is fed to a steam turbine, generating additional power, see Figure 3.

IGCC is capable of giving even higher efficiencies and lower emissions than other clean coal technologies such as CFBC or pressurised fluidised bed combustion (PFBC) with average efficiencies predicted to be over 43 per cent. Emissions of SO_2 can be significantly lower with sulphur capture efficiencies of over 99 per cent achievable.

IGCC technology can be regarded as being at the introductory commercial scale. The largest plant to date is under construction in Spain. The plant, based on Prenflo gasification technology, will have a capacity of 340 mWe and will burn hard coal.

Of the advanced technologies CFBC can be regarded as commercially established technology and demonstrated for use with coal up to a scale of 250 mWe. This scale of utility operation is consistent with the typical block size of Indian power plant which is 210 mWe. Development of CFBC technology is still underway.

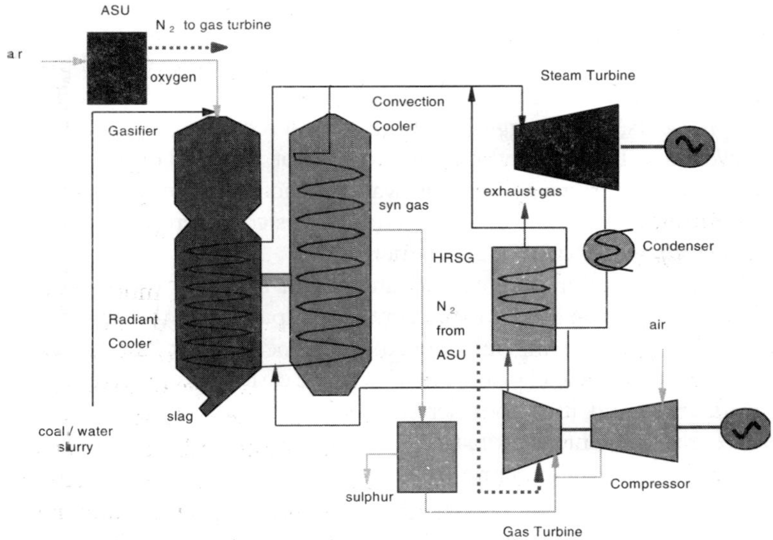

FIGURE 3: SCHEMATIC REPRESENTATION OF AN IGCC PLANT

Manufacturers are now designing boiler units of 500 to 600 mWe. Units of this scale are expected to be commercially available between 2005-10. Currently there are at least three CFBC plant in India, two have been operational since 1995. CFBC units are particularly suitable for low grade fuels such as high ash Indian coals and lignites without significantly affecting efficiency.

CFBC plant also have advantages over pf plant in that their emissions of SO_2 and NO_2 are significantly lower. The capital cost of CFBC is comparable to that of pf plant, without systems for de-SO_2 and de-NO_2. Retrofitting older existing power blocks with CFBC units could be a good near term option to reduce emissions. The costs of these retrofits could be minimized by retaining the existing steam turbine units. If new environmental legislation in India requires reduced emissions of SO_2 and NO_2 the capital cost of installing CFBC compared to pf fitted with FGD and low NO_2 burners will be significantly lower.

There are considerable cost advantages for CFBC over IGCC. The technology therefore represents a good near term solution to meet increased power demand but with reduced environmental impact. The introduction of CFBC technology would not significantly reduce ash disposal issues.

PFBC technology is not considered to be best suited for high ash coals and lignites. One plant has been installed in Spain operating on a relatively high ash coal (36 per cent ash). However, the plant has experienced a number of operational difficulties namely: Fuel feed problems, in-bed agglomeration and ash removal problems from the cyclones. The plant efficiency has also not achieved expectations, one of the contributing reasons was the fact that the plant was a reboilering demonstration. The technology is considered to be more suitable for better quality lower fuels.

IGCC does offer potential advantages in terms of much higher efficiencies and the lowest environmental impact of all the new clean coal technologies being introduced. Efficiencies up to 45 per cent are predicted for IGCC plant. IGCC is at the early stage of commercial introduction and it is considered that it will be at least five years before the current demonstration scale plants indicate sustained operability and can generate sufficient confidence in their reliability to warrant large scale introduction by utility power companies worldwide. There is considerable interest in India in IGCC. One IGCC project is now under construction, which is a cogeneration project at Gujarat which will burn lignite. The plant will produce

52 mW of electricity and 30 mW of steam for the Sanghi cement works. In addition, Bharat Heavy Electrical Ltd have been developing an Indian IGCC process. Two further projects are also under consideration at Sabarmati by Ahmedabad Electric Co. and by Oswal Agro Ltd.

CONCLUSION

1. To meet its increased energy demand from population growth and economic expansion within tight economic constraints India must increase its use of natural resources for energy production.
2. India is currently the third largest coal producer in the world after China and the USA. Coal is currently the primary energy resource in India accounting for 56 per cent of India's primary energy consumption. Coal is the dominant energy resource in the electricity production sector. Coal fired plant represent some 64 per cent of the installed capacity in India and 69 per cent of the electricity generated.
3. The most abundant indigenous fossil energy resource is coal. Oil and gas resources are limited and indigenous supply cannot meet existing demand. Imports of oil and gas will be required although this will place a heavy burden on India's balance of payments. Nuclear and renewable energy resources cannot be expected to increase significantly to offset the need for coal.
4. Coal demand is expected to double from 325 mt/y now to 690 mt/y by 2010. Most of the increase in coal use will be in the power sector
5. The increased use of coal will lead to an increase in environmental pollution unless measures are taken to reduce the environmental impact of coal use. Measures could include: Coal washing, increased ash utilization, use of more efficient coal burning technology.

NOTE

1. On an average, 1 million ton coal equivalent (or mtce)=0.7 million ton oil equivalent.

REFERENCE

IEA (1998), *Energy Statistics and Balances of non-OECD Countries, 1995-6*, International Energy Agency, Paris.

Advanced Technologies for Higher Efficiency in Petroleum Exploration and Production

PHILIPPE ROGIER

MAJOR TRENDS IN THE UPSTREAM SECTOR

Developments in the world energy situation over the past 20 years have shown that hydrocarbon use should continue to expand substantially over the next 25 years, in the absence of a substitute which could amply meet world energy needs. World hydrocarbon demand will grow because of pressure from the newly industrialized countries for which these energy sources are the easiest to develop.

In the long term, this increase will inevitably pose problems for Europe and also India which are and will remain largely dependant on hydrocarbon imports. The only answer is to pursue efforts to boost exploration activities and to develop technologies so as to renew hydrocarbon reserves and make available abundant and diversified oil and gas supplies at the lowest possible cost.

To start with, it is interesting to have a quick look at the evolution of the petroleum industry over the last few decades.

Up to the seventies, the upstream petroleum sector lived in a technically routine way where scientific knowledge and innovation had little room to expand in a rather conservative and lucrative industry, developing its activities mainly in the United States and the Middle East.

Then, the situation changed. There were several reasons for that:

- First, many producing countries had taken control of their oil and gas resources through total or partial nationalization of oil companies. As a result, the large multinational petroleum groups began to search for new reserves to replace the nationalized ones.
- Second, the two oil shocks of 1973 and 1979 gave strategic importance to any discovery and development of reserves outside

of the traditional zones of production (Middle East and, more generally, OPEC countries).

- Third, with the sharp increase of the price per barrel between 1973 and 1981, the upstream activities of the oil companies became by far the major source of income.
- Fourth, after the price drop of 1985-6, the priority of the oil industry was to adapt 'frontier' oil production developed when prices were high to the new market conditions.

These main factors led the major operating companies to change the way they carried out their exploration-production activities, with an increasing trust in R&D to tackle problems. The scientific and technical progress that followed had a net impact on reserves and costs.

These efforts led to the rapid development of zones where the petroleum potential was known, but had been difficult to develop until then, such as the North Sea and Alaska. Between 1973 and 1983, the production of Alaska thus rose from 72 to 625 mbbl/year, and the offshore production of western Europe went from 25 to 1,100 mbbl/year. In addition, a few other countries such as Brazil, India, Malaysia, West Africa and Yemen became attractive areas.

As a consequence, the share in the world oil production of non-OPEC countries (excluding former Soviet Union) increased from 29 per cent to 44 per cent, production by OPEC countries was divided by two, and its relative share decreased from 55 per cent to 33 per cent .

The period from 1985 to 1995 was very illustrative of the capacity of the petroleum industry to reduce overall technical costs, after the price drop of 1985-6, to adapt to the new market conditions. This meant improving productivity and making technological progress so that the cost of this expensive oil could be brought within range of normal oils (maximum US $10 to US $12/barrel) compatible with the new crude prices.

By changing its organization and focusing its efforts on the most promising approaches for reducing technical costs, by optimizing techniques, by using the power of computer processing, the industry managed to significantly lower its technical production costs within the space of just a few years. Most of this production was thus kept and even further developed.

This reduction in technical costs allowed the industry to:

- Diversify its zones of production, thus enlarging its playing field,
- develop technologies for exploration and production in deep sea areas (far beyond 200 metres water depths),
- substantially reduce the investments needed for exploration and production for comparable targets.

A good example of this profound change in the oil situation is the production in the North Sea which, year after year, is reaching new records, despite the fact that ten years ago it seemed to be in decline. This turnabout was possible due to two main reasons:

- Production at a very large number of new fields, even modest ones, which would not have been considered in the past. So far about five hundred small hydrocarbon discoveries have been listed of which close to 150 are marginal fields meant to be developed.
- The prolonged life of big existing fields thanks to better reservoir management and tie up of additional satellite reserves.

The reduction in technical costs was reinforced by substantially shortening the necessary time between the discovery and the start of production. In just a few years, it has been reduced from 5/7 years to 2/3 years, taking advantage of the existing facilities and of the increased speed of the laying of pipes.

Indeed, technical progress and increases in productivity taken together have allowed oil companies to reduce their overall technical costs by US $1/boe each year on an average since the beginning of the 1990s (exploration costs + depreciation + operating costs).

Between 1985 and 1995, the situation has changed considerably due to the combined effect of technological progress and the industry's gains in productivity.

Non-OPEC production of expensive oil, which had production costs of between US $12 and more than US $20/barrel in 1985, experienced a drop in costs to below US $10/barrel. In addition, far from shrinking, this production expanded by 200 million tons. The gap in production costs between the most expensive non-OPEC fields and the large Middle Eastern fields was reduced considerably, from a ratio of 1 to 10 in 1985 to 1 to 3 or 4 today.

Today, at the present level of crude price, cost cutting remains a must and many specialists expect this situation to last.

To maintain their competitivity, oil companies are thus trying to sustain their short-term profits to the maximum, while increasing returns on long-term investments as much as possible. Reducing operating costs, development time and installation costs were one of the methods used to achieve this.

Many oil operating companies think however, that great improvements are still possible through the optimization of the work process as a whole. In-house, the companies are restructuring their organization towards their core business, thus sharply reducing their staff. On the outside, they are forging new relations with petroleum supply and service companies favouring integrated services, such as a complete geophysical survey (data acquisition, processing and interpretation), or the carrying out of a drilling and competition programme as a whole rather than service contracts.

Petroleum supply and service companies are now acting as a general contractor in place of the petroleum operator, even investing in to the short-term R&D for the operating companies. Turnkey contracts are increasing, as well as alliances among oil companies and petroleum supply and service companies in capital and operating expenditures. By this new type of management, operators hope to reduce their expenditures even further. However, it is very likely that the improvements achieved will quickly level off.

NEW TECHNOLOGICAL ACHIEVEMENTS IN EXPLORATION-PRODUCTION

The technological achievements of the past ten years though very substantial, have only come half way. It is important to understand that further cost reduction and higher productivity will continue largely to stem from a better scientific knowledge and the use of new technologies. In the years to come, several major technological objectives have been identified for implementation by many companies (Figure 1).

Nobody knows exactly how much oil and gas remain to be discovered, but one can say that the more one searches for them the more one will have the chances to find them.

For 50 years, many assessments of ultimate oil reserves have been made. They evolve somewhat in time, going from 500 Gbbl in the 1940s to an average of 2,000 Gbbl in the 1980s. The most recent figures range from 1,700 Gbbl to nearly 3,000 Gbbl.

- Basin modeling in under-explored and frontier areas.
- 3D seismic survey and imaging.
- Integrated reservoir studies.
- Horizontal and multibranch wells.
- Deep offshore drilling and subsea completion.

Source: IFP/Strategy & Corporate Planning Division, 1998.

FIGURE 1: ADVANCED TECHNOLOGY FOR HIGHER EFFICIENCY IN E&P

For the most pessimistic observers, the renewal of reserves of liquid hydrocarbons is going to be, in the coming years, the main challenge. For gas, for which the current lifetime of reserves is more than 60 years, it is less critical. In the future, petroleum discoveries will be likely to be smaller and smaller. Whereas the average size of fields in the world has been 35 mbbl to date, the fields of tomorrow will be many times smaller. According to these observers, they will require exploration and development expenditures that will be too high to mobilize the resources they contain, as they will be situated in more and more geologically complex zones and in deeper and deeper formations. These views do not take into consideration the impact of scientific and technical improvements and the pace at which they are applied in the industry. In addition, the opening up of new business deals resulting from privatization and more flexible contractual agreements are attracting more exploration activities.

Whatever the doomsayers think, the oil and gas industry has made some quite remarkable strikes. For instance, between 1990 and today, close to 20 giant fields were discovered with huge reserves of oil, gas or condensates.

Successful operations carried out recently in countries being opened up to foreign oil companies include the following:

- In Latin America, the discovery in Colombia of the giant fields Cusiana-Cupiagua, Volcanera, Opon and Copporo. While in Brazil the discovery of Reconcador in the offshore Campos basin and in Venezuela important oil reserves have been discovered in the eastern basin.

- In western Europe, Great Britain was particularly rewarded with the discoveries made in west of the Shetland Islands, an area where water depths however are twice those of the North Sea.
- In north Africa, exploration in Algeria was particularly fruitful, as around 1.5 Gbbl of oil and condensate were discovered in the last few years, thanks, among other things to modern seismic interpretation and basin modelling coupled with the new exploration policy implemented since 1991 with close to 30 foreign companies sharing efforts in the National Algerian Company.
- Exploration has also been successful in other countries, such as Angola, Congo, Egypt, Indonesia, Nigeria, and Norway, often in known production areas. The impressive results over the last eighteen months are the discoveries of six giant fields in deep sea waters offshore Angola.

INCREASING THE RATE OF SUCCESS IN EXPLORATION/DELINEATION WELLS

Twenty years ago, the success rate of exploration and delineation wells was 1 out of 10. Today, it is estimated to average 1 out of 5. This rate can be improved even further. Yet the reasons for failure in exploration and delineation drilling have been clearly identified on the whole. Half the time, they come from wrong seismic analysis and poor structural imaging, in 25 per cent of the case, they are due to unexpected reservoir properties (lack of knowledge about quality and heterogeneity), and in the remaining 25 per cent to a poor analysis of the basin potential.

The reduction of exploration risks requires, above all, a better understanding of petroleum systems, to help with the development of high-performance methods and ways of assessing the final potential of sedimentary basins, and to improve the structural representation of the subsoil. This lies in a greater integration of different disciplines such as geology, geophysics and geochemistry through basin modelling and the development of 3D seismic method. These techniques are not only applied to petroleum basins in which the potential has been recognized, but also to the exploration of new provinces. Even if till now many oil companies prefer, because of the low price of crude oil, to concentrate their activities in known, mature and low-risk areas, the exploration of new provinces or little-known basins must not be neglected. It may prove to be very profitable.

By providing a three-dimensional image, this technique helps

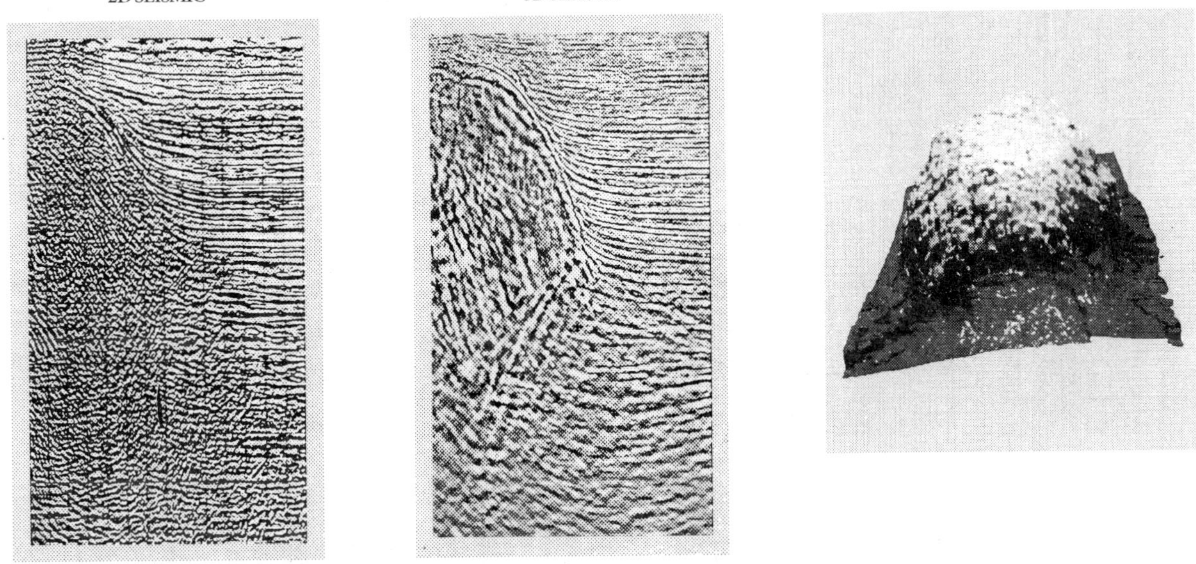

Source: IFP/Strategy & Corporate Planning Division, 1998.

FIGURE 2: 3D SEISMIC AND IMAGING

reveal new structures, even very small ones, even in areas which have already been well explored. It is possible to drill with a much greater chance of success (Figure 2).

The improvement of seismic imaging, the availability of work stations which can process large volumes of data, the development of the 3D seismic method and parallel processing have brought about a very significant improvement in reservoir cartography and geological models. In time, they should make it easier to delineate fields, and to optimize reservoir management, thereby reducing the number of wells and with them the corresponding expenses. This more sophisticated evaluation capacity comes at a time when the industry is exploring smaller and smaller targets and working with more and more complex structures. These technologies have to be integrated into a multidisciplinary approach that is more widely adopted by exploration-production teams.

OPTIMIZING FIELD EXPLOITATION AND RECOVERY RATE

Increasing the recovery rate is an extremely important goal. On a global scale, increasing the recovery rate by 1 per cent means gaining an extra two to three years of consumption. Thirty years ago, the field recovery rate was not more than 15 to 20 per cent on a world scale. Today the world average is between 30 and 50 per cent, with vast differences according to the fields and the production areas.

The recovery rate is no more than a few per cent for some heavy oil fields (for example giant Emeraude field in Congo or Faja Orimoco in Venezuela) but may exceed 50 per cent for some light oil fields developed with current techniques.

A better recovery rate goes via a better reservoir characterization. Visualization of the structure and the quality of the reservoir will lead to the optimization of both location and architecture of the wells to be drilled, to the better use of improved recovery techniques, in brief to a considerable improvement of drainage. With the more frequent use of horizontal and multibranch wells, the description of the reservoir and its heterogeneities will become supercritical and will require sophisticated softwares to interpret seismic data and advanced reservoir simulators.

Integrated studies of reservoir are more and more recognized as an efficient approach combining different disciplines named as geosciences. This concept was developed in the late 1980s. It arose from the evidence that no single discipline could provide solutions to reservoir characterization problems.

Integration of geology, geophysics, reservoir engineering and related technologies such as drilling technology and information technology has to be achieved at three equally important levels:

- in the company organization with creation of integrated teams, common working rooms and change in culture and practice;
- in the data management with investments in checking, cleaning and building consistent and accessible data base through modern data depository, working stations networks;
- in the working concept to allow in-depth integration which requires adequate algorithms, tools and methodologies.

Despite the results already achieved, one is still far from the peak. An increase in recovery rates from 30 per cent to 45 per cent is possible over the next twenty years as long as significant R&D work continues. The importance is clear. The R&D effort keeps up with the challenge of generating an additional 70 billion to 100 billion tons of reserves (compared with proven current reserves of 135 billion tons).

One of the recent and most efficient methods for increasing the recovery rate is horizontal drilling, sometimes combined with stimulation methods. This important concept holds the promise to help develop many horizontal wells with multiple, lateral branches, substantially improving productivity and also reservoir drainage (Figure 3).

Another method which is developing rapidly is gas injection, which significantly improves reservoir sweep efficiency and which now seems to be an economical technique to complement water injection.

The optimization of field recovery rates has already progressed very significantly in the North Sea. This optimization should be applied as widely as possible because it could push back the decline of the fields in question by almost ten years.

REDUCING THE COST OF DRILLING

Drilling remains the most expensive item on the upstream investment budget. Over the past few years, new technologies have appeared offering significant cost reductions while maximizing the productivity

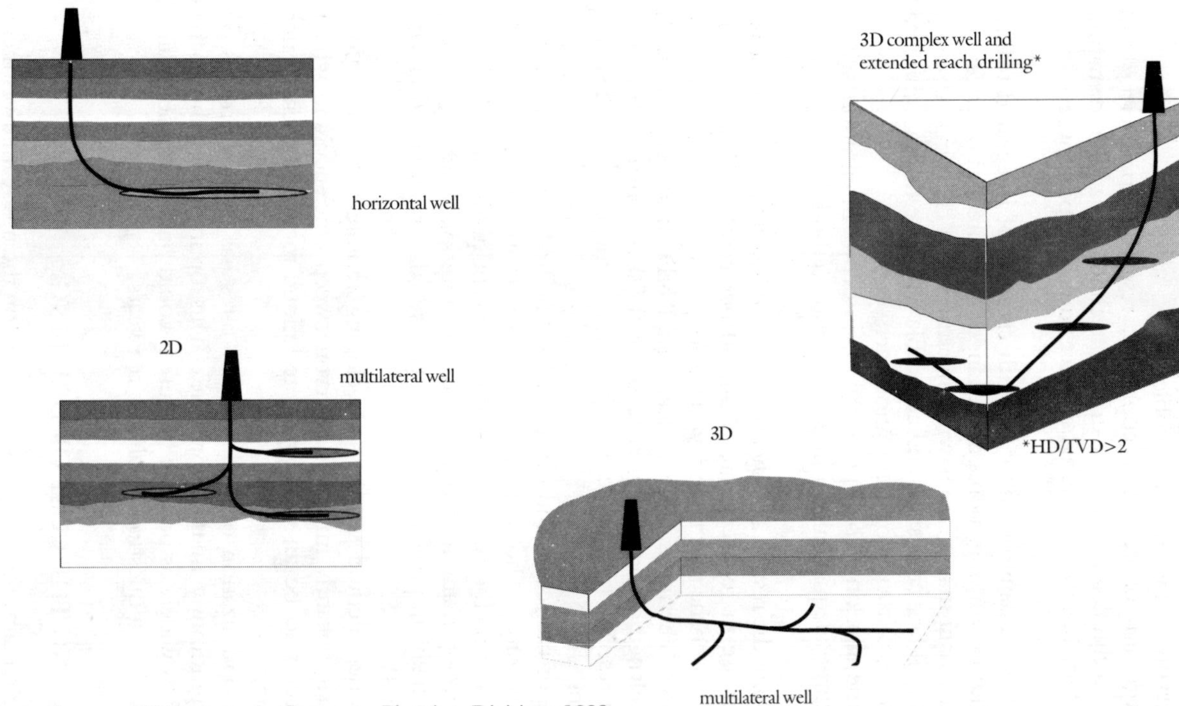

Source: IFP/Strategy & Corporate Planning Division, 1998.

FIGURE 3: DRILLING ADVANCED WELLS

of wells and the recovery rates. The use of new drilling bits, the improvement in drill strings and automation, the development of downhole motors, and MWd (measurement while drilling), are some new technologies among others that have reduced the time of drilling.

In exploration, the use of slim hole drilling, which reduces investment and operating costs by close to 40 per cent while protecting the environment better, should make it possible to significantly reduce drilling costs further.

For production, multilateral drilling, mentioned earlier, highly deviated drilling and extended reach drilling, with horizontal displacements of 7,000 to 10,000 metres, not only helps improve reservoir drainage but also reduce the number of wells or make it possible to operate from a single well with substantial savings, particularly for offshore drilling (Figure 4).

PRODUCING DIFFICULT OR MARGINAL FIELDS

As for most large offshore basins, the North Sea has entered the stage of maturity. While the advantage is very good geological knowledge and substantial infrastructure (platforms, pipelines, terminals, etc.), the disadvantage is smaller discoveries. The exploiting of the new, 'marginal' or 'satellite' fields, which has already begun in the North Sea, will become a major technological challenge.

The development of these reserves, which are divided into numerous small deposits, will require flexible, inexpensive and reusable techniques. For these fields it is essential to accelerate production while minimizing capital expenses, in light of the uncertainty regarding their profitability.

The North Sea, which has a production network installed for the large first generation fields, can set a good example with regard to development of marginal fields. So far, close to five hundred small hydrocarbon discoveries have been listed. Among these, close to 150 deposits representing 3.8 billion barrels of reserves, can be considered marginal fields because of their size and especially because of the costs involved, which are close to the threshold of economic viability.

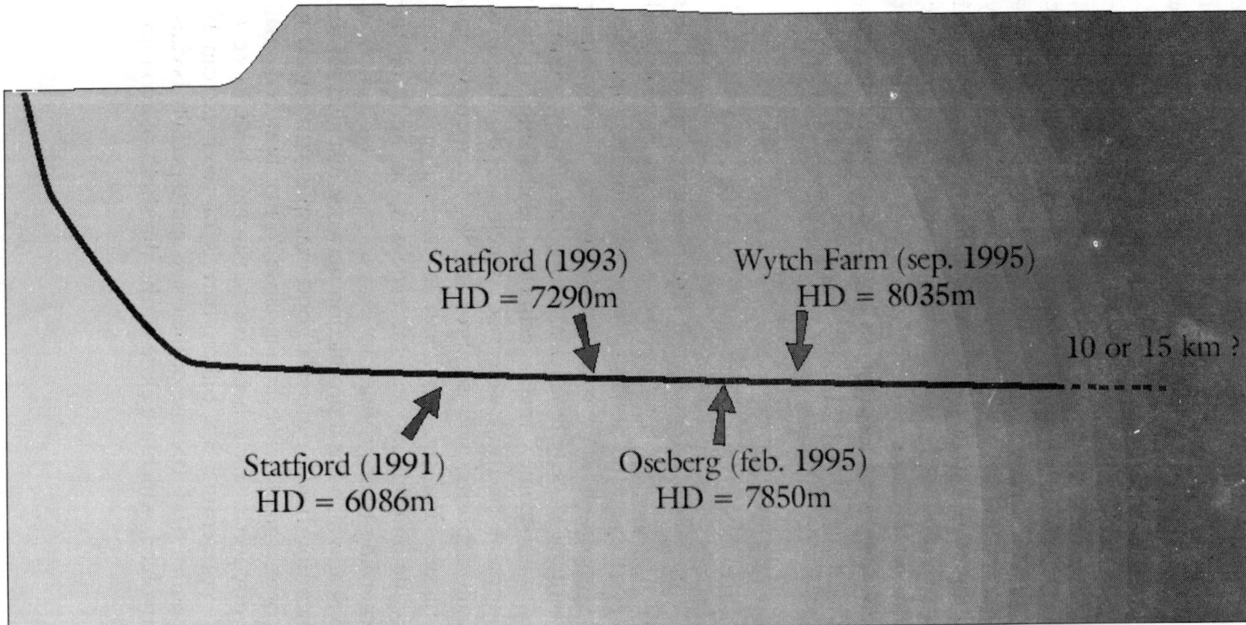

Note: HD = horizontal displacement.
Source: IFP/Strategy & Corporate Planning Division, 1998.

FIGURE 4: EXTENDED REACH DRILLING

DEVELOPING NEW OFFSHORE PRODUCTION SYSTEMS

The development of technologies specially designed for deep offshore work allows the industry to venture into this huge domain on a large scale. These include floating production systems (semi-submerged, FPSO, and tankers) with subsea completions and sometimes tension legs platforms (TLP).

With these technologies, water depth is no longer a real technical or economic obstacle, opening up a large new area for the industry (Figure 5).

Deep sea prospects seem highly attractive today, for the major players and in a growing number of regions: Gulf of Mexico, Brazil, west of the Shetlands Islands, north of Norway's offshore area, the Barents Sea, western Africa and South-East Asia.

For instance, the Marlim oil field in Brazil, put on stream by Petrobras in 1994, is located under 1,027 metres of water. More recently in late 1995, Shell decided to start producing the Mensa gas field at a water depth of 1,600 metres in the Gulf of Mexico, where production should come on stream next year. This is also a good example of how lead time has been shortened, even for a field that will in fact be a technological challenge. Offshore western Africa (Angola, Congo, and Nigeria) the new discoveries are located in water depths ranging from 500 to 1,700 metres.

In 1994, deep sea production started, providing 1 mbbld of the world's oil supply in 1995. It could amount to 3.5 mbbld at the turn of the century.

Success in meeting these challenges requires in particular the development of multiphase pumping and transportation, mainly in offshore areas. The goal is to integrate, into the production design and architecture, all the techniques that have to be mastered for the multiphase pipelining of all the effluents produced. The main aspects of this problem are the modelling of flows, the pumping and flow-metering, and the prevention of hydrate deposits (Figure 6).

Multiphase pumps such as POSEIDON pump developed at IFP can be used on any kind of oilfield to increase the oil production rate, to restore the production of shut-down wells, to market gas of low pressure wells instead of flaring and to maintain the production rate of declining oilfields.

Likewise, flexible flowlines have become an important element in offshore production systems. Research is being done on the behaviour

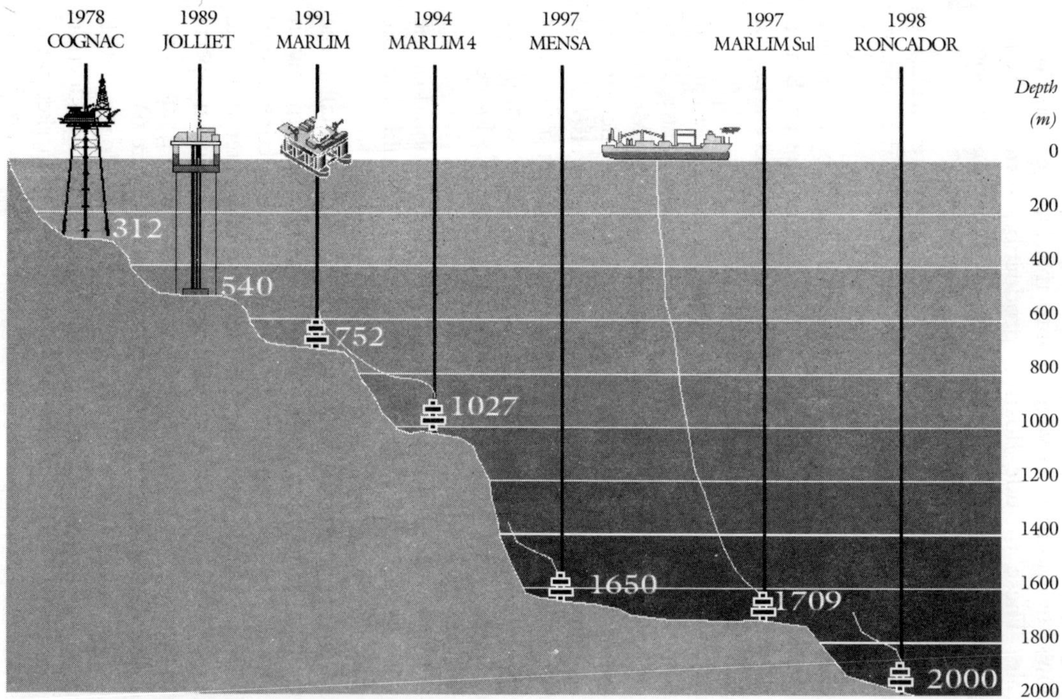

Source: IFP/Strategy & Corporate Planning Division, 1998.

FIGURE 5: DEEP OFFSHORE RECORDS PRODUCTION

of materials, the lightening of flowlines, and other technical issues such as insulation (Figure 7).

INTEGRATING THE UPSTREAM ENVIRONMENT

The rapid evolution of legislations concerning the environment in recent years has given rise to a great deal of research concerning the replacing of oil-base drilling fluids by non-polluting fluids. Various products or associations of products are now available on the market, such as water-base fluids and vegetable oil-base fluids.

Likewise, drilling fluids should be improved by continuously controlling the properties of the fluid during operations.

THE FUTURE OF R&D IN THE OIL AND GAS INDUSTRY

All petroleum and gas regions in the world will continue to need more innovative technologies coming from scientific and technical R&D. Here are a few examples:

- In North America, operators are making use of the most recent progress in geosciences to better understand and exploit the potential of infrasaliferous formations in the Gulf of Mexico. They will make use of the latest offshore techniques to develop deep water resources.
- In Latin America, where countries and their national companies are opening up and offering many exploration blocks, the explorationists will have to apply the most advanced exploration tools and methods, in particular in the subandean basins where all types of complex geological settings and traps occur.
- In West Africa and Brazil, deep water exploration and development of their coasts in the Atlantic Ocean will also make use of the most recent offshore technologies (drilling platforms, and subsea completion).
- In Asia and Latin America, many countries attempt to either maintain their production level by improving the oil recovery rate of mature fields, or tackle new propective petroleum systems in poorly explored zones.
- In the North Sea, one of the challenges is the development, at an acceptable cost, of the 5 to 6 Gbbl of oil in marginal fields, situated less than 30 km away from existing installations. Simplified

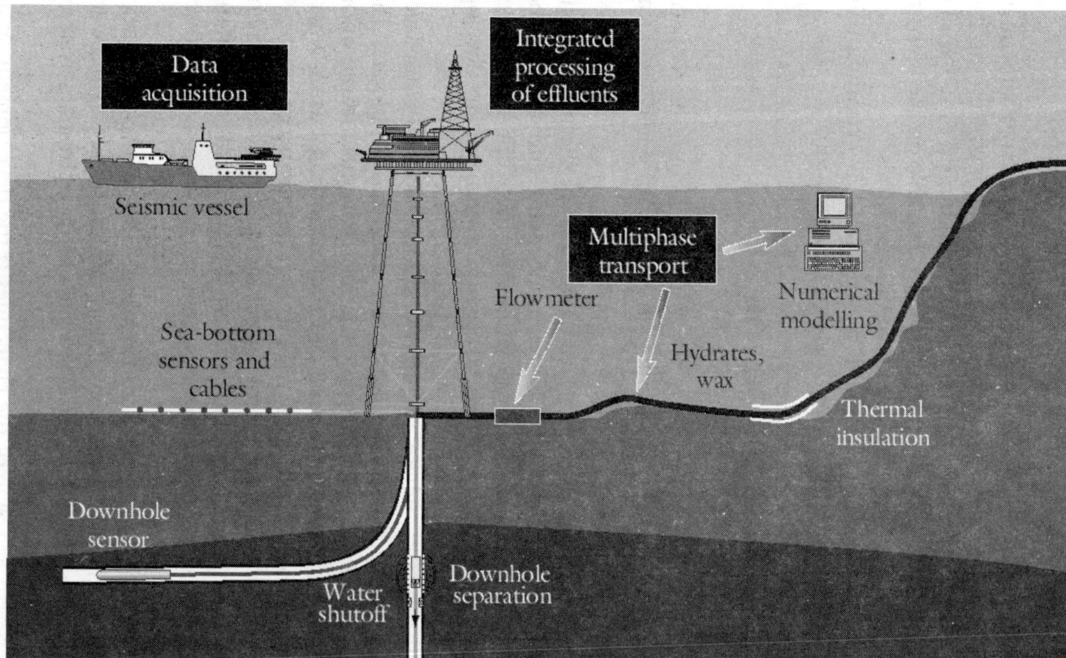

Source: IFP/Strategy & Corporate Planning Division, 1998.

FIGURE 6: RESERVOIR AND PRODUCED-FLUIDS MANAGEMENT

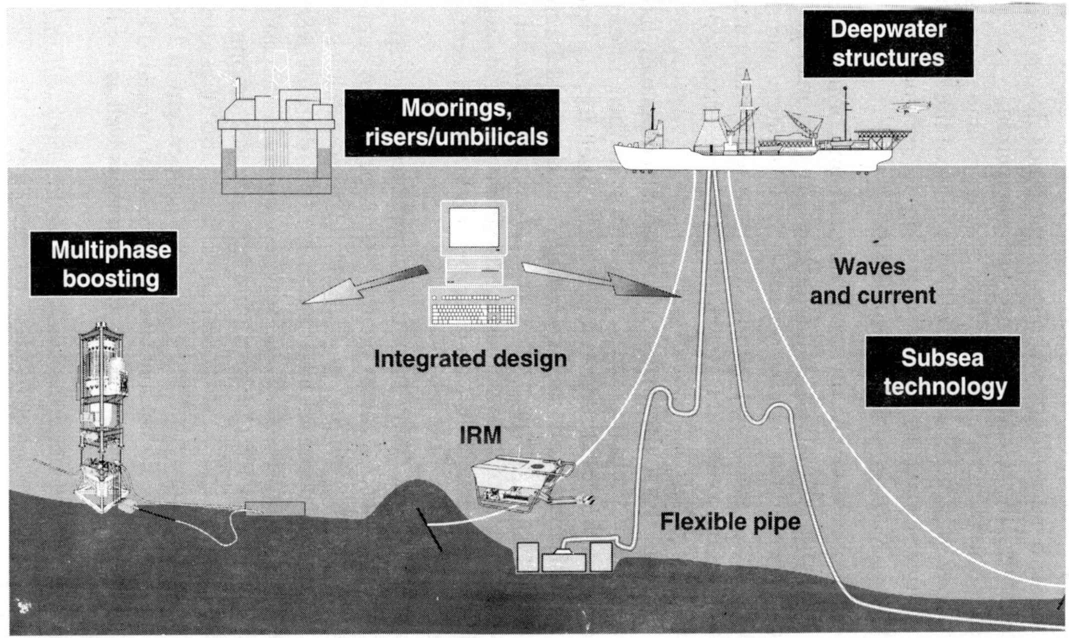

Source: IFP/Strategy & Corporate Planning Division, 1998.

FIGURE 7: ULTRA DEEP WATER PRODUCTION

design, floating production storage, offloading systems (FPSO) and multiphase pumping will be used.

- In the Middle East, maintaining of the production rate of large fields will require use of well stimulation techniques and improved recovery. This will demand a better description of the reservoir combined with a good understanding of the fluids flow, so as to avoid damaging the reservoirs by too fast a depletion.
- Likewise, concerning the CIS, existing reserves and potential ressources are very large, and the country will need the whole set of technologies, ranging from exploration to production, to rehabilitate its upstream petroleum industry.

In a context of a relatively low crude oil price and of increasing efforts to maintain profitability, oil companies have to manage to reduce their expenditures. A goal-oriented R&D strategy, aiming both at increasing reserves and cutting costs, has to be maintained with the appropriate means. How will this R&D be organized in the future?

In the last ten years, the major international companies have drastically decreased their personnel, particularly in their research teams. Between 1985 and 1994, Exxon, BP and Shell for example, reduced their staff by one-quarter to one-half. This downward trend did not just involve only these major companies. The number of employees of a sample of 11 other large petroleum groups, shows a cut by half in ten years, with a decrease by almost 40 per cent of R&D expenditure from 1985 to 1995.

As already discussed, many operating companies now want to opt out from the role of general contractors to petroleum supply and service companies, resulting in a transfer of responsibilities and competence. In the field of oil and natural gas, the share of R&D assumed by the petroleum supply and service industry is increasing. Since 1980, the load of R&D expenditure has increased among the US petroleum supply and service companies. The ratio of research expenditure versus turnover has increased from 1.6 per cent in 1980 to 3.7 per cent in 1994. By comparison, this ratio has remained less than 1 per cent for the 11 operators of the sample, as well as for BP, Shell and Exxon.

It is hardly probable, none the less, that this industry will make up, by increasing its own expenditure, for the drop in the R&D budgets of the major petroleum operators.

In the opinion of most oil companies, the objective is not to skip out on R&D but rather see it become more efficient, better integrated and more quickly applicable. They favour in-house applied research having short-term goals and results, and would rather subcontract research having more long-term goals and results to outsiders or collaborators.

In this situation, a question can arise: If the oil companies do not carry out enough in-house long-term research, who will do it? Service companies, national laboratories, or petroleum research institutes? Most technological and scientific progress currently comes from these different organizations, and it is true that cooperation with oil companies is equally important as it is fruitful.

Is it possible to expect national laboratories and petroleum research institutes, which generally have limited access to the field, to undertake by themselves a large share of this research and to validate it by new tools and methods?

Finally, how will the value of an innovation and its application be assessed by the operating companies, in the absence of the high-level in-house competent talent?

One way to deal with these questions is to favour and implement co-operative programmes and joint industry projects through partnership between petroleum companies, services companies and research organizations. Partnership can be organized in a very flexible manner (international research consortium, bilateral agreement, R&D contract, or technology licensing) according to the subject to be tackled. As soon as partners concerned start looking at the same overall objective with a clear and fair understanding of their respective capabilities with a definite trust in the positive impact of advanced technology in the petroleum activities, R&D will start to benefit all the world players.

CHALLENGES IN INDIA'S OIL AND GAS UPSTREAM SECTOR

As outlined in other articles, the demand for hydrocarbons has steadily been increasing for the last ten years while the supply from indigenous petroleum resources has not been keeping the same pace. This situation is not going to improve, on the contrary it is worsening with the demographic trend and the increasing need for energy in a country where low per capita consumption is a clear feature (Figure 8).

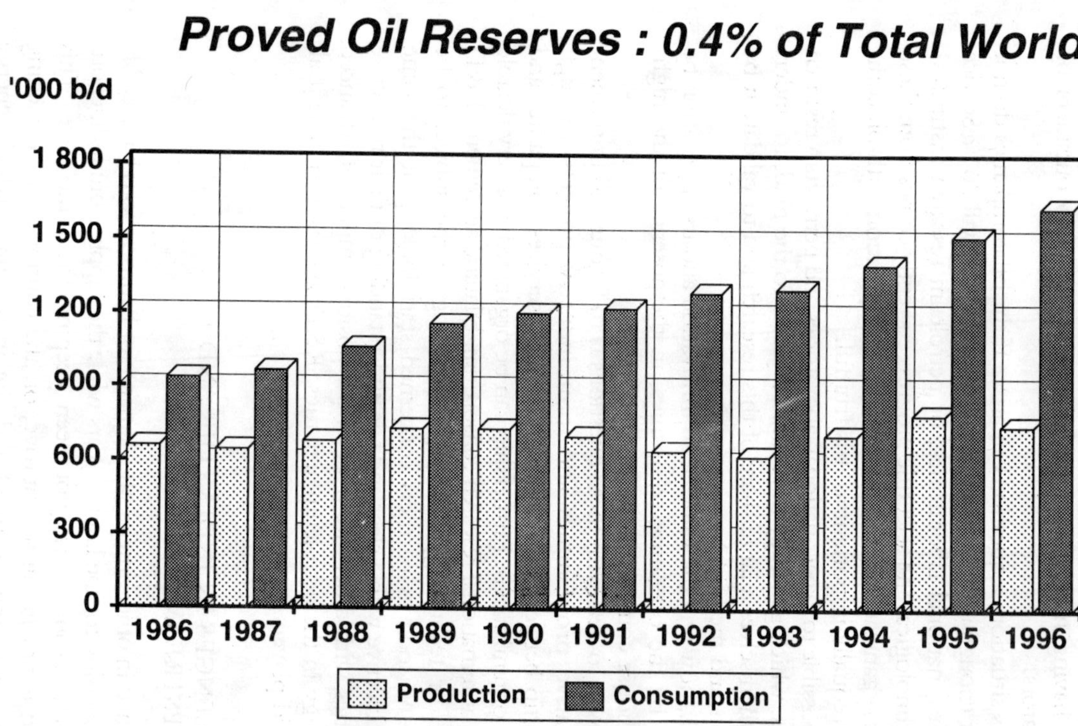

Source: *BP Stat Review*, IFP/Strategy & Corporate Planning Division, 1998.

FIGURE 8: EVOLUTION OF OIL PRODUCTION/CONSUMPTION IN INDIA

To meet the shortfall in indigenous production, India resorted in the short medium term to import petroleum products while in the medium long term, she planned to maintain or improve production rates from existing fields and to promote exploration (Figure 9). Here lies technology for a higher efficiency in exploration-production activities combined with new policies at the national level and at the company level.

The New Exploration Licensing Policy (NELP) is meant to attract investment in the exploration business. It included in its initial wording a series of elements that were not attractive enough for the international companies to bid for, especially the small blocks that were offered in second category zones of interest. At the same time, a number of countries in a similar situation were offering far better terms and conditions in geologically attractive basins. The revised NELP, expected to be adopted soon, should have a better impact. In the meantime, the two national oil companies might initiate a series of actions that would facilitate technical discussions with potential foreign investors and lead them to revisit some selected basins where new prospects could possibly be identified.

In other countries of the world, in Western Europe, Africa or Latin America examples are many, where this strategy lead to very positive results even in mature exploration areas or those considered as such (Algeria, Austria, Egypt, and Venezuela, etc.).

One of the first and somewhat important task is to build up a clean, fully checked, coherent data base, fed with data filed and stored generally in a number of offices with teams scattered across the company. From this database it would then be possible to reconsider exploration work according to new geological concepts to be tested through sophisticated basin modelling systems and softwares. Obviously, the building up of the database will induce, in selected zones, the scanning of thousands of well logs or seismic profiles for later easy retrieval. The reinterpretation of the existing data compiled can be conducted with the assistance of explorers whose knowledge of many basins and geological settings in the world are of prime value.

The declining production of the existing fields in particular the main fields of the Bombay offshore basin (Bombay High, Neelam, Heera and other smaller ones) is of great concern. The nature of the geological layers made of fractured carbonate where the oil is trapped makes it difficult to exploit the fields. There are many similar examples

Zones	Proved Reserves	
	Oil& gas (Bboe)	Oil& gas (Btoe)
Bombay Offshore	24,6	3,37
Cambay	6,4	0,87
Assam	4,6	0,63
Krishna-Godavari	2,2	0,30
Cauvery	0,5	0,07
Others	0,3	0,05
Total	38,6	5,29

Source: Ministry of Petroleum & Natural Gas, IFP/Strategy & Corporate Planning Division, 1998.

FIGURE 9: MAIN PRODUCING ZONES IN INDIA

elsewhere in the world. Today, thanks to advanced technology in seismic acquisition, processing and interpretation as well as in reservoir engineering and simulation tools, one can tackle the problem of adverse production behaviour through the powerful analysis of reservoir characterization. This is a key factor which not only helps identify the causes but also suggests appropriate remedial measures. These include, for instance, the design of additional drainage pattern of non-recovered oil and the integration of innovative pumping systems or additives for improved fluid flow in the production scheme of the field.

The new 3D seismic survey shot over the Bombay High field would provide an impressive set of data that will be very useful to interpret structure imaging and reservoir characterization. Similar exercise could be initiated for the other main producing fields. Any attempt to slowdown their declined production would require special efforts to carefully look at the reservoir characteristics by multi-disciplinary teams combining all available geoscience disciplines and expertises in an integrated study approach.

Frontier exploration is another stake for the Indian petroleum industry. Among possible new prospective zones, the potential of deep and ultra deep offshore (beyond 200 metres of water down to 1,500-2,000 metres) should be investigated. Primarily along the eastern coast (Cauvery, Khrisna-Godavari, Mahanadi basins) in the Bay of Bengal. Other offshore frontier areas might also be identified along the western coast of Kerala or Bombay. All of these potential prospects require the acquisition of reconnaissance seismic surveys along with regional investigation profiles going from known onshore areas to long distance offshore targets. This kind of frontier exploration can now be considered since deep offshore exploration, and its development are no longer limited by technical constraints as very successful results have been obtained in geological settings elsewhere in the world that may well exists over the Indian territory (fluvio-deltaic deposits off the huge Ganga river mouths for example).

There are still many onshore basins and areas that are under-explored or not yet recognized for their hydrocarbon potential. Thrust zones such as the Himalayan foothills may be considered as speculative since very little work has been conducted on it so far. Areas in the foothills in other part of the world have often been found to be very attractive with highly producing areas like in Latin America along the Andean range (Venezuela, Colombia, Equator,

Peru, Bolivia, etc.). New seismic techniques, modern geological concepts, structural interpretation assisted with adequate modelling softwares are the tools that can be used efficiently today to enhance exploration efforts with the help of foreign companies ready to share risk and money with the Indian partners in the search for new oil and gas reserves in India.

The Security of Supply Issue: The Growing Dependence on the Middle East

GULSHAN DIETL

'Energy security' is a widely used term but is much less precise. Coined in 1950s to mean safeguarding adequate supplies in the event of war, it has moved beyond the military aspect to include long-term economic safeguards against the effects of oil price shocks as well. The relation between energy import dependence and energy security has been a persistent theme in the international energy debate. On the one hand, it has been argued that there is no direct link between energy import dependence and energy security. While on the other, however, arguments that increased dependence on imported energy is a threat to security have provided a driving force for energy policies and strategies in the past.[1] The debate has a specific context—the global energy dependence on the Middle East. This article attempts to examine the issue with reference to India.

SECURITY OF SUPPLY FROM THE MIDDLE EAST: AN APPRAISAL

Several events in the past twenty-five years have led to major supply disruptions from the Middle East: the 1973 oil embargo, the Iranian revolution, the eight year long Iran-Iraq war, Iraq's invasion of Kuwait and the consequent embargo on supplies from Iraq and Iraqi occupied Kuwait, etc. The 1973 embargo lasted six months at the height of which the net loss of supplies was 4.4 mbbld, or only about 9 per cent of the total 50.8 mbbld that had been previously available. Confusion in the market, coupled with widespread uncertainty about the future supply of Middle East oil, led to panic buying, further exacerbating the shortage.

The Iranian revolution in 1978-9 removed about 3.7 mbbld of oil for six months. By late 1978, a strike by the oil workers virtually shut down production and halted exports. Panic spread following the fall of the Shah in January 1979. This precipitated panic buying in the West and Japan. Spot market prices increased and oil companies scrambled to build stocks in anticipation of further price increases. The result was an artificial increase in world demand of 3 mbbld above actual consumption.

In September 1980, Iraq invaded Iran, producing yet another serious disturbance in the Gulf. There was an upward pressure on the prices which rose from US $14 billion at the start of 1979 to more than US $35 billion in January 1981. The crude prices remained high throughout the early stages of the war. Together, the Iranian revolution and the Iran-Iraq war, magnified uncertainty and speculation regarding the future availability of oil from the Gulf.[2]

On 2 August 1990, Iraq invaded Kuwait. The day marks a complete U-turn in the narrative of oil embargoes. Since then, each successive embargo has been imposed by the consumers against the procedures—rather than vice versa as was the case till then. The United Nations embargoed oil from Iraq and Iraqi occupied Kuwait which totalled some 4.3 mbbld representing almost 7 per cent of world supplies. The crude prices shot up from US $16 billion in July 1990 to US $36 billion in September.

After fighting what it claimed to be the 'mother of all battles' on the wrong side, Iraq was subjected to the mother of all resolutions in the form of UNSC resolution 687. It imposed sanctions on Iraq till the time that Iraq recognized Kuwait and its UN-demarcated borders; paid up compensation to Kuwait; returned the Kuwaiti prisoners of war and properties; improved human rights situation in the country; destroyed its nuclear, biological and chemical war potential and the missiles to deliver the same.

In August 1996, the United States expanded its own unilateral trade embargoes against Libya and Iran to any country or company investing more than US $40 million in their oil and gas sectors and non-compliance was threatened with various forms of penalization. At the G-8 summit in London in May this year, Clinton has promised to seek Congressional approval for his waivers to the European companies in breach of the embargo. His move may have been motivated by a desire to avoid confrontation with the European Union as also to give a signal of approval to the moderate regime of President Mohammad Khatami in Tehran.

Article 153 of the Iranian constitution specifically forbids 'any form of agreement resulting in foreign control over the natural resources'. In case of a change in government in Tehran, the hardliners are determined to expel foreign companies and adopt a tough posture on the 'constructive dialogue' with Europe. In the eventuality, the investments by the French Total, Russian Gazprom and Malaysian Petronas oil companies, to develop South Pars gas fields in Iran may not usher in an era of normalization in Iranian oil economy and supply as is expected.

Political stability is an important ingredient in the oil production and price stability. A brief overview of present circumstances to determine future outlook is in order.

Non-participatory politics and rentier economy—hallmarks of the oil producing states—are undergoing a subtle but steady change. Today, the rents are falling in absolute amount. They are falling short of the domestic needs and aspirations even more. The state dipped into its accumulated surpluses, ran deficits, curtailed outlays, borrowed nationally and internationally and shuffled its overseas assets for a while. Today, it is compelled to seek revenues from its citizens. In short, it may have to behave like any other normal state. Once the citizens pay to run it, the state will inexorably open up to their scrutiny. And then the state will inevitably invite them to be participants and partners in economic decisions.[3]

Even if one rules out a violent change in any of these states, the whispers of democratic expression are growing louder across the region. Simultaneously, there is a distinct upsurge in national identity that does not depend solely on the depleting oil resources. A Kuwaiti princess and poetess has expressed the nationalist yearnings in these few pithy words:

> 'My country, I hardly recognize it.
> Is it the bazaar, the bounced check, the gambling houses?
> Is it the Kuwait people strangled by its Mafia in broad daylight?
> I refuse to allow oil to be my destiny.'[4]

Confronted with staggering economic, political and social challenges, the elite in these states have neither been honestly responsive to their people nor convincingly reassuring to their foreign consumers. With the exception of Brunei and Bhutan, all the ruling monarchies are located in the Arab world, and apart from Morocco and Jordan, all of them are situated on the western shore of the Gulf. All twelve of them are incorporated into the Gulf Cooperation

Council. The question of succession in each one of them is a crucial one. In Saudi Arabia, even if there is a smooth succession after Fahd, the political uncertainty does not clear up. Considering the age, the rules of Abdullah and Sultan are bound to be short. Three royal successions in a brief period are, in turn, bound to provoke ferment within the royal family and activate younger aspirants. In Oman, the Sultan is a bachelor. In Qatar, King Hamad has deposed his father only recently.

To date, the domestic dissent has not targeted energy infrastructures in any of the Middle East oil producing states. It has, however, plunged an entire state into a prolonged state of turmoil as in Algeria or has resorted to terrorist attacks on the US military presence as in al-Khobar in Saudi Arabia. Disruption of energy supply in order to snap the ties between the ruling elite and their foreign protectors needs to be examined in this context.

A radical change in the territorial integrity of Iraq and navigability of the Strait of Hormuz may have serious consequences for the supplies from the region. A closer look at these two flashpoints is in order. The post-Gulf War Iraq is an isolated, embargoed state. Its territory is divided along sectarian-ethnic faultlines. North of the thirty-sixth parallel are the Kurds in the allies' security zone and south of the thirty-third parallel are the Iraqi Shias in the Allies' no fly zone. It is a highly precarious balance that could easily tilt, undermining the very existence of the state of Iraq. In the event of the balance tilting, there would be no immunity for the territorial sanctity of the neighbouring states.

The Shias are estimated to constitute a majority of Iraqi population. The southern parts of the country are almost totally Shia. The Kurds are estimated to be 4 million. Whereas the Shias have a friendly, porous border with Iran; the Kurds have maintained a fraternal/fratricidal relationship with 10 to 12 million Turkish Kurds in a traditionally no man's land. The Kurds are in a strong position *vis-à-vis* the Iraqi state on two grounds; one, the area possesses vast oil fields together with a network of oil pipelines; and two, the Iraqi, National Congress operates from there.

At the end of the Gulf War, the Kurds had pushed for a thirty per cent share of all oil export revenues. The UN Secretary General Kofi Annan's proposal after the end of the latest Iraq crisis (October 1997-February 1998) included a separate disbursement of increased oil income to the Kurdish governorates of Dahuk, Arbil and

Sulaymaniya. Baghdad reacted by rejecting any plan that did not involve centralized control over the whole country. But any future expansion or post-Saddam privatization of oil production and export facilities is bound at some point to ignite a new regional push for revenues independent of Baghdad.[5]

The Strait of Hormuz saw a lot of action during the Iran-Iraq war and was a virtual battleground during its tanker war phase. From July 1987 till the ceasefire in August 1988, the US reflagged and escorted eleven Kuwaiti oil tankers in and out of the Gulf and put together a formidable naval presence to ensure their safe passage. It was the biggest show of the US military muscle beyond its borders after its withdrawal from Vietnam.

Currently, about 20 per cent of the world's supply of crude oil transits through the Strait. The Saudi east-west pipeline (Petroline) with the capacity of 5.1 mbbld which runs across the state to the port of Yanbu on the Red Sea was built to bypass the Hormuz. Today, moves are afoot to export the Kuwaiti oil through a pipeline to Saudi Arabia, and the United Arab Emirates (UAE) oil through a pipeline to the Omani terminal at Mina al-Fahal near Muscat—with a possible spur to Qatar.

And finally, there is another important psychological element that triggers insecurity regarding supplies from the Middle East. Markets tend to think of the region as an area where events in one country can easily impinge on the fortunes of others, more so than other parts of the world. Because of the political and military interdependencies among producers in the Gulf region, events in the Middle East will threaten larger quantities of oil and hence produce larger price reactions than one would expect from disruptions in other parts of the world.[6]

PRODUCTION AND DEMAND IN INDIA: AN APPRAISAL

The discovery of hydrocarbons off the Indian west coast in 1974 dramatically changed the nature of domestic petroleum production, which had been dominated by the onshore oilfields of Assam and Gujarat. Within five years, offshore oil constituted 37.58 per cent of total domestic production and 15.86 per cent of total demand. Three years later it surpassed the onshore production and constituted 61.14 per cent of total production and as much as 38.48 per cent of total demand. In 1989-90, it provided 21,716 mt of crude oil, accounted for 63.71 per cent of total domestic production, and as much as 40.53 per cent of the total demand. The production of 13,088 bn.m^3 of natural gas in the same year constituted 77.04 per cent of total domestic production, which met about 80 per cent of the total demand.[7]

Expectations that output of oil and natural gas would continue to rise were dashed thereafter. In fact, there was a net decline in the output of crude to 27 mt in 1992-3. Production of natural gas too suffered concurrently as associated gas constituted a large proportion of total output. Free gas supplies were not available in the required volume and they were not effectively exploited in areas like Tripura, where there were problems in establishing projects which would ensure regular offtake of natural gas.[8] During 1993-4, at least 10.4 per cent of gas produced was flared, as satellite oilfields were not yet connected to integrated production system. In the north-east, the percentage was as high as thirty.

Indigenous crude oil production is expected to pick up in the coming years and is likely to peak at a level of around 44 mt by the turn of the century, if no further accretion of reserves takes place. This would imply a reserve to production ratio of 18 years at the current levels of recoverable reserves. The natural gas availability from indigenous sources is expected to go up from the current level of 18 bn.m^3 to 23/30 bn.m^3 by 2001-2. At the current level of gas production of 18.6 bn.m^3 per annum, the reserves are likely to last for 40 years.[9]

The level of energy consumption in India is extremely low as is indicated by the per capita energy consumption which currently stands at 226 kgoe as compared to 7,759 kgoe in the USA. Even as it is projected to increase by nearly 145 per cent by the year 2010, the average will still be about a fifth of what an average American consumes today. The energy consumption has gradually increased from 64.9 mtoe in 1973 to 112.6 mtoe in 1983 and to 201.9 mtoe in 1993 indicating a constant annual growth of around 6 per cent as against the world average of 1.5 per cent. Oil consumption grew at annual rate of 5.9 per cent in 1973-83 and 5.3 per cent in 1983-93. The share of oil in the total basket of primary energy decreased from 32.4 per cent in 1973 to 30.9 per cent in 1993.[10]

Earlier, the rise in demand for petroleum products was mainly due to the growth of the transport sector, but now it is evident that increased use of gasoline for transport purposes, naphtha and natural gas for manufacturing fertilizers; and HSD and furnace oil for power generation are together responsible for the rising demand.[11] By the first half of the next century, India is expected to be one of the top five consumers of petroleum products, even ahead of industrialized countries like France and the UK, and just behind Russia and China. According to the *Oil and Gas Financial Review*, by the year 2010, China and India are expected to have overtaken Japan as the two largest consumers of primary energy, followed by South Korea, Indonesia and Taiwan.[12] The existing primary energy demand is forecast to go up from 250 mtoe to 700 mtoe. The natural gas consumption is forecast to go up from 17.4 bn.m^3 in 1994 to 78.6 bn.m^3 in 2010.[13] The demand for LPG is anticipated to go up by four times by 2010 from the present level of only 3.11 mt.[14]

Import dependence in the circumstances, will steadily rise. In the most optimistic situation, domestic production of crude would meet only 44 per cent of the demand at the end of the century. This would go down to 33 per cent by the year 2005 and 27 per cent by the year 2010. The rest of the expected crude requirement of 159 mmt will have to be met by import. In case of natural gas, against the indigenous availability of 23/30 bn.m^3, the registered demand is approximately 96 bn.m^3 by end of this century. Thus, there is likely to be a shortfall of 66/73 bn.m^3.[15]

ENERGY DEPENDENCE OVER THE MIDDLE EAST

Physical shortages coupled with higher prices of oil can be brought about by oil supply disruption, cause serious damage to the economy of an oil importing country. This can reduce output and operation in the industry sector, and can bring about loss of GNP and employment. Physical shortages of gasoline and electricity, in turn, reduce energy supply to consumers and affect civil and economic life negatively. Additionally, higher oil prices, often increasing the amount of import payments, make the importing country's balance of payments worse. Higher oil prices, increasing input costs causing upward pressures on general prices, can raise inflation in the importing country.[16]

Every oil shock in the Middle East has had an inevitable adverse impact on Indian economy. During the 1973 oil crisis, India's energy import bill rose by over 50 per cent. The direct overall adverse impact of 1990-1 on India's balance of payments in that fiscal year was estimated at Rs. 5,180 crore. In 1991, India was to import 1.5 mt of crude from Kuwait and 6.25 mt from Iraq. That figure included 4.5 mt of oil that the Soviets were to transfer to India against rupee payment. Of the total of 7.75 mt only 3 mt had been delivered by the time the UN imposed sanctions. Thus, India had to shop for the extra 4.75 mt of oil in spot markets at a much higher price and against foreign exchange payment.[17]

In July 1996, the Indian government increased the price of all petroleum products—except kerosene, LPG and HSD—in an effort to reduce deficits in the oil pool account. In September, the US fired 44 missiles at the Iraqi targets in response to a fighting between the two rival groups of Iraqi Kurds. The Iraqi oil did not come on the market as a consequence and the world crude prices went up from US $18 billion to US $24 billion. The Indian government's calculation was totally upset: the Ministries of Oil and Finance made ominous predictions that the oil pool account deficit—rather than going down from Rs. 5,500 crore where it stood in March 1996—would go up to anything between Rs. 15,500 crore to Rs. 20,000 crore by March 1997; assuming that the world oil prices would not go up and the rupee would not be depreciated any further.[18]

India imported 27.34 mt of crude oil out of which 22.1 mt were from the Middle East and 12.27 mt of petroleum products out of which 10.7 mt were from the Middle East in the fiscal year 1994-5.[19] In the fiscal year 1996-7, Saudi Arabia and Kuwait provided 15.1 per cent each, UAE 9.9 per cent and Iran 4.6 per cent of the total Indian imports of raw materials and intermediate,[20] which constituted 82 per cent, 96.3 per cent, 85.7 per cent and 81.2 per cent respectively of the total exports from these countries to India. The country ran an adverse trade balance with each of the four: With Saudi Arabia the negative balance stood at US $1,715.3 million, with Kuwait at US $1,808.4 million and with Iran at US $578.9 million.[21] The trade balance with the OPEC as a whole showed a consistent deficit from 1980 onwards and stood at Rs.11,457 crores in 1994-5 with imports at Rs. 19,011 and exports at Rs. 7,554 crores. The figures constituted 9.2 per cent of India's total exports and 21.4 per cent of India's total imports.[22]

Middle East has been a source of investment in India, mainly in the refineries. The total investment of about US $694.44 million is committed by the Oman Oil Company, Kuwait Petroleum

Corporation and Saudi ARAMCO.[23] The situation is still unclear as the Oman Oil Company is expected to drop its joint venture with Hindustan Petroleum Corporation even as ARAMCO and Hindustan Petroleum have recently decided to expand the capacity of their joint venture refinery in Phulo Khari in Punjab from 6 mt to 9 mt at a cost of US $2.5 billion. The most noteworthy Indian investments in the region are four fertilizer joint ventures in Jordan, Oman, Iran and the UAE which will use cheap gas or abundant phosphates to produce locally for exports to the Indian market.[24]

In addition, the construction of submarine pipelines for the transportation of natural gas to India from the Gulf has been proposed. These plans revolve around three major projects with Oman, Qatar and Iran. In June 1993, the Indian and Omani governments agreed to the preparation of a feasibility report on the construction of a 1,450 km submarine pipeline from Oman to Gujarat, on the west coast of India. An ambitious project valued at US $5 million, the subsea pipeline would be sunk to depths of up to 3.5 km, which is deeper than any other wide diameter gas pipeline in the world. The scheme faces huge technical challenges while some doubts have arisen due to insufficient confirmation of gas reserves in Oman. The second project involves a pipeline from Qatar possibly linking up with the Indo-Omani pipeline.[25]

The third project involving a 42 in. pipeline stretching 2,000 km from Iran to India has become a bone of contention between India and Pakistan. The Indian defence experts reject the option of an overland route through Pakistan, as it empowers Pakistan to cut off supplies to India whenever it wants. International guarantees can reduce, but not eliminate, the chances of such a cut off. Pakistan however favours the overland route as this will assure its own gas supplies while giving it a stranglehold over supplies to India. India favours the laying of the pipeline through the Pakistani exclusive economic zone. Pakistan declines to permit it citing various techno-economic, defence and strategic reasons. It says that the project will cost one and a half times more if laid under water, with the estimated cost touching US $ 10 or 12 billion.[26]

Narsi Ghorbal, an Iranian expert, has sought to argue the case for an onshore route on two counts: one, that international investors would favour only a foolproof or investor friendly project; and two, that an offshore project could be easily sabotaged by a politically rival country. 'But an onshore project cannot be destroyed easily as the nation through which the pipeline passes will have to bear responsibility for the same.'[27] In early 1997, India, Iran and Pakistan agreed in principle to officially pursue the matter with urgency.[28] Nothing has so far emerged on the matter.

In May 1997, India's four principal oil and gas companies—Gas Authority of India, Oil and Natural Gas Corporation, Indian Oil Corporation and Bharat Petroleum Corporation—came together to set up Petronet-LNG. Since then, there has been a spate of LNG related projects. One, the Petronet-LNG has identified six locations in India where it can set up LNG terminals. Two, it has invited global bids for a tender to supply LNG. The shortlisted companies which were asked to submit detailed proposals, have already done so. Under a memorandum of understanding signed early this year, the Qatar General Petroleum Corporation has committed to draw up an LNG supply agreement with the Gas Authority of India. The Enron's well advanced proposal for LNG facilities at Dabhol, British Gas's proposal at Pipavav, Total's two joint ventures with Hindustan Petroleum and the Tata Electric Company; and the TIDCO tenders at Ennore outside Chennai are other LNG proposals under way.[29]

ENERGY DEPENDENCE: GROPING FOR STRATEGY AND ITS IMPLEMENTATION

Energy security has two aspects: (a) mitigation of the consequences of temporary shortages due to supply disruptions, and (b) development of long-term policies to avoid shortages due to medium or high price rise. India is still groping for a well rounded strategy to meet these contingencies. A well balanced portfolio that spreads risks over a number of options seems to enjoy consensus at official and non-official levels at present.

Maintaining strategic reserves will help the country tide over a short-term crisis. A high powered committee that was appointed to look into the matter, recommended in its report, *Hydrocarbon Perspectives 2010*, that the reserves should be managed by a common agency in view of economies of scale and operational flexibility. The committee suggested that the reserves be developed only for the mass consumption products, namely motor spirit, HSD, kerosene and LPG and asked the government to enact necessary legislation in this regard.

As for the tankage, the committee estimated that a tankage of approximately 24 mint would be required for reserves adequate for 90 days. Among various options, it suggested long-term leasing of required tankage to minimize the financial impact.[30]

A group of energy experts has called for supplementing the creation of strategic reserves by seeking agreements with trading partners like Malaysia, Indonesia and Singapore to mobilize supplies from their stocks for a few weeks.[31]

A long-term policy will have to be two-fold—demand side management and supply side management. The demand side management seeks to improve energy efficiency without compromising on growth and aiming to arrest the degradation of the environment. It could be pursued at three levels: (a) command, e.g. statutory obligation for energy conservation; (b) persuasion, e.g. TV and mass awareness campaigns; and (c) market, e.g. tax on energy consumption.

The eighth plan 1992-7 for the first time provided a capital outlay of Rs.1,000 crores for energy efficiency measures with the targets of energy saving of 5,000 MW and 6 mt in power and petroleum sectors respectively.[32] The state intervention aimed at energy conservation and alternative energy development is cost ineffective at this point of time but will become relevant as and when the oil prices firm up.

The supply side management is essentially multi-pronged; a few of its components are discussed as follows:

(a) Acceleration of surveys in unexplored acreage to establish potential reserves. The number of wells drilled per 1,000 sq. km in India is only 20 compared to the world average which exceeds 100. There are 26 basins in the country out of which six basins and a number of other areas remain totally unexplored. Even in offshore, deeper waters have yet to be explored.[33] *Approach Paper to the Ninth Five Year Plan, 1997-2002* recommends acquisition of acreage in other countries as well.[34]

(b) Enhancement of refining capacity. It has several advantages: Handling of large crude volumes is easier than small quantities of different products; transportation is easier and cheaper; more value addition takes place, and it safeguards energy security.

(c) Encouragement of private sector participation. In the course of the ninth plan, the government proposes to set up appropriate regulatory mechanisms in view of greater participation in the energy sector.[35]

(d) Incentives for foreign investments. The OPEC producers may be willing on several counts: Fiscal deficits, persistent low prices, creating value-added to their natural resources and the recent decline in LNG plant construction costs. India has succeeded in inviting some investments in the refinery and LNG sectors though not enough. The search for investment need not be confined to the OPEC sources.

(e) Introduction of market determined pricing mechanism. The government does not propose to go the whole way on the issue. *Approach Paper to the Ninth Plan, 1997-2002* states categorically, though, that 'the administered pricing mechanism will be replaced by a more rational pricing system reflecting the cost of supply'.[36]

(f) Research and Development in exploration and production. The government is committed to increased R&D efforts across the energy sector.[37]

(g) Development of infrastructure like pipeline networks and port facilities.

(h) Long-term contracts with gas rich states in the Middle East for imports and joint ventures in fertilizer and petrochemical sectors. The prospects of all the three major gas pipelines are still not clear.

(i) Diversification of supply sources to Central and South-East Asia. Turkmenistan and Kazakhstan in Central Asia and Malaysia and Indonesia in South-East Asia are prospective candidates in this context. A pipeline network linking India, Bangladesh and Burma is also being explored.

(j) Finally, a steady growth in exports. Unless the country's exports also increase at the same pace, the import bill will absorb even more of the export earnings than its already high share of 32 per cent. Apart from the balance of payments problem, it would make India more vulnerable to sudden spikes in oil prices, with a consecutive increase in the prices of other commodities and may have a serious bearing on energy security. Whereas the official report visualizes the oil price of US $22 per barrel in 2010 and considers an annualized growth of 8.7 per cent to be sufficient to meet it, the non-government energy experts prefer a 13 per cent export growth that would give a reasonable cushion to withstand the high oil price such as US $26 per barrel which they consider more likely.[38]

Of these, points (a), (d) and (h) are particularly relevant in the context of Indo-Middle East relations. Whereas the Ninth Plan recommendation to acquire acreage in other countries could be taken up with cash-strapped and embargoed countries like Iran, Iraq and Libya; the search for investments could fruitfully be directed at Saudi Arabia, Kuwait and Qatar. Import of LNG involves huge initial outlay and vast infrastructure. More than that, however, it involves sustained engagement with the exporting and transiting countries. The Indo-Iran gas pipeline that would transit through Pakistan illustrates the point. The Middle East specific points can best be pursued within an overall policy framework and not independently of the rest of the recommendations.

CONCLUSION

Enhancement of domestic production and diversification of supply sources, in the ultimate analysis, will not make a radical difference in India's energy dependence on the Middle East. An energy policy, in the circumstances, will have to proceed from this basic given. Various government agencies and non-government experts have made valuable recommendations to head off short-term crises and long-term problems. Some of them have been incorporated in the Ninth Five Year Plan that will run through 2002. What is still lacking is a comprehensive energy strategy with set targets to be achieved within a specific time frame that the government is committed to and the people are aware of. Whereas significant strides have been made in domestic exploration, production, refining, infrastructure network and so on; long-term contracts for LNG supplies and construction of gas pipelines have not been properly attended to. In the meanwhile, the social, economic, political and security problems in the Middle East are steadily worsening; and any complacency regarding secure supplies is unwarranted and unwise.

NOTES

1. Ken Koyama, 'Growing Energy Demands in Asian Countries: Opportunities and Constraints for Gulf Energy Exporters', in *Gulf Energy and the World: Challenges and Threats* (Emirates Centre for Strategic Studies and Research, Abu Dhabi, 1997), p. 59.
2. M.T. Freund et al., 'Annex: Identifying Future Courses for Crises', in Clawson, Patrick L., ed., *Energy and National Security in the 21st Century* (National Defense University Press, Washington, DC, 1995), pp. 151-84.

3. Gulshan Dietl, 'Changing Profile of the State in the Gulf Region', *India International Centre Quarterly* (New Delhi), Vol. 24, no. 1, Spring 1997, p. 157.
4. The Kuwaiti Princess Suad al-Sabah, quoted in Ghassan Salameh, 'Hangover Time in the Gulf', *The Middle East Report* (Washington, D.C.), March-April 1986, p. 42.
5. Maria Kielmas, 'Iraqi Oil: Waiting for Sanctions to Go', *Middle East International* (London), 13 March 1998, p. 15.
6. *Political, Economic, Social, Cultural and Religious Trends in the Middle East and the Gulf and Their Impact on Energy Supply, Security and Pricing* (James A. Baker III Institute for Public Policy, Houston, April 1997), p. 3.
7. Rahul Roy Chaudhury, *Sea Power and Indian Security* (Brassey's, London, 1995), p. 89.
8. *The Hindu* (New Delhi), 1 December 1996.
9. *Hydrocarbon Perspective 2010: Meeting the Challenges* (Report of the Study Group, New Delhi, 1995), pp. 3-4, 3-5 and 1-6.
10. Ibid., pp. 1-2.
11. *The Hindu* (New Delhi), 9 December 1996.
12. Hirofumi Kanai and Gainer Kwan, 'Future Markets of LNG in Asia', in Michaela Crisell, ed., *International Oil and Gas Financial Review 1997* (Euromoney Publication, Essex 1997), p. 108.
13. Ibid., p. 110.
14. *Hydrocarbon Perspective 2010*, no. 9, pp. 1-9.
15. Ibid., pp. 3-9. The official forecasts by the Government of India regarding demands in the gas sector being higher than those quoted in the *International Oil and Gas Financial Review.*
16. Koyama, no. 1, pp. 59-60.
17. K.R. Singh, 'India and West Asia: Retrospect and Prospects' (Paper presented at a seminar on *India's Foreign Policy: Challenges and Prospects*, Rajendra Prasad Academy, New Delhi, 14-15 October 1996), p. 10.
18. Shebonti Ray Dadwal, 'India's Energy Situation: Crisis in the Making', *Strategic Analysis* (New Delhi), June 1997, pp. 374-5.
19. Ministry of Petroleum and Natural Gas. Indian Oil Corporation, quoted in *Middle East Economic Digest* (London), 16 February 1996, p. 15. According to the *Energy Statistics Yearbook 1995* (United Nations, New York, 1997), India imported 27.7 mt of crude out of which 6.8 mt from Saudi Arabia, 2.1 mt from Iran and 6.8 mt from the UAE in 1994. In 1995, India imported 30 mt of crude out of which 6.9 mt from Saudi Arabia, 3.2 mt from Iran and 6.8 mt from the UAE, pp. 176-9.
20. *Foreign Trade, November 1997* (Economic Intelligence Service, Centre for Monitoring Indian Economy Private Ltd., Bombay), pp. 223, 265, 271, 277, 291.

21. Trade balance with the UAE is not specified. *Monthly Review of the Indian Economy, March 1998* (Economic Intelligence Service), p. 174.
22. *Indian Petroleum and Natural Gas Statistics 1994-5* (Ministry of Petroleum and Natural Gas, Government of India, New Delhi, 1996), p. 70.
23. *Middle East Economic Digest,* 16 February 1996, p. 14, Roy Choudhury, no. 7, p. 90.
24. Ibid.
25. *Middle East Economic Digest,* 16 February 1996, p. 14, Roy Choudhury, no. 7, p. 90.
26. Gulshan Dietl, 'Quest for Influence in Central Asia : India and Pakistan', *International Studies* (New Delhi), Vol. 34, no. 2, April-June 1997, p. 136.
27. *The Statesman* (New Delhi), 3 October 1995. On the pipeline controversy, see also Swaminathan S. Anklesaria Aiyar 'Case for Mad Pipeline', *The Times of India* (New Delhi), 18 August 1996 and 10 December 1996.
28. *Observer of Business and Politics* (New Delhi), 13 February 1997.
29. Deepak Mehta, 'Foreign Investors prefer the Petronet-LNG option', *Petroleum Economist* (London), April 1998, pp. 44-6.
30. *Hydrocarbon Perspective 2010*, no. 9, pp. 1-16.
31. Jyoti Parikh, Kankar Bhattacharya, B. Sudhakar Reddy and Kirit S. Parikh, 'Energy System: Need for New Momentum', in Kirit S. Parikh, ed., *India Development Report, 1997* (Indira Gandhi Institute of Development Research, Oxford University Press, New Delhi, 1997), p. 89.
32. *Eighth Plan Document, 1992-7* (Government of India, New Delhi) p. 82.
33. Vijay Kelkar at the Lovraj Kumar Memorial Lecture, August 1997. Quoted in Dadwal, no. 18, pp. 376-7.
34. *Approach Paper to the Ninth Five Year Plan, 1997-2002* (Planning Commission Reprint Document, Centre for Monitoring Indian Economy Private Ltd. Bombay, February 1997), p. 53.
35. Ibid., p. 54.
36. Ibid., p. 53.
37. Ibid., p. 54.
38. *Hydrocarbon Perspective 2010*, n. 7, pp. 3-12 and 'Energy System: Need for New Momentum', no. 31, p. 89.

Linking Demands and Supplies: Regional Energy Cooperation in South Asia

GILLES BOQUÉRAT

The SAARC countries are characterized by a still relatively low per capita use of commercial energy, varying from 33 kilograms of oil equivalent (kgoe) in Nepal to 260 kgoe in India. Yet one notices a steady increase in consumption due to rising incomes, urbanization and a growing energy intensity in the agricultural and industrial sectors. The per capita consumption has more than doubled in Bangladesh and in Nepal between 1980 and 1995 and has increased by around 80 per cent in the case of India and Pakistan. Only Sri Lanka has experienced a comparatively lower growth with an average annual rate of 2.7 per cent (against 9.3 per cent in the case of Nepal).[1] These figures only give a partial image of energy consumption since a substantial part of the total energy consumed in the countries of South Asia is still met through traditional non-commercial sources of energy, namely, fuel-wood, agricultural wastes and animal dung. Although inevitably bound to decline, but rather slowly due to a recurrent poverty preventing large inter-fuel substitution in rural areas, this reliance on traditional fuels combined with high population growth rate has led to over-exploitation of forest resources for fuel-wood and consequently induced depletion of forests cover far in excess of their regeneration (the exception being Bhutan which can report a large forest and woodland cover and a low rate of deforestation).[2]

To meet the challenge of development, the South Asian countries have become net energy importers for oil resources which are locally far inadequate—even non-existent in Bhutan, Nepal and Sri Lanka—to match production with consumption. In 1996, self-sufficiency in oil was of the order of 41 per cent for India, 19 per cent for Pakistan and only 4 per cent for Bangladesh.[3] In consequence, oil accounts for a disproportionate share of total energy imports

TABLE 1: COMMERCIAL ENERGY CONSUMPTION IN 1995

(in PJ)

1995	*Commercial Energy Consumption*		*Traditional Fuels*	
	Total	*Imports as % of CEC*	*Total*	*% of Total Consumption*
Bangladesh	349	22	336	49
Bhutan	3	(*)	13	81
India	10,513	13	3,065	23
Nepal	23	83	234	91
Pakistan	1,357	37	335	20
Sri Lanka	93	83	97	51

Note: (*)For Bhutan, the amount of commercial energy produced is twice the amount of commercial energy consumed.

Source: Based on *World Resources 1998-99*, United Nations Statistical Division (New York, 1998), p. 332.

(see Table 2). Greater exploitation of national energy reserves after the oil crises of the seventies has not substantially reduced the vulnerability of South Asian economies to the foreign exchange constraints which might result from political upheavals in the volatile Gulf region.

Given the nature of the supply-demand imbalance and the declared objective of the SAARC to promote and strengthen collective self-reliance, one could have expected regional cooperation in energy to have been prominent in SAARC activities. Questions related to energy did find place in two technical committees—one on rural development and the other on science and technology—under the Integrated Programme of Action (IPA) initially adopted in August 1983. But it remains that out of twelve technical committees, none has dealt specifically with energy.

Subsequently, workshops, seminars and meetings of experts were held on renewable energy resources, energy modelling techniques, biomass gasification, solar thermal technology, etc.[4] These were non-controversial subjects but also relatively marginal since the emphasis on renewable energy sources such as solar, both thermal and photo-voltaic, biomass based systems and mini-hydel systems, though desirable, it will probably never account for a large share of total energy production, even if the development of cost effective technologies in this field can be of some interest in remote areas.

Energy related issues were also taken up in two regional studies, both completed in 1992. The first one, the SAARC regional study

TABLE 2: NATIONAL COMMERCIAL ENERGY BALANCES

Bangladesh: National Commercial Energy Balance, 1995
(in thousands tons of oil equivalent = ktoe)

ktoe	*Coal*	*Oil*	*Gas*	*Electricity*	*Nuclear*	*Hydro*
Indigenous production	0	107	7,437	0	0	32
Imports	0	2,557	0	0	0	0
Exports	0	129	0	0	0	0

India: National Commercial Energy Balance, 1995
(in thousands tons of oil equivalent)

ktoe	*Coal*	*Oil*	*Gas*	*Electricity*	*Nuclear*	*Hydro*
Indigenous production	1,35,686	36,660	15,591	0	1,824	7,174
Imports	5,455	48,884	0	144	0	0
Exports	43	3,486	0	11	0	0

Pakistan: National Commercial Energy Balance, 1995
(in thousands tons of oil equivalent)

ktoe	*Coal*	*Oil*	*Gas*	*Electricity*	*Nuclear*	*Hydro*
Indigenous production	1,361	2,821	12,331	0	133	1,966
Imports	721	12,841	0	0	0	0
Exports	0	579	0	0	0	0

Source: International Energy Agency, Paris.

on the causes and consequences of natural disasters and the protection and preservation of the environment, stressed the necessity to develop technical cooperation for information exchange and technological transfer programmes in the field of alternate and renewable energy systems, energy conservation, monitoring of environmental impacts of energy producing systems. As a matter of fact, the countries of the region exhibit growing environmental stress and needs to focus attention to reduce energy intensities and improve the low efficiency of energy use resulting from substantial losses in generation, transmission and distribution of power and from obsolescent plants and poor maintenance.

The second SAARC regional study was on greenhouse effect and its impact on the region. It emphasized the need for carbon emissions reduction strategies in the energy sector involving the switch-over to less carbon or no carbon emitting fuels. CO_2 emissions had increased by 160 per cent in South Asia between 1980 and 1995.[5]

To reduce the use of coal and fossil fuels, the study recommended to develop at the regional level an energy master plan with an emphasis on maximizing the use of clean energy, e.g. hydroelectricity and wind or solar energy. Electrical energy could have a significant replacement value as an environment-friendly source of energy as fossil fuels increases global warming. For this, South Asian countries were encouraged to come together and 'utilize the potential hydropower, involved in the huge water resources in the upper catchment areas of Bhutan, India and Nepal to the common benefit of the region'.[6]

Five years later, the heads of state or government of the SAARC countries, at the Male summit of May 1997, expressed the urgent need for the implementation of the recommendations of these two studies. So little had been achieved during the first decade of SAARC that a paper submitted by the Coalition for Action on South Asian Cooperation (CASAC) to the commemorative session of the council of ministers in New Delhi in December 1995 proposed to look at possibilities of sectorial cooperation in energy at the earliest opportune moment. Cooperation could be in three directions: Joint exploration for fossil fuels, increasing production from available reserves and trade. More recently, the report of the group of eminent persons, whose mandate was to assess the progress made by this Association since its inception, was released during the tenth summit of the SAARC held in Colombo in July 1998. In their conclusion, it was noticed that energy was regrettably an area still outside the SAARC umbrella.

At present regional trade in energy is minimal. In fact, the South Asian countries have little surplus of commercial energy to export. India, the third largest world producer of coal, exports small quantities to Bangladesh, Nepal and Bhutan which taken all together account for much less than India's imports of coking coal.[7] After independence, Pakistan depended almost entirely on Indian coal, but reciprocal recriminations related to the implementation of the successive trade agreements, and a general climate of political mistrust led Pakistan to import coal from other countries, notably from Britain, at exorbitant cost whereas coal from India could be had at much cheaper rates. Energy resource development had even some unforeseen transnational implications when in the early sixties the Karnafuli hydroelectric scheme, in what was then East Pakistan, led 40,000 Chakmas tribals, driven away from their land by the construction of the Kaptai dam, to settle down in the North-East Frontier Agency (Arunachal Pradesh) of India. This dam still remains for Bangladesh the only source of hydroelectricity.

Pakistan and Bangladesh do not export their main indigenous resource, i.e. natural gas. Being self-sufficient, Pakistan could have exported gas to India but for the will to save on its main indigenous energy resource and the deleterious political relations. Since Pakistan will probably have to resort to gas imports before the end of the next decade, the interest of the supplying country, which could be Iran or Central Asian Republics, would be to have a pipeline connection extended up to India, requiring cooperation between New Delhi and Islamabad for preventing any disruption of supplies *en route*.

The situation could be different in the case of Bangladesh. Given the volume of gas recently discovered and estimation of reserves onshore and offshore, there could be more than enough to fulfil domestic demand in a country where a large majority of the country's 125 million inhabitants still lack electricity. There is a possibility of gas exports to India undermining the traditional Bangladeshi's opposition to giving valuable national resource away to a towering neighbour. The warming of political relations after the coming into power of the leader of the Awami League, Sheikh Hasina, in June 1996, reflected in a historic thirty year Ganges water sharing treaty with India followed by the repatriation of Chakma refugees from their decade old exile in India, has replaced the older stance adopted by the Bangladesh National Party of former Prime Minister Khaleda Zia. Bangladesh could export gas or electricity from gas-fired plants to India as it would fit into New Delhi's larger plans for energy security in the twenty-first century. Although there is still no definite governmental policy on this politically sensitive issue, the need to remedy the large trade imbalance with India and the pressure from oil industry executives will probably dictate the timing of gas exports. Large foreign companies—the UK's Cairn Energy, UNOCAL from the United States and the Royal Dutch/Shell—have already moved into Bangladesh. West Bengal could first benefit of such imports and this would be an environment friendly substitute for coal transported from Bihar or Orissa. As India can also anticipate gas reserves in Tripura in excess of local requirements, gas pipelines could be laid across Bangladesh and the Ganges basin. A memorandum of understanding has been signed between the Indian

Oil and Natural Gas Commission and the UNOCAL to supply gas from Tripura to Bangladesh and from Bangladesh to India through a pipeline.

In the meantime, there could a power swaping arrangement between the two countries. Dhaka has proposed to supply power from its eastern zone to Tripura and in return has asked India to supply 200 MW from its coal-based power plant at Farakka. Both countries have agreed to prepare a feasibility report for interconnection of power systems. During a meeting between the Indian and Bangladeshi Foreign Secretaries held in June 1998, India had proposed to Bangladesh to address its adverse trade balance by actively cooperating with it in the oil and gas sector. As a value added means of exporting their natural gas and of creating jobs, Bangladesh can also think of providing eastern India with fertilizers, eventually through the establishment of joint production facilities.

The possibility of building transmission links between India and Pakistan, with the support of the Asian Development Bank, has also been mentioned. Discussions between Indian and Pakistani officials under a broad memorandum of understanding were conducted during the winter of 1998-9 for the export of electricity generated by different independent power producers (IPPs) to meet the shortfall in the northern states of India. If the availability of 300 MW of power for export to India for the next ten years, which could be increased to 600 MW as per availability during certain period of time, is established, the negotiations have so far fell flat because of differences which have cropped up regarding the electricity prices demanded by Pakistan and offered by India.

To face the dependence on imports of 'extra-regional' commercial energy in a region where the total population is likely to double within the second quarter of the next century, the most promising energy surplus flows from the virtually untapped Himalayan potential for hydroelectricity generation, besides the use of water resource for irrigation and navigation purposes. Consumption of electricity has increased on an average of 11.5 per cent per year between 1985 and 1995 and critical power shortages still retard the growth of South Asian economies. Electricity could be traded among the South Asian countries benefiting the buyer countries by solving energy deficit and by way of reduction in transportation costs because of the relative geographical proximity as well as the seller countries in view of the extended market. For the Himalayan kingdoms of Nepal and

TABLE 3 : ELECTRICITY CONSUMPTION AND TRADE IN 1995

In 1995	*Electricity Consumption*		*Elect. Cons./Population*		*Trade (million kWh)*	
	(TWh)	*% Change since 1985*	*(kWh/ Capita)*	*% Change since 1985*	*Import*	*Export*
Bangladesh	7.45	121	62	82	0	0
Bhutan	n.a.	n.a.	n.a.	n.a.	4	1,717
India	341.51	129	367	88	1,675	130
Nepal	0.85	166	39	105	110	42
Pakistan	41.19	125	317	66	0	0
Sri Lanka	3.94	90	217	66	0	0
Asia*	942.00	149	551	105	-	-

Note: *Asia does not include DPR of Korea and Vietnam.

Source: Figures based on *Energy Statistics and Balances of Non-OECD Countries 1994-5* (Paris, 1997), pp. 354-419 for columns 1 to 4 and on *World Resources 1998-99*, op. cit., for columns 5 and 6.

Bhutan, landlocked and classified as least developed countries, large hydropower projects are a way to earn much needed foreign currency.

Bhutan possesses a potential in theory for generating about 20,000 MW of energy (of which 11,000 MW is identified hydropower potential). Nepal can generate some 83,000 MW of which about 42,000 MW are economically exploitable, specially through the harnessing of the perennial rivers of Mahakali, Karnali, Gandak and Kosi. The irony is that Nepal is the only country of the region which has the highest dependence on traditional sources of energy which count for 91 per cent of total energy consumption in 1995, while sitting on a formidable reserve of hydroelectric power still remaining out of reach for a major part of its population: In the mid-nineties, only 15 per cent of the total Nepalese population had access to electricity.[8] India also has a vast potential of hydropower, awaiting exploitation in the north-eastern region which has been assessed at 84,000 MW at a 60 per cent load factor, of which about 27,000 MW accounts for in the state of Arunachal Pradesh alone. Yet, only 1 per cent of the total resource has been tapped so far. India has a relatively low thermal-hydel mix with a ratio of around 76 to 24 whereas the required mix should be 60 of thermal and 40 of hydel.[9] In 1996, hydroelectricity accounted for only 16 per cent of total domestic electricity generation in India.

Regional cooperation in the area of water resources has so far failed to make any headway as an integration scheme. Although the water resources was cited by King Birendra, at the time of the

TABLE 4: SOURCES OF ELECTRICITY IN 1996 *(in %)*

1996	*Hydropower*	*Coal*	*Oil*	*Gas*	*Nuclear Power*
Bangladesh	6.4 (24.8)	–	6.5 (26.6)	87.1 (48.6)	–
Bhutan	n.a.	n.a.	n.a.	n.a.	n.a.
India	15.9 (39.0)	73.2 (49.9)	2.8 (7.7)	6.2 (0.8)	1.9 (2.5)
Nepal	90.2 (82.3)	–	9.8 (17.7)	–	–
Pakistan	40.7 (58.2)	0.8 (0.2)	30.8 (1.1)	26.8 (40.5)	0.8 (0.0)
Sri Lanka	71.8 (88.7)	–	28.2 (11.3)	–	–
South Asia	19.1 (41.5)	62.6 (43.0)	6.2 (7.4)	10.3 (5.9)	1.7 (2.2)

Note: Figures in parenthesis are for 1980.
Source: *World Development Indicators 1999*, The World Bank (Washington, 1999), pp. 153-4.

twenty-sixth session of the Colombo plan consultative committee in December 1977, as a potential area for joint ventures with other South Asian countries, it has been however considered too contentious a subject to be included in SAARC's regular agenda and cooperation in the development of Himalayan hydraulic resources has remained only bilateral. At the time of the SAARC Bangalore summit of 1986, the leaders of Bangladesh, India and Nepal had agreed to collaborate in studying the prospects of the multiple uses of the water resources for their common benefit, but the tripartite talks got bogged down, partly because of the Indian exaggerated sense of alarm over the politically-guided multilateral approach.

The most fruitful collaboration has been the one between New Delhi and Thimphu. Bhutan has shortages of money, manpower and machinery to build and operate its hydroelectric potential resource. Also, India has assisted Bhutan, since its first five year plan (1961-2/1965-6), in rural and urban electrification with the establishment of small, medium and large power projects and setting up of transformers and electric lines across the country. The fact that the latter has never really challenged the former's political and economic ascendancy over the Himalayan kingdom has certainly helped collaborative endeavours. India imports electricity generated in western Bhutan with the construction of the 336 MW run-of-river hydroelectric plant located at Chukha. This project had been agreed in March 1974 and commissioned in 1986-8. It was carried out with Indian technical and financial assistance (60 per cent of the project's cost was given as grant and the remaining 40 per cent as loan) and includes a buy-back arrangement. Hydropower investment not only involves a large sum of money but the foreign exchange component may work out to be more than 70 per cent in Bhutanese context, as the majority of construction materials, machines and labour have to be imported. Only cement, sand, stones, boulders and timber can be made available locally for the construction purposes.[10]

In spite of shortcomings regarding the terms and conditions for the transfer of electricity (India being the only importer of Bhutan's hydroelectricity, the bargaining power is limited), the Chukha hydropower station on the Wangchu river is the most successful effort at cooperation between India and her neighbours in the energy sector.[11] It has provided the eastern regional electric grid of India (West Bengal, Orissa, Bihar and Sikkim) with sorely needed additional capacity. Besides, Bhutan could in the future seek India's assistance for routing electricity through sub-stations in West Bengal or Meghalaya to Bangladesh. Such cross-border grid would also allow India's north-eastern region to be connected to the rest of the country via Bangladesh. More imports from Bhutan would follow the completion, expected by the end of 2004, of the largest project in Bhutan—the 1,020 MW Tala powerhouse—and other smaller hydroelectric projects implemented with Indian assistance like the 60 MW Kurichu project. Even if Bhutan had been able to reduce the share of oil in primary energy supply due to the commissioning of the Chukha hydel project,[12] these hydropower plants are less justified by domestic demands—Bhutan's prospects for development are not commensurate with its generation potential—than by being a main source of revenue: 80 per cent of the total hydroelectric energy output is being exported to India (see Table 3). The Chukha scheme has provided most of the impetus for economic growth during the second half of the eighties and electricity sales to India constituted in the early nineties about one-third of all Bhutan's domestic revenues.[13] During a visit to Thimphu in October 1998, the Indian Union Minister of Power, Mr. Kumaramangalam, proposed to develop river based programmes. With India estimated to be short of 30,000 MW by the time the Tala project is completed, a ready customer stands beyond the border.[14]

As a monopoly buyer, India can be tempted to dictate its conditions specially when the partner-country is ill-equipped in terms of technical expertise and negotiating experience and when the leadership in landlocked country with minimum elbow room for independent action to harness the resource is ready to provide concessions in exchange for political support. Nepal is also unable to take up large development projects on its own and must go for funds and technological expertise either to India or to multilateral agencies and other donor countries. Even if India is not directly involved, the latter, both on ground of riparian rights and financial viability, would want Nepal to come to an agreement with its southern neighbour on the purchasing of surplus power and water sharing rights. Profitable exploitation of the vast hydroelectric resources remains largely a pipe dream since only 257 MW, or 0.6 per cent of the economically exploitable hydroelectric potential, has been connected with the national grid as of 1997 and electricity, whatever its origin (thermal, hydro, solar), accounts for 1 per cent of total energy consumption.[15]

Collaborative agreements with India have long been prevented by the feeling in the minds of Nepalese of unfair deals in the harnessing of the common Himalayan river wealth. The first post-independence river water development scheme was the Kosi barrage which was agreed in April 1954 and was designed to yield power, irrigation and flood control benefits for both countries. This agreement was subsequently amended in 1966 in order to acknowledge Nepal's complaints, some politically motivated, about a project furthering India's own interests at the expense of the legitimate rights of Nepal. The Gandak scheme of December 1959 was also criticized for falling short of Nepal's expectations on the dividends resulting from the project.[16] These barrages constructed on the common border, funded by India—Nepal's contribution was essentially to provide land, raw material or labour force, have cast a shadow on subsequent negotiations.

The impression of unequal allocation of benefits has been carried for so long that the question of the exploitation of common rivers has always been very sensitive and politically controversial. Suspicion and occasional strains in the bilateral relations during the thirty years of the Panchayat system were an impediment in further joint endeavour, delaying the realization of the Karnali, Pancheshwar and Rapti multipurpose projects. The return to a multi-party democracy did not dispel all mistrust. The harboured grudge was reflected in Article 126 of the Nepalese constitution of 1990 which requires a majority of two-third of the members present at a joint sitting of both Houses of Parliament for the ratification or approval of any treaty or agreement, with long-term implications, on natural resources and the distribution of their uses. In case of any treaty or agreement which does not affect the nation in the long term, the ratification or approval may be done by a simple majority of the members present at the House of Representatives. Conceived as a means to prevent a government from succumbing to external pressure, the Supreme Court in December 1992 reproached Girija Prasad Koirala, the then Prime Minister, for his non-observance of this constitutional provision regarding the controversial decision on the Tanakpur barrage taken during his visit to Delhi one year earlier and which allowed India the use of 577 metres of Nepali territory to complete the construction of the left aflux bund of the barrage. The barrage was built, along with a power station, by the Indians during the last years of the Panchayat régime on the Mahakali, a border river on major stretches between the two countries. In the general elections of November 1994, the row over the Tanakpur understanding and the supposed Koirala's 'sell out' to India was a contentious issue which was exploited with success by the communists for gaining electoral mileage.

The Narasimha Rao government succeeded in winning the confidence of Nepal's main political parties and in ending the long stalemate on jointly harnessing water resources with the signing in February 1996 of a treaty on the integrated development of Mahakali River 'on the basis of equal partnership', comprising the Pancheshwar multipurpose project which India had wanted for long and allowing for a higher amount of electricity offered to Nepal from the Tanakpur powerhouse as well as a more equitable sharing than before in regard to the utilization of waters from the Sarda barrage which was built after an agreement in 1920 between Nepal and then British India. The estimated nine billion units of electricity generated by the Pancheshwar high dam would be consumed mostly by India, consequently Nepal—which is entitled to 50 per cent share of the waters—shall expect to gain revenues from the selling of a portion of its share of the energy produced. At present, Nepal is still a net importer of electricity. In February 1996, an umbrella agreement was also signed between the two countries allowing any governmental, semi-governmental or private enterprise in India or Nepal to buy or sell power to each other and determining to that effect their terms and conditions.

After a heated debate and the unanimous passage of a binding 'scripture' redefining water rights, the Mahakali treaty was finally ratified in September 1996 by a more than two-thirds majority by the joint upper and lower houses of the Nepali Parliament as per the

the constitutional requirement of Article 126. The instruments of ratification were exchanged with the Indian government on 4 June 1997, but without including the provisions of the aforementioned scripture. Ever since, the Mahakali treaty has sharply divided the Nepali political community leading to a current impasse on its implementation.

Any agreement on the utilization of border rivers should not be seen in isolation but linked with landlocked Nepal's key requirements like transit facilities and market for Nepali products. Nepal and India have also had further discussions on the development of multipurpose projects on the Karnali and the west Rapti rivers. Electricity imports from Nepal could surely help to mitigate the acute power shortage faced by the northern grid in India but this leads one to question the viability of the Uttar Pradesh and Bihar state electricity boards (SEBs) as reliable customers when the energy pricing system is still based on large subsidies.[17] Nepal submitted an approach paper at the SAARC council of ministers meeting in December 1996 on the feasibility of sub-regional cooperation among Nepal, Bhutan, Bangladesh and India to improve the climate for economic integration. A 'northern quadrilateral network', which could develop cross-border energy projects, would not necessarily be at variance with the SAARC charter since Article 7 allow two or more SAARC member states to embark on collective economic cooperation on specific projects of exclusive concern to them as long as it is not opposed by the other member states.

To conclude, regional cooperation in energy has been impeded by the limited base of exportable resources required to meet the large and growing energy supply-demand gap, by the relative scarcity of financial resources needed for large investments in transportation and infrastructure development and above all by populist rhetoric and political suspicions arising from collateral issues and past wrongs. If some collaborative ventures in energy have been successful at the bilateral level, SAARC has been shying away from taking any initiative in energy production and power exchange for an optimal operation of subcontinental resource endowments. Regional energy cooperation has not been taken up for its intrinsic value but as part of a larger political framework of bilateral relations setting the tone for possible negotiations. The time is yet to come when mutual trust and co-operation would translate into a profitable interdependence. It is all the more regrettable that in view of the wave of liberalization, the wooing of the private sector and the drive towards attracting foreign investments, the policy-makers are converting themselves to the urgent need to improve the infrastructure as part of an holistic approach to economic development.

NOTES

1. *World Development Report 1998-99*, World Bank (New York, 1999), pp. 208-9. Malaysia, for instance, has a commercial energy use per capita of 1,655 kgoe.
2. See 'Profile of environmental degradation', *Human Development Report 1998*, UNDP (New York, 1998), pp. 180-1.
3. International Energy Agency, Paris.
4. Integrated approach to energy problems, research and development in non-conventional and renewable sources of energy, utilization of agro-waste products for the production of energy were among the areas identified by the study group on scientific and technological cooperation for further consideration at its first meeting in June 1982. The SARC Technical Committee on Rural Development identified 'Rural Energy' as a field of research at its third meeting held in Dhaka in October 1985 and a workshop on this subject took place in Islamabad in February 1986. One year later, 'Rural Energy' was discussed during a workshop in New Delhi on transfer of technology.

   The second meeting of planners which took place in Islamabad in October 1987 identified energy as one of the important areas for possible cooperation. A meeting of experts on energy modelling techniques was held in New Delhi in June 1989. It was then recommended to develop a networking arrangement for ensuring regular exchange of information and expertise among institutions working in the field of energy modelling techniques. Meanwhile, the report of a seminar on regional cooperation for the protection of the environment in South Asia held in February 1989, mentioned the fact that in view of the close links between environment and energy needs, it would be useful to develop a programme of cooperation in the field of non-conventional energy sources, including systematic exchange of information, exchange of specialists, research programmes, etc. The SAARC secretary general, in its report of November 1990 on the activities of the association, was of the view that cooperation in energy conservation and energy modelling techniques can be usefully brought within the purview of the technical committee on science and technology.
5. *World Development Report 1998-99*, World Bank (New York, 1999), p. 209.
6. SAARC regional study on greenhouse effect and its impact on the

region in: *South Asian Survey*, 1 (2), July-December 1994, p. 305. Subsequently, the SAARC fund for regional projects commissioned a study on hydel power project in Bhutan and Nepal which is yet to be completed.

7. In 1996-7, the share of Bangladesh in India's coal exports was 61.1 per cent (nearly 70 per cent of Bangladesh's total coal imports), Nepal 34.3 per cent, Bhutan 4.5 per cent and Sri Lanka 0.1 per cent. CMIE, Economic Intelligence Service, *Foreign Trade*, November 1997, p. 38.
8. *Economic Survey*, Fiscal Year 1996-7, HMG, Ministry of Finance, Kathmandu, 1997, p. 62.
9. *The Asian Age*, 12 February 1999. Two large hydel power projects are to be developed in Arunachal Pradesh, the 13,400 MW Dihang and the 7,300 MW Subansiri multipurpose projects.
10. B. Tamang, *Hydropower Development in Bhutan*, National Environmental Commission, Thimphu, 1993, p.12.
11. For a Bhutanese analysis, see Bhim Subba, 'Tapping Himalayan Water Resources: Problems, Opportunities and Prospects from a Bhutanese Perspective', in *Water Nepal*, 4 (1), September 1994, 209-17.
12. Oil share in primary energy supply fell from 82 per cent in 1984 to 34 per cent in 1989. *Regional Report: South Asia*, World Energy Council, London, 1992, p. 28.
13. *Bhutan: Round Table Meeting, 1992*, Planning Commission, Royal Government of Bhutan, 1991, p. 2.
14. *Kuensel*, 31 October 1998.
15. *Economic Survey*, Fiscal Year 1996-7, HMG, Ministry of Finance, op. cit., p. 58.
16. For discussions regarding the Kosi and Gandak water resources development schemes, see B.C. Upreti, *Politics of Himalayan River Waters*, 1993, pp. 102-8.
17. Of some relevance is, for instance, the threat of the state-owned National Thermal Power Corporation to stop supplying power to the eastern region from its Farakka, Talcher and Kahalgaon power stations due to mounting arrears of the SEBs of West Bengal, Bihar and Orissa. *The Hindustan Times*, 12 October 1998.

Meeting India's Energy Needs: What Role for Central Asia?

FRÉDÉRIC GRARE

Ensuring a secure, affordable energy supply is certainly one of the most pressing issues India will have to confront in the years to come. India is already faced with occasional energy shortages, and will have to address the question of restructuring its energy sector in the context of a chronic lack of capital to realize the necessary investments. In the near future India will thus have to satisfy its growing energy needs through alternative sources of supply, although this will create an additional burden on its balance of payments.

According to the Tata Energy Research Institute (TERI), India's reserves of crude oil were 727 million tons in 1996.[1] Due mainly to technical problems in the Bombay High offshore fields, domestic oil production declined from 33,021 thousand tons in 1990/1 to 26,950 thousand tons in 1992/3.[2] The decline was reversed in 1994 and India's domestic production rose to 33,826 thousand tons in 1997/8[3] but the country is increasingly dependent on oil imports. Gross imports of crude oil rose from 13,624 thousand tons to 34,494 thousand tons between 1975/6 and 1997/8.[4]

With the Indian economy growing at over 5 per cent per annum, energy demand is currently growing faster than in past decades. Moreover, with the country's population projected to reach one billion by the year 2000, and with rising incomes, this trend can be expected to accelerate. While recent on and offshore discoveries are already contributing to domestic production, the cost of developing new fields is relatively high, especially for the capital-poor Indian public oil sector. The consumption of refined products is also substantially higher than India's refinery capacity. Although it has expanded in the recent past, this capacity remains around six million barrels per year. Further expansion could raise the capacity to 10 million barrels per year at the turn of the millennium, but this is not likely to eliminate the need for imports. India remains self-sufficient in natural gas but the projected increases in demand for gas will inevitably require imports in this sector as well.

This situation raises a number of issues, ranging from the current structure of the Indian energy sector and its efficiency, to the pressing problem of finding alternative sources of supply. These issues are closely linked. Because of heavy subsidies for some groups of customers, the administered price mechanism and the government's inability to take rational decisions against the interests of certain political groups and lobbies, India's public energy sector is particularly inefficient. According to K.R. Pachauri and Maithili Iyer, 'the energy intensity of GDP in India is almost thrice as high as that in Japan and almost forty per cent higher than in the United States'.[5] Moreover, government policies aimed at reducing the gap between demand and supply have led to massive increases in imports without sufficient efforts to attain optimal resource utilization. This approach has created an additional burden on the balance of payments.

This is not only a matter of concern for the present. It raises important questions about the sustainability of India's economic growth in the future. What is at stake is not only the country's economic well-being and its social cohesion, but also its capacity to take on the role of regional giant to which it aspires. The government has repeated its willingness to address the problem by bringing prices progressively into line with real costs. Prices of oil and gas have already been raised,[6] and the administered price mechanism is supposed to be dismantled during the coming ninth and tenth economic plans. But it will take time before the Indian public energy sector can generate the profits required for massive investment in domestic production. India will therefore remain heavily dependent on imports for the foreseeable future.

At the same time, a major post cold war event has been the emergence of Central Asia and the Caucasians as a new focal point of international relations. Following the break up of the Soviet Union, international attention—including that of India has been drawn to the massive and largely untapped resources of this region which is said to be the third largest oilfield in the world. If this hypothesis is confirmed, the emergence of Central Asia as a major new producer of oil and natural gas could provide India with an additional source of supply. Most hydrocarbon projects in the region are, for the time being, looking towards the West. But a comparison between the demographic and economic growth rates of Asia and the West clearly indicates that the major increase in energy demand in the next ten years will come from Asia, in which India, already the fifth economic power in the world, could assume a major role. And if that is the case, the coming decades could well witness a reorientation of world energy flows in which Central Asia could play a role.

The present article focuses on the relations between India and Central Asia, and, precisely, on the possibility for the latter to supply energy to India. It concentrates on the security of India's energy supply for oil and gas and tries to answer the central question: What role can Central Asia play in meeting India's energy needs? The article argues that many political hurdles would have to be overcome for India to import energy through the necessary pipelines. But Central Asia could prove an interesting option, which would, in the context of India's long-term energy policy, provide a valuable source of supply diversification. However, the article argues that India and Pakistan have a common interest in that specific context. Following an examination of India's past and present strategic interests as well as its disputes with each of the countries concerned by the opening up of Central Asia, the article suggests that the involvement of India in Central Asia's energy development schemes would be a guarantee for each of the region's actors. Furthermore, given the right conditions and political will, the energy question could well become a factor of regional integration.

THE SECURITY OF INDIA'S ENERGY SUPPLIES

India's growing dependence on energy imports, particularly oil, has generated increasing concern about the security of supply. The problem has both political and economic dimensions.

POLITICAL DIMENSIONS

India's major sources of import of crude oil are located in the Persian Gulf region, essentially in Saudi Arabia, the United Arab Emirates and Iran. Iraq, long an important supplier, has not figured among India's major sources of energy, as a result of the international embargo imposed on the country since the end of the Gulf War. In this context, there are three main potential threats to the security of India's supplies: (1) The possibility of social and political instability in the Arab monarchies; (2) the potential concentration of a substantial part of the regional reserves in the hands of one single regime, as it happened during the Iraqi invasion of Kuwait; (3) and military action that would interrupt the oil flow from the Gulf. These three potential threats are considered more fully further.

(1) The possibility of social and political instability of the Arab monarchies is certainly a factor to be taken in consideration. As Gregory Gause has noted,

> Things have changed in the kingdom [Saudi Arabia], and in the Gulf as a whole. The welfare states built in the 1970s, with seemingly limitless resources for very small populations, are now strained by high population growth rates and flat oil prices. Indigenous middle classes, created by state education and employment policies, expect remunerative employment and increasingly seek an outlet for their hope of political participation.[7]

In fact, every Gulf country is confronted with the same problem: How to do more politically but economically. For the first time in more than two decades, Gulf regimes have to live within their means and face relatively hard economic choices. They are being forced to cut government expenditures and raise revenues at a time when their populations are growing rapidly. It is estimated that they will double in 40 years at current growth rate.[8]

Yet economic difficulties are probably not the most pressing issue. Since the Gulf War, political discontent has been more open and public than at any other time in the history of the Arabian peninsula. The nature of reactions has varied in each country, depending on the effectiveness of popular representation. In Saudi Arabia, India's main

TABLE 1: INDIA—IMPORTS OF CRUDE OIL AND MAJOR SOURCES OF IMPORT OF CRUDE OIL (*in million tons*)

Year	*Total*	*Iran*	*Saudi Arabia*	*Iraq*	*Kuwait*	*UAE*	*USSR/ Russia*
1971	12.72	9.96	2.74	0.02	n.a.	n.a.	n.a.
1976	14.03	7.16	4.37	0.46	0.01	1.03	1.00
1980	15.98	2.43	3.12	6.90	n.a.	1.41	1.83
1985	14.81	5.70	2.60	0.90	n.a.	1.70	2.00
1990	20.80	3.16	6.78	2.38	0.73	3.83	2.31
1992	25.50	2.96	8.11	–	(3.0)	6.17	0.06
1994	27.895	3.13	6.8	–	n.a.	6.8	n.a.

Source: K.R. Singh, India: Commercial Energy, Domestic and Foreign Policy Options, unpublished.

oil supplier, Islamic activists have attacked the religious credentials of the ruling monarchy. Opposition has remained limited, but violence has been used on some occasions. More important than the physical consequences of a few terrorist attempts however is the fact that the religious nature of the opposition makes it difficult for the regime to answer without putting into question its own legitimacy.

Such problems do not present an immediate threat to the stability of the Gulf monarchies. Yet they are likely to become more and more pressing if the monarchies do not move toward greater openness, allowing their citizens more opportunities for free expression and social organization. This is especially relevant at a time when the percentage of the young generation who has received a formal education is greater than ever. If not satisfied, demands for greater participation could lead to instability that could jeopardize oil supplies or substantially raise the cost of oil for importing countries.

(2) The concentration of a substantial part of the region's oil reserves in the hands of one regime would not necessarily represent economic catastrophe for India. Because it was supposed to lead to higher prices, Iraq's annexation of Kuwait, which doubled the reserves of the former (to 200 billion barrels), was often presented as a global economic threat. But it has also been argued that it would have had no influence on the international oil market, because Iraq desperately needed to sell as much oil as possible to maximize revenues at a time when the country's financial situation was catastrophic.[9] Over the long term, however, this argument could be reversed. After it recovered from the war Iraq would have been in a position to push up international prices according to its own economic and political interests. Such a situation would clearly present the constant possibility of blackmail by the dominant producer, increasing India's foreign exchange burden and also affecting its foreign policy by forcing it to depend increasingly on continued presence in the region of the only remaining superpower for the security of its supplies.

It is true that the present heavy involvement of the United States in the Gulf area, which could be reinforced as the importance of the Gulf in the world oil supply increases in the years to come,[10] renders this scenario very unlikely for the time being. It should nevertheless be taken into consideration given the internal evolution of several Arab monarchies, as described earlier. For example, terrorist attempts aimed at weakening the legitimacy of the existing regimes, but directed against Western presence on the Arab soil, such as the bombing of the US military facilities in Riyadh in November 1995 and in Daran during the summer of 1996, could lead the United States, given the sensitivity of their public opinion, to reconsider their position and withdraw along the lines that were theirs before the Gulf War. If this were to occur, the first scenario of social and political instability (described earlier) would become relevant. Moreover, the current situation—with or without Iraq—is not totally free of risks for India. For example an agreement between the producers to increase oil prices would pose serious challenges.

(3) In the third scenario, military action that would interrupt the flow of oil from the Gulf, is related to the 'tanker war' that occurred during the Iran-Iraq war. In an attempt to internationalize the conflict, Iraq launched a missile on a Kuwaiti ship. At the time superpowers reacted in order to prevent internationalization of the conflict and re-establish the free flow of oil out of the Gulf. A similar scenario appears very unlikely in the near future. Neither of the former belligerents is currently in a position to attack the other and this situation is reinforced by the American policy of dual containment. Yet there is still debate about Gulf security, especially the challenge posed by Iran. For example, Jamal Al-Suwaidi has suggested that Iran's continued occupation of Abu Musa (islands belonging to the United Arab Emirates), Iran's ongoing programmes to develop a conventional military arsenal and acquire weapons of mass destruction, and Iran's active role in attempting to destabilize Arab Gulf governments are all potentially destabilizing.[11] In examining the reasons behind Iran's desire to acquire both conventional and unconventional weapons, he argues that although present-day Iran is unlikely to attack any of the Gulf Cooperation Council states or take any action which could generate a retaliation by a GCC-Western coalition, the situation could change if Iran perceived any weakening in Western commitment to Gulf security. The motives that might lead to such a change have been alluded above.

Although these scenarios are improbable in the present context they serve to underline India's vulnerability to events affecting the Middle East. Moreover, they do raise one crucial fact: India's energy security *de facto* depends, like that of the rest of the world, on the capacity of the United States to maintain its predominance in the region. In this connection, it is worth noting that the economic structure of the United States makes it prefer relatively moderate prices—but ones high enough to ensure the survival of its own petroleum industry. This latter aspect goes against India's direct interests.[12]

TABLE 2: A COMPARISON OF ALTERNATIVE OIL PRICE PROJECTIONS

Source	*1995*	*2000*	*2005*	*2010*	*2015*	*2020*
OWEM Reference Case (1996 $/bn.)	17.2	17.6	19.4	21.4	23.6	26.1
IIASA/IEW poll response (medians), January 1996	20.5 (1990)	19.0	–	26.0	–	33.3
P.R. Odell, 'Is Middle Eastern domination of the international oil market inevitable?' IIASA International Energy Workshop, Laxenburg, Austria, 1995	15.8 (1993)	16.5	–	18.3	–	21.0
International Energy Outlook, 1996, EIA/DOE	16.8	19.3	21.9	23.7	25.4	–
World Energy Outlook/IEA, 1996	16.3	17.0	17.0-25.0	17.0-25.0	–	–
Petroleum Economics Ltd., Oil and Energy Outlook to 2010, December 1995	16.4	14.7	14.6	12.3	–	–
Data Resources Incorporated, Oil Market Outlook, October 1995	16.5	16.8	20.8	23.2	24.8	–
Petroleum Industry Research Associates Inc. 'World and US Oil', October 1995	17.7	14.7	15.4	–	–	–
The WEFA Group, 'US long-term economic outlook', 4th Quarter 1995	17.2	19.6	21.3	22.1	–	–
Gas Research Institute, 'Baseline projection of the US energy supply and demand', October 1995	–	16.2	16.2	16.2	16.2	–
National Economic Research Associates Inc. 'NERA Energy Outlook', February 1996	16.9	21.6	27.1	21.5	–	–
EC 'European Energy to 2020', Spring 1996	17.6	21.10	–	29.0	–	31.0
Bonner & Moore Associates, in Arab Oil and Gas, 1 February 1996 (1995 $/bn.)	17.1	17.2	18.5	–	–	–
Median Growth in forecasts other than OWEM	1995-2010: 0.9% p.a.			2010-20: 1.4% p.a.		

Source: *Oil & Energy Outlook to 2020*, January 1997, OPEC Secretariat, Vienna.

ECONOMIC DIMENSIONS

Projections concerning the price of oil are as important, if not more important. Petroleum is currently priced extremely low, but it could increase under certain conditions, some of which are enumerated above. There is thus a need for India to diversify its sources of supply.

THE NATURAL GAS OPTION

Natural gas is increasingly seen as an interesting energy option by Indian decision-makers since it is both cheaper and cleaner than oil. Several supply options have been explored, but the highly ambitious projects proposed to increase the quantity of natural gas delivered to India but have been abandoned or postponed for financial, political and technical reasons. Various projects are described further.

(1) In 1990, the construction of a gas pipeline linking Bandar Abbas to Calcutta was proposed. Its capacity would have been of 36 billion m^3 per year. Western provinces of Iran would have received 10 per cent of the gas and Pakistan 20 per cent with the balance going to India. The cost of the pipeline was estimated at US $12 billion. The project was later abandoned.[13]

(2) The same year, an Australian company, Broken Hill Petroleum, presented a pipeline plan for the export of Iranian gas to the west coast of India. Starting in the Qeshm island, the gas pipeline would have followed the Iranian and Pakistani coasts to India. The gas from the offshore South Pars field could have subsequently been linked to this line. The project was abandoned when company management changed.[14]

(3) In early 1992, a Japanese company, Chiyoda Corporation, proposed the construction of a multi-gas suppliers and users grid from the Mediterranean to India, designed to transfer 20 million m^3 of gas annually by a 48 in. diameter pipeline. The networks based on the construction of a natural gas pipeline loop over the Middle East and transportation grid to Europe across North Africa (Morocco and Tunisia), also included a gas pipeline from Iran to India as well as a base from which liquified natural gas (LNG) could be exported to East Asia.[15] Initially estimated at US $38 billion, the project was dramatically reduced in September 1993, and the proposed gas pipeline to India was not pursued.

(4) Another proposal still being discussed, proposed by the Oman

Oil Company, concerns a 1,200 km gas pipeline from Sur in the Oman straight to Gujarat in India via the Indian Ocean. Despite its route through water at depths of 3,000 metres,[16] it was announced in November 1993 that the project was technically feasible. It does present however enormous engineering challenges. A gas pipeline has never been built in such deep waters. Another export project, concerning LNG for East Asia but also taking India into account, is also being considered by Oman. But it is unlikely that sufficient gas supplies would be available for both projects.[17] In both cases India's gas supply would be subjected to the same types of technical hazards.

IS CENTRAL ASIA A POTENTIAL SOURCE OF DIVERSIFICATION?

Central Asia's potential as an energy supplier is in no way comparable to the Gulf one. As noted by some analysts, such as Raja Mohan 'the estimated 200 billion barrels of hydrocarbon reserves there are nowhere near the size of the known reserves in the Arabian peninsula and the Persian Gulf.... Even with significant new discoveries in its basin, the Caspian Sea is unlikely to emerge as an alternative to the current global energy dependence on the Persian Gulf.'[18] However, Central Asia does have the natural gas reserves that could satisfy some of future needs. The problem there is essentially political: Both of the possible supply routes—one from Turkmenistan, the other from Iran—involve Pakistan (and in the first case Afghanistan), and are therefore subject to a number of hazards.

THE AFGHANISTAN-PAKISTAN OPTION

A proposal of the Centgas consortium initiated by the Saudi company Delta Oil and American Unocal, which was suspended in August 1998 for security reasons after the American bombing of the *mujahedin* camps in Afghanistan, could resume despite Unocal withdrawal from the consortium. The project initially consisted of a double pipeline to export hydrocarbons from Turkmenistan. An oil pipeline, which could transport some 50 million tons of oil per year, would have linked the Turkmen oilfield of Chardzou, to a new terminal located on Pakistan's Indian Ocean coast. From there the oil could be exported to the rest of the world, including India.[19] A gas pipeline could transport some 20 billion m³ annually from the

Dautelabad gas field in south-east Turkmenistan to Multan (Pakistan) through Herat and Kandahar (Afghanistan). The gas pipeline could be linked to India at a later stage.[20] Two main obstacles currently stand in the way of progress on this project and are likely to remain a liability for any further development: The state of the Indo-Pakistani relations and the persistence of the Afghan conflict.

The Afghan conflict deserves particular attention in the context of the Caspian Sea energy issue. Like most other conflicts, the Afghan war has both internal and external repercussions. In addition to being the site of the struggle between the various factions to control Kabul and the country, Afghanistan is also the place where regional and sometimes extra-regional countries play out their own stakes. Often, these are external to the conflict as such, but they provide countries that become involved with an incentive to fuel the conflict. From this perspective, the continuing war in Afghanistan is tied to the unresolved Pashtounistan issue, Pakistani ambitions in Central Asia, and persisting Indo-Pakistani rivalry. Russia's position *vis-à-vis* Central Asia and the Caspian Sea, as well as the policy of the United States toward Iran also play a major role.

Because of the interest expressed by Delta and Unocal as well as Argentina's Bridas in building a pipeline from Turkmenistan to Pakistan (and eventually India) via Afghanistan, 'the Kingdom of Insolence' as Barry has referred to,[21] is considered by some as a key, sometimes even the most promising one, to unleashing Central Asia's energy potential. Moreover, in view of the current determination of the United States to block a southern route through Iran, the Afghanistan-Pakistan corridor seems to be the only alternative. Success will depend on several factors, notably stability in western Afghanistan, the attitude of Pakistan, and the ability of the project's sponsors to secure financing for their initiative. Western Afghanistan has been relatively peaceful for the past few years, and this situation was reinforced by the Taleban's take-over in Kandahar, in the fall 1994. The likelihood of major investments in pipeline projects will also depend, however, on the ability of the Taleban to maintain control and develop an effective administration, not only in the west and south-west but in the whole country.[22] For the time being, and despite the major advance of the Taleban during the summer of 1998, the continuation of the civil war will prevent further development of this route.

It may be argued that the problem is not so much insecurity in itself, but rather the impossibility of securing financial guarantees—no international financial institution is willing to support the consortium until there was an internationally recognized government. In other words until the Taleban was recognized as the legitimate government in Afghanistan, which is unlikely in the present situation, pipelines projects via Afghanistan are unlikely to go ahead.

It is also noteworthy that India and Pakistan have found themselves in opposing alliances throughout the Afghan conflict, which is a reflection of their deeper antagonism. India consistently supports all opponents of Pakistan's proxies in Afghanistan, but in doing so India has constantly undermined its own chances of obtaining access to the valuable hydrocarbon resources of Central Asia. This too could drastically change if peace were restored in Afghanistan.

The Iranian Option

Iran plays a particular role in India's energy equation: It is both a producing and, indirectly, a transit[23] country. Located in the Gulf, Iran is also a potential bridge with Central Asia.[24] Iran has been a major supplier of oil to India since the late 1960s (see Table 1).[25] Both countries are now willing to expand their relations to include the transfer of natural gas from Iran[26] to India. Talks between the two countries began in April 1993, and negotiations led to the signature of a memorandum of understanding in December 1993. India's Minister of Oil and Petroleum announced that Iran had promised to deliver about 707 billion m^3 of natural gas per year to India,[27] but none has been delivered thus far.

On 24 January 1998, the Australian company Broken Hill Proprietary Petroleum and the National Iranian Gas Company announced that 15 billion m^3 of gas from the South Pars field would be allocated to Pakistan and that they intended to build a 2,500 km gas pipeline from Assaluyeh, in the south of Iran, to Multan in Pakistan, which could be linked to India in a second phase. The estimated cost was around US $2.7 billion. At this stage, India was not really concerned. But the project added a new dimension to an already complex situation, creating a rivalry between two routes, the Iranian and the Afghan, and between two countries, Iran and Turkmenistan. The Iranian route was politically more secure, but more expensive while Turkmenistan could offer a better price for its gas but was politically risky due to the Afghan situation. It would be naive not to see this as a important determinant of Iran's behaviour in Afghanistan although clearly it is not the only motivation for Iran to support the anti-Taleban forces.

Competition between the two routes can be interpreted as a contradiction between the long-term perspectives and the present reality. All the companies involved in the region are targeting the Indian market, which is considered the most important emerging market in the world. With the exception of LNG, which is extremely costly, every project aimed at exporting Iranian or Central Asian gas to India has to pass through Pakistani territory, either onshore or offshore. Without a significant improvement in the relations between the two countries that would foster a real cooperation, these companies must settle for the Pakistani market to make their investments profitable. Until 1997, the energy deficit in Pakistan was such that it was possible to envisage several projects. But recent discoveries of gas in Baluchistan have modified this perspective. Although it is difficult to determine precisely the importance of the fields, the Pakistani Ministry of Petroleum and Natural Resources now envisages only one project, with a second postponed until 2007.

The Iranian option would not significantly alter the security of India's energy supplies. Iran has expressed willingness to promote structures of regional cooperation and a set of pipelines for the production and distribution of natural gas from Central Asia, Iran and the Arab world to the region, and also to Europe, the Far East and South Asia.[28] While this corresponds with India's own aspirations, it also underlines her vulnerabilities. Not only is Iran part of the Middle East problem, described above, and thus subject to an American embargo, but also internal instability seems to be increasingly growing. Unemployment is now estimated at above 30 per cent, and per capita GDP stands at only US $1,540. Inflation is at approximately 50 per cent and the country's foreign debt is over US $30 billion.[29] At least one quarter of oil revenues—Iran still relies on oil for some 85 per cent of its foreign currency—are required to service the country foreign debt. Iran's present isolation has probably protected it from the escalation of a major crises (such as in 1992, when riots by the poor engulfed several large cities), but large parts of the population, especially the young remain alienated from the regime,[30] and the status quo cannot be expected to continue indefinitely. Whether change will occur gradually or through a more radical and violent process remains to be seen. The first of these two hypotheses cannot be taken for granted, however, and it is noteworthy that Indian officials take the possibility of destabilization of Iran seriously.

The export of natural gas from Iran to India also raises a set of bilateral political issues between Iran and India, including Iran's support of Pakistan's position over the Kashmir issue and the latter's alleged support to some activist groups in the valley[31] has been a point of contention between the two countries, although not to an extent that would have precluded the development of their relationships in other fields. It could be argued that during the last two years relations between Iran and India improved as they deteriorated between Iran and Pakistan as a result of growing sectarian violence in Pakistan. Ironically, in purely geopolitical terms this situation should be favourable to India's interests. Considered through the energy prism, however, India, despite its excellent relations with most Central Asian countries, is now a victim of Pakistan's growing isolation in the region.

THE ROLE OF EXTERNAL POWERS

RUSSIA'S INTEREST IN THE REGION

Although its influence and power in Central Asia is declining, Russia still remains an important regional player because of its control of the flow of oil and gas from the Caspian and Central Asia. Russia has clearly demonstrated that it will not allow the power vacuum in the post-Soviet era to be filled by outside interest groups. The country's emerging energy security doctrine emphasizes the need for the commonwealth of independent states (CIS) to work toward the reintegration of industries and pipelines, and to 'secure CIS markets' through 'energy diplomacy' in order not to lose out to Western investors as they move into the region (Azerbaijan and Kazakhstan, for example). As underlined by Elaine Holoboff, 'Moscow is desperately afraid that it will be permanently left out of major international oil and gas projects in the near abroad. Should that occur, Russia's regional hegemony could ultimately be challenged by powerful oil rich neighbours some decades down the road'.[32] But what Russia fears most in the relatively short term is the Western political influence that would inevitably go with the transfer of capital and technology necessary to develop Caspian's energy potential. Russia's approach to energy relations with its southern neighbours is thus structured around two major issues.

The first has to do with access to new supplies and exploration opportunities. Moscow has made it clear that its political and commercial interests must be taken into account in any major oil or gas exploration projects in what it calls its 'near abroad'. For example the Caspian Sea legal regime has yet to be resolved. Until the break-up of the Soviet Union in December 1991, the Caspian Sea was the exclusive domain of two bordering states, Iran and the USSR. The Soviet Union de facto controlled most of it, and its naval domination was total, although no formal treaty was ever signed between the two countries. The collapse of the Soviet Union created a number of new states bordering on the Caspian, and has led to the emergence of conflicting interests in the dispute over the legal status of the Caspian Sea.[33] Moscow's desire to prevent the exploitation of the Caspian's resources without its participation is obviously the key to its position. Until a mutually acceptable solution to the Caspian Sea issue is found and agreed by all bordering states, Russia has the possibility to block the implementation of any major oil or natural gas project.[34]

The second issue is related to the existence of effective means of transport that would open up Central Asia and link it to the countries bordering the Indian Ocean. Not only is Russia insisting that it must be made a party to any agreement on sharing the oil and natural gas resources of the region, but it is also seeking to prevent the construction of pipelines transporting Central Asian oil and natural gas to the markets.[35] (Russian support for the anti Taleban opposition in Afghanistan may also be interpreted from this perspective, although it is not the only factor affecting its position). While it is not directed against India, such Russian move clearly affects the interests of a long-term ally.

Pakistan, the United States and India's Energy Interests

Equally important, although again in a paradoxical way, is the attitude of the United States. As discussed earlier, national interests of the regional powers involved can explain the rationale behind the alliances in Afghanistan. But it is the US policy that conditions most of the projects aimed at opening up central Asia (through a western or a southern route). For example, it was the US bombing of the *mujahedin* camps in Afghanistan, and not the Afghan situation per se, that led to the suspension of the Centgas project, thus putting an (temporary) end to Pakistan's expectations and Indian hopes. Interestingly, the US did so by acting in favour of India's traditional geopolitical interests.

One objective of Pakistani decision makers in seeking access to Central Asia was the revitalization of the privileged relationship that the country enjoyed with the United States during the Soviet invasion of Afghanistan. At that time, Pakistan was the proxy of the United States in an anti-Soviet operation aimed at keeping Moscow in Afghanistan where it would incur military, economic, political and diplomatic damage in what was then perceived as imperialist aggression of a non-aligned country. The United States made Pakistan a 'front line state' and closed its eyes to Pakistan's military nuclear development programme. Pakistan, traditionally a second rate ally was propelled to the top of the US hierarchy of priorities. At the same time India was diplomatically neutralized by the move of the USSR. With the Soviet withdrawal from Afghanistan, Pakistan's strategic importance for the United States was diminished. But in Pakistan, the emergence of the newly independent oil and gas producers of Central Asia was perceived as an opportunity to revitalize the country's relationship with the United States, provided that Pakistan could become the preferential export route from Central Asia. Pakistan's dilemma was clear in a move for which the rationale was anti-Indian, but the most likely consequence of which could be beneficial to India.

Peace in Afghanistan was, however, a precondition for Islamabad's project to materialize. Having failed to bring peace to Kabul through its proxy (Hekmatyar), Pakistan turned to the Taleban in the fall of 1994. It did not create the militia but provided significant support in the form of ammunition and military training until it conquered some 80 per cent of Afghanistan by the summer of 1998. But the United States, which had seem to support, (at least implicitly) the Taleban and Pakistan until the beginning of 1997, openly declared that they were strongly opposed to a Taleban government which the US Secretary of State, Madeleine Albright, said they would never be recognized by the United States. US bombing of the *mujahedin* camps was not seen as an anti-Pakistani move, but instead a clear sign of total disregard for Afghanistan and, at the same time, for the commercial interests of Unocal in the region. Already isolated since its nuclear tests in May 1998, Pakistan was deserted by what it considered its best ally in the region.

As suggested earlier, the result placed India in a dilemma. From political and military perspectives, the total isolation of Pakistan was a complete success. But considered through the prism of India's energy needs, it was a blow to longer term interests.

ENERGY AND RELATIONS BETWEEN INDIA AND PAKISTAN

Any project aimed at importing hydrocarbons from Central Asia to India must face the reality of antagonism between India and Pakistan (as well as Pakistan's own regional problems, in which India plays a major role but which go far beyond the bilateral relations between the two countries). The main obstacles are political and psychological.

The source of Indo-Pakistani antagonism is deeply rooted in South Asia's historical legacy and more specifically, in the trauma of an unfinished partition. Not only were some 5,00,000 people massacred and more than 13 million displaced, but the two countries were left with a number of unresolved issues that generate conflicting claims by the two successor states. The Kashmir issue soon became the core of their dispute and was the cause of two wars (in 1948 and 1965) between the two countries. A third war was fought in 1971 in the wake of the partition of East Pakistan, which was to become Bangladesh.

The psychological bases of rivalry relate to Pakistani resentment of what it perceived as an Indian aspiration to leadership and commanding role for itself in the region, because of its size, population, industrial and technological advancement, and military power. Together all these factors have resulted, among other things, in a regional arms race which culminated with the explosion of nuclear devices on both sides of the border in May 1998.

Since the Simla agreement following the 1971 war, a normalization process has taken place between the two countries. But given their long history of acrimonious relations and the fact that several bilateral disputes are still unresolved, normalization has been a very slow process with sporadic interruptions and reversals. Three times in 15 years (1984, 1987 and 1990) the two neighbours came close to war while reconciliation looked possible at least twice (1988-9 and the very beginning of Nawaz Sharif's tenure as Prime Minister).[36] But no significant result has been achieved thus far.

As indicated above the Central Asian policies of India and Pakistan always been mutually exclusive. Similarly, throughout the Afghan conflict, they consistently supported opposing factions. This attitude, which made sense from the regional geopolitical perspective, runs counter to their interests in the energy sector. Both India and Pakistan face the dilemma of having to choose between geopolitics and geo-economics.

Awareness seems to be growing in both countries of their real community of interests in the energy sector. Just like India, Pakistan is faced with a chronic and growing deficit in energy. Just like India it considers natural gas a cheaper and cleaner alternative that can decrease its dependence on oil. An to a greater extent than India, Pakistan considers Iran and Central Asia serious potential sources of supply. All studies concur that the joint use of pipelines to import natural gas would allow vast economies of scale, resulting for India and Pakistan in a substantial reduction of the unit price of gas. Moreover, the construction of the necessary pipelines would present no major technological challenges. As a matter of fact, energy is regularly on the agenda of negotiations between the two countries. Pakistan's promise to delivery electricity to India was one of the most substantial results of the February 1999 summit between Prime Ministers Nawaz Sharif and Atal Behari Vajpayee, and may have paved the way for future oil and gas pipelines between the two countries,[37] hadn't the last episode of the war over Kashmir pushed back the two countries relations by some years.

PROSPECTS FOR DIVERSIFICATION OF INDIA'S ENERGY SUPPLIES

What are the prospects for diversification of India's energy supplies from Central Asia? In the short term they are not very bright, despite recent improvements in both the Afghan situation and the bilateral relations with Pakistan.

THE END OF THE AFGHAN CHAOS?

It is already clear that the so called 'peace process' initiated in Ashkabad on 14 March 1999 has failed. Whatever the result of the now traditional summer offensive of the Taleban, it is likely to remain extremely fragile for some time. Several scenarios can be envisaged. First as has happened in the past, personality conflicts could lead to new eruptions of violence. Second the Taleban movement itself may not be as homogeneous or unified as it has seemed. Moreover, there are already signs that the movement has lost dynamism. Tribal, clanic or local logics could well lead to its implosion in the future.

Moreover, despite the declaration of goodwill by most regional capitals, it is difficult to determine the extent to which they are ready to accommodate (what will be mainly) a Taleban government. The advance of the 'student' militia during the summer of 1998 had provoked a virtually unanimous rejection by the regional powers. Although it is in their interests to open southern corridors bypassing Russia, the course of their future relations with Afghanistan is still unclear.

Caspian Uncertainties

The political stability of most of the Caspian producers cannot be taken for granted in the short and medium term. Azerbaijan has experienced three presidents in six years, and remains vulnerable to the persistence of the Nagorno-Karabakh conflict and to Russian attempts at destabilization. Turkmenistan is also very fragile experiencing growing social problems due to the inability of the regime to satisfy the basic needs of the population. Due to the absence of a real 'civil society', social mobilization has been so far limited, but this situation cannot be expected to last indefinitely. Its leadership is pressing to have the exploitation of its hydrocarbons started as soon as possible but so far, with limited success. In Turkmenistan, the hold on power of President Nyazov will depend to a large extent on the export of Turkmen gas making his country the 'Kuwait of Central Asia'. But the timing of the oil and gas companies differs from that of the producing states, and the latter may not be in a position to wait for the international prices to be high enough for the companies to consider new exploitations profitable. Turkmenistan's GDP lost some 30 per cent between 1993 and 1995, an additional 3 per cent in 1996, and between 15 per cent in 1997. The situation in Turkmenistan will continue to deteriorate if the country does not find a market for its gas, and President Nyazov's 'Central Asian Kuwait dream' could well turn into a political nightmare.

PERSISTENT DEMAND

Does the uncertainty of the situation mean that India should abandon any idea of developing relations with the region in the field of energy? This would be going too far, too fast. As time passes, the need for new energy sources will continue growing for both India and Pakistan if they want to improve (or even maintain) current economic growth rates. Moreover, their present economic difficulties as well as their common environmental problems give them additional incentives to cooperate in the search for cheaper and cleaner energy sources.

EXTERNAL INTERESTS

It is clear that the Central Asian hydrocarbon exporters desperately need new markets. These are likely to emerge in Asia, because the Western markets are close to saturation with gas. Oil and gas companies are aware of the stakes, and have targeted the Indian market, building their regional strategy according to this goal.

The international community should also recognize that regional cooperation in the field of energy would not only help stabilize the individual states, because of the revenues that it would inevitably generate, but also the entire region because of the interdependence that it would foster.

THE CASPIAN SEA AND ITS ENVIRONS: AN INTEGRATED PERSPECTIVE

DELINKING THE KASHMIR ISSUE FROM OTHER RELATIONS WITH PAKISTAN

Normalizing relations between India and Pakistan is certainly the central feature of any attempt to establish some form of energy cooperation between India and Central Asia. India made the first step in this direction with the adoption of 'unilateralism', a policy first conceived by P.V. Narasimha Rao's government in 1992-3. A significant move along these lines was made by India in February 1994 with the suggestion of a new regime of confidence-building measures between the two countries. Within the new regime, each country would commit not to employ its nuclear capability against the other, to disengage its force from the Siachen Glacier, and to contribute to the establishment of better communication between their armed forces by exchanging information about troop movements and exercises.[38] This policy, further refined and continued by the United Front government in 1996, also contained an important element of 'economic diplomacy' aimed at creating a stake in trading with India for the Pakistani establishment[39] by allowing Indian traders to import items from Pakistan without waiting for reciprocal measures. Over a period of time, it was supposed to automatically improve the climate between the two countries. Although Pakistan welcomed the 'economic diplomacy' measures adopted by India it responded negatively to the more political 1994 proposals, arguing that unless the Kashmir issue was tackled first, there was no point in discussing other issues it considers peripheral. Pakistan maintains this position to this day. The situation is further complicated by the international dimension of the Kashmir issue. Due to Pakistan's efforts, the Kashmir problem is now on the agenda of the Organization of Islamic Conference (OIC). However, all the major international actors (including China, Pakistan's ally), have now recognized that Kashmir is a bilateral issue between Pakistan and India. Clearly Kashmir is the core of any normalization process between the two countries and, by extension, the key to any regional integration.

To a large extent however, and despite the recent 'Kargil affair', Kashmir is a domestic Indian problem as much as a bilateral Indo-Pakistani one. Without renouncing its own claims, much could be done by India to reduce the importance of the Kashmir issue in the relations between the two countries. Some elements bear mention in this context.

(1) The current phase of the revolt against Indian domination was launched independently in 1989 by a Kashmiri organization, the Jammu Kashmir Liberation Front (JKLF). It was only later that Pakistan came to support it, before switching its support to other groups such as the Hizbul Moujahedin and other movements because the JKLF was judged too independent (because it was struggling for the independence of Kashmir and not for its reunification with Pakistan). In other words the uprising was first a local movement that enjoyed if not some support, at least the sympathy, of the population. Pakistan did not create the problem but it tried to instrumentalize the revolt for its own objectives.

(2) The population soon became disenchanted with Pakistan and its proxies in the Kashmir valley. The Indian armed forces played a

role in this process by trying to split the rebellion along two lines: The relatively secular, independence seeking JKLF and the fundamentalist, pro-Pakistan groups led by the Hizbul Mujahedin.[40] On one hand, New Delhi repeatedly showed willingness to talk to the JKLF. On the other, it specifically targeted the pro-Pakistan groups making them the heroes of the revolt but showing (through repression of large parts of the population) that the suffering in Kashmir came from these groups and, indirectly, from Pakistan.

(3) The Kashmiri population is tired of the violence, killings and other disruptions of normal life. Participation in the last elections was a success for New Delhi despite the reservations one can legitimately have about its real freedom. The results provide evidence that the Kashmiri population would gradually accept to remain in the Indian federation providing that it were given more autonomy and integrated in the Indian economy (and, of course, if repression ended and the Indian troops withdrew).

The point here is not to deny the responsibility of the militant groups in the current situation, but to reduce it to its real proportions. Because the militancy is being deprived of any popular support, Pakistan would also lose in terms of propaganda and means of action. The recent 'Kargil affair' and its subsequent developments only demonstrated that Pakistan had politically lost the battle for Kashmir. The massive infiltration of moujahedins in the summer of 1999 was the only way to revitalize the issue and a tacit admission that the internal guerilla movements had failed. None the less it is true that the claim over Kashmir finds support across the whole political spectrum in Pakistan and it is unlikely to abandon it in the near (or even more distant) future. The best possible outcome for the years to come would be a decline of the political relevance of the Kashmir problem in Pakistan's internal politics to a level that would allow any Pakistani government to delink it from other issues.

This would have important repercussions for the energy issue. Importing oil and natural gas from Central Asia would be facilitated politically, since it would be acceptable for Pakistan and India to have one or several pipelines across the territory of the other. Crossing the continental shelf (or even Pakistan's territory) would be possible. This would also have some financial consequences—with political constraints put aside, economic considerations would lead the choices.

Delinking Kashmir from other issues would also have repercussions in the Afghan conflict. Throughout the conflict, India and Pakistan found themselves in opposite alliances. India supported Karmal and

Najibullah during and after the Soviet occupation when Pakistan was backing the Islamic resistance; India assisted Massoud when he opposed Hekmatyar, Islamabad's protégé at the time who was later replaced by the Taleban. Although India's involvement has been limited, it has been a consistent projection of its rivalry with Pakistan. Delhi's willingness to have a reverse alliance with Afghanistan against Pakistan, and its desire to deny Islamabad any access to Central Asia were, along with Kashmir, among Indian motivations. Reminiscence of the cold war logic, consisting of helping Moscow prevent Washington's establishment of some form of political containment in the southern republics of the CIS, also play a role.

Considered only in the context of the energy issue, however, the Afghan conflict takes on a different perspective. India, Pakistan, and to some extent the United States share a common strategic interest in getting access to Central Asia's oil and natural gas. The fact that Pakistan and India have a common interest in developing their energy links with Central Asia has been so far overshadowed by their rivalry over Kashmir, but with the latter put aside or at least delinked from other issues, the incentive for cooperation appears clearly.

The regional picture would then take on a totally different shape. Not only would it help stabilize the Afghan situation, but India could also become a facilitator in the opening up of Central Asia to the rest of the world. India was a long-term ally of the former Soviet Union and still shares strategic interests with the Russian federation. Both countries recognize that instability in Central Asia would affect their national security interests. Rightly or wrongly, both fear a potential spillover to their own Muslim minorities, should Central Asia be destabilized by some form of Islamic fundamentalism. In the Central Asian countries themselves, while there is some mistrust of Pakistan's use of Islam for political purposes,[41] there appears to be considerable goodwill for secular India. It would also be in Delhi's interest to develop closer relationships with all these new members of the OIC in order to weaken Pakistan's position in the organization. Moreover, India's participation in regional energy projects would provide Russia with guarantees that Central Asia would not be left to the sole influence of the United States and its proxies, Pakistan and Saudi Arabia. The opening up of Central Asia through a southern route would thus be made more acceptable for Russia. In turn, and given the right conditions in Afghanistan itself, the building of a permanent infrastructure of pipelines would create the kind of organic links on which regional cooperation could be built.

Several short-term arguments can also be made in favour of the construction of joint pipelines.

First, there are precedents of pipelines being built, linking countries at war or having tense relationships. The gas pipeline linking the Soviet Union to Europe, built during the cold war in 1984, is only one example of such a situation. Second, there are ways to limit the damage and the consequences of potential supply interruptions. Technologically, the choice of dual technology, or the creation of links with networks using LNG can be used to prevent or limit such damages. And political means and legal techniques can also be used, such as the 'take or pay clause' for the intermediary. For example in this case Pakistan would purchase the entire quantity of gas consumed by itself and India, and would be constrained to sell the balance to the Indian consumers. Agreements implying the end of all supplies by the producing country to Pakistan if the latter interrupted it deliveries to India could be envisaged. It should be added that it is in the interests of New Delhi to develop closer links with members of Economic Cooperation Organization (ECO) to counterbalance the influence of Pakistan.

CONCLUSION

None of these scenarios can be taken for granted. While the prevailing chaotic regional situation does not necessarily mean that the worst should be assumed, a positive evolution of the situation, such as that described above, is far from being guaranteed. Central Asia certainly has the potential to become a source of supply diversification for India, but given the uncertainties the region carries as many risks as the Persian Gulf.

Much will depend on the political willingness of many actors, regional and extra-regional, as well as on factors over which India cannot always influence. India's presence in some energy deals with Central Asia could ensure Russia that the region would not be left to the sole influence of the proxies of the United States—but the US policy in the region will certainly play its role. Whether its desire to get access to the Central Asian republics will lead to policies that will antagonize Russia so much that any further development will be blocked by the latter, or whether it will gradually evolve towards a more cooperative approach from which everybody will benefit, is still an open question. Of great importance also is the US attitude towards Iran. Normalization of relations between the two countries would radically change the current situation, creating new opportunities for India.

But India has problems of its own that are all crucial for any further development of its relations with Central Asia. Pakistan is obviously the most important, since it conditions the construction of the pipelines from both Iran and Turkmenistan. India has taken steps to improve relations and could certainly even do more without harming itself, but Pakistan's situation is still uncertain. The present government in Islamabad is relatively open to discussion and the business sector is keen to develop better relations with India. But the present economic situation is disastrous, and the Prime Minister, whose legitimacy is wide in the Parliament but not so well certain across the country, will have to take other political forces into account.

Therefore, the process of opening up Central Asia through southern routes will be a very slow one, if it ever occurs. Whatever its future development, however, it should not be expected to become more than a possibility for diversification of India's energy supplies. For the time being, Central Asia is no more, but should be no less than an option. As time passes, India's (and Pakistan's) needs for alternative sources of energy supply will continue to grow, strengthening the incentives to cooperate. South Asia as a whole will face growing energy needs that it will not be able to satisfy by itself, and a valuable opportunity for greater co-operation could emerge from this common basic need. India certainly has the willingness, and some of the means, to initiate such a process. As noted by a commentator, 'the time has come for India to develop an integrated perspective on the Caspian Sea basin and its environs'.[42]

NOTES

1. *TERI Energy Data Directory and Yearbook, 1998-9*, p. 53.
2. Op. cit., p. 55.
3. Op. cit., p. 55.
4. Op. cit., p. 62.
5. K.R. Pachauri, Maithili Iyer, 'Energy Issues in India', *Revue de l'Energie*, No. 470, juillet-août-septembre 1995, pp. 485-90, p. 487.
6. See Timothy Mapes, 'Hard Climbout of a Crisis', *Far Eastern Economic Review,* 21 November 1996.
7. Gregory F. Gause, 'The Gulf Conundrum: Economic Change, Population Growth, and Political Stability in the GCC States', *The Washington Quarterly*, 20:1, pp. 145-65, p. 146.
8. Gregory Gause, op. cit., p. 153.

9. Louis Blin, *Le pétrole du Golfe*, Paris, Maisonneuve and Larose, 1996, p. 22.
10. According to the International Energy Agency, petroleum production in the OECD countries will gradually diminish to just under 14 million barrels per day in 2010. Most of this increase will come from the United States. During the same period, production in the rest of the world will increase, mostly in two regions, the Middle-East and Latin America. In 2010, the Middle-East and Venezuela alone, are expected to produce a little less than the total global requirement of petroleum, that is, approximately 45 million barrels per day. International Energy Agency, *Perspectives énergétiques mondiales jusqu'en l'an 2010*, Paris, 1993, pp. 31-5.
11. Jamal Al-Suwaidi, 'Gulf Security and the Iranian Challenge', *Security Dialogue*, 1996, Vol. 27(3), pp. 277-94, p. 277.
12. On this particular aspect, see Blin Louis, op. cit., pp. 21-31.
13. Ghorban Narsi, 'The Evaluation of Recent Gas Export Proposals in the Middle East', *The Iranian Journal of International Affairs*, Vol. VII, No. 2, Summer 1995, pp. 449-65, p. 450.
14. Narsi Ghorban, op. cit., p. 45.
15. Narsi Ghorban, 'The Evaluation of Recent Gas Export Pipeline Proposals in the Middle East', *The Iranian Journal of International Affairs*, Vol. VII, No. 2, Summer 1995, pp. 449-65, p. 452.
16. Narsi Ghorban, op. cit., p. 452.
17. International Energy Agency, *World Energy Outlook*, Paris, 1995, p. 204.
18. Raja Mohan, 'Caucasian fire Circle', *The Hindu*, 20 March 1997.
19. In the medium term, the project (suspended in August 1998 but about to resume) is planned as part of a much broader one, the 'Central Asian Oil Pipeline Project'. Through a grid of pipelines, this project would transport oil from Turkmenistan, Uzbekistan, Kazakhstan and the West of Siberia to the Indian Ocean. UNOCAL, Delta Oil Company, *Central Asian Oil Pipeline Project.*
20. UNOCAL, Delta Oil Company, *Turkmenistan-Afghanistan-Pakistan Gas Pipeline Project.*
21. Michael Barry, *Le Royaume de l'insolence*, Paris, Flammarion, 1984.
22. See also John Roberts, *Caspian Pipelines*, London, The Royal Institute of International Affairs, 1996, pp. 69-71.
23. Iran has already concluded oil swap agreements with Azerbaijan and Kazakhstan. While most of the demand comes from the more populated north of the country, which is supplied mostly by Iran's neighbours, its own oilfields are located in the south, from where oil can easily be sent by tanker to the international oil markets. Royalties are then retroceded to the producing countries according to their share in the exports. Similar agreements exist for gas with Turkmenistan. See also, Frédéric Grare, 'La nouvelle donne énergétique autour de la Mer caspienne: une

perspective géopolitique', *Cahiers d'études sur la Méditerranée orientale et le monde turco-iranien* (*CEMOTI*), No. 23, Fall 1996.

24. In this context, the alliance between Iran and Russia, although not related only to the energy issue, should not be misinterpreted. Iran's current dispute with the United States overshadows the fact that their interests coincide on the energy issue. Iran will support Russia's position on the legal status of the Caspian Sea, legal only as long as it is prevented from participating more actively in exploitation of the Caspian resources by the United States. It should be recalled that Teheran did not protest in September 1994 when the so called 'deal of the century' was signed by Azerbaijan. In November 1994, Iran even obtained a quarter of the 20 per cent share Azerbaijan had in the consortium in charge of exploiting Azerbaijani oilfields. Only since April 1995, when it was excluded from the consortium under American pressure, did Iran reiterate its support for Russia's position on the legal status of the Caspian Sea. It was obvious that if Iran were offered the possibility to become one, if not the main, exporter of Central Asia's hydrocarbons, it would most probably renounce its support of Moscow in this area.
25. Iran also helped India in the construction of the Madras oil refinery. See K.R. Singh, 'Indo-Iranian Relations in the Nineties: Defining Parameters and Framework', in Girijesh Pant, P.C. Jan and A.K. Pasha (eds.), *Contemporary Iran and Emerging Indo-Iranian Relations*, New Delhi, Neelkant Publishers, 1996, pp. 103-109, p. 106.
26. According to K.R. Singh, Iran has probably the largest proven natural gas reserves in the Gulf region amounting to approximately 20,000 trillion m^3 per year. Its present natural gas production is more than 58 billion m^3 per year. K.R. Singh, op. cit., p. 106.
27. K.R. Singh, op. cit., p. 107.
28. See Narsi Ghorban and Mohammad Sarir, 'Oil and Gas: An Outlook for Future Co-operation among the Persian Gulf States', *The Iranian Journal of International Affairs*, Vol. V, Nos. 3 & 4, Fall/Winter 1993-4, pp. 738-53.
29. According to Hazhir Teimourian, these statistics would have been worse if Iraq had been present on the oil market. Fortunately for Iran, Iraq's absence coincided with cold winters in the West and an economic boom in South-East Asia. Hazhir Teimourian, 'Not Looking Forward to a New Era in Iran', *The World Today*, May 1997, pp. 125-7, p. 127.
30. Iran's population has nearly doubled in 17 years, from 34 million to 64.7 million, and 45 per cent of the population is under fourteen years of age. Hazhir Teimourian, op. cit., p. 127.
31. See Kalim Bahadur, 'Pakistan as a Factor in India-Iran Relations', in Girijesh Pant, P.C. Jain and A.K. Pasha, op. cit., pp. 119-24, p. 123.
32. Elaine Holoboff, 'Russia's Draft Energy Security Doctrine', *Jane's Intelligence Review*, January 1997, pp. 19-22, p. 22.
33. For a discussion of the legal status of the Caspian sea, see Romano

Cesare, 'Quelques considérations sur le statut juridique de la Mer Caspienne', *Cahiers d'études sur la Méditerranée orientale et le monde turco-iranien* (*CEMOTI*), No. 23, Fall 1996.

34. Other means of pressure have also been used. During the negotiations for the construction of an oil pipeline to transport Kazakh oil, Moscow made it known to Almaty that 'unless the pipeline crossed Turkey as the Kazakh wanted and not Russia, the latter would be unable to transport the 4,00,000 barrels that Kazakhstan is currently trying to export', Ian Cuthberson, 'Notre destin est en train de se jouer en Asie centrale', *Le temps stratégique*, September 1995, pp. 30-45, p. 35. Moscow went as far as threatening of regional destabilization from apparently uncontrollable forces, Elaine Holoboff, 'Russia's draft energy security doctrine', op. cit., p. 20.
35. This attempt to impose a single direction for the pipelines north via Russian territory is viewed by some authors as an aggressive device to give Russia tremendous control over the flow of oil and gas to Western markets, potentially making the West more vulnerable to Russia's political whims. Although there is undoubtedly some truth in this argument, it should not be exaggerated. Moreover, Western attempts to establish direct links with the Caspian energy producers can be interpreted as a means for the West to acquire both economic and political influence in the newly independent states, gradually depriving Russia of influence in its former empire. As noted by Ajay Darshan Behera, 'US interests in Central Asia are similar to Russia's. While, unlike Russia, it cannot lay historical claims, it definitely has the capacity and will to make every effort to insinuate itself as the principal broker for the region on the lines of the role it has defined for itself in the Gulf. It would not only like the export routes to be controlled by anyone other than itself, but also the control over the oil reserves will help the US to perpetuate its influence over Russia and the emerging powers like Europe, Japan and China'. Ajay Darshan Behera, 'The Battle for Kabul: Interplay of Geopolitics and Cold War Logic', *Strategic Analysis*, January-February 1997, pp. 1371-87, p. 1374.
36. Shekar Gupta, *India Redefines its Role*, Adelphi Paper 293, Oxford University Press, 1995, p. 53.
37. Ahmed Rashid, 'Shotgun Marriage', *Far Eastern Economic Review*, 4 March 1999, p. 19.
38. Shekhar Gupta, op. cit., p. 54.
39. Sreedhar, 'Indo-Pak Relations in Post Benazir Period', *Strategic Analysis*, March 1997, pp. 1689-98, p. 1695.
40. Shekhar Gupta, op. cit., p. 30
41. Most of the mullahs expelled from Central Asia after 1991 where either Saudi or Pakistani.
42. Raja Mohan, op. cit.

Institutional Stakes in India's Oil and Gas Restructuring

U. SUNDARARAJAN

India's oil and gas industry is undergoing a major metamorphosis. After two decades of intense regulation, this US $ 30 billion industry is now entering into tumultuous phase due to deregulation.

I would like to share with the reader some experiences in the process of restructuring. Before I do so, let me give an overview of the industry.

CONSUMPTION

Three characteristics are typical of the Indian energy sector—the high energy intensity, the low per capita consumption and the lagging domestic production.

While the energy intensity of developed nations is less than one, the rate of increase in the consumption of primary energy in India is higher than that of its GDP. The growth in the demand for petroleum products over the last 15 years has increased at an average rate of 6.1 per cent. This is four times the world average. For every 1 per cent increase in national income, the consumption of petroleum products has increased by 1.1 per cent.

The per capita oil consumption in India is only 70 kgoe, which is one of the lowest in the world. With the increase in the income levels, the per capita consumption is likely to double by the end of the next decade. Considering the high population base, even a small increase in the per capita consumption will translate into a phenomenal jump in the overall demand. This itself shows the enormous potential for growth in the sector.

In the process of development, the type of energy consumed is also undergoing a considerable shift with non-commercial forms of fuel like wood gradually getting displaced with commercial fuels like coal, oil, and gas. It is expected that the share of non-commercial fuel in the energy basket will eventually reduce from the present level of almost 40 per cent to 25 per cent. This qualitative change in consumption will also add to the demand for hydrocarbons.

Coal remains the predominant source of primary energy in India accounting for nearly 57 per cent of the total consumption. Hydrocarbons are the second largest contributors with a share of approximately 40 per cent, of which oil comprises 32 per cent and gas 8 per cent. Over the next few years, the share of oil is likely to decrease and correspondingly the share of natural gas is likely to go up.

OIL

The consumption of petroleum products increased from 22.3 million tons (mt) in 1973 to 85 mt in 1997-8. That is, in about 24 years after the first oil shock, the demand went up by almost four times. On a growth in GDP of 7 per cent, as is envisaged now, it is estimated that demand will reach a level of 113 mt by the year 2001-2 and about 155 mt by the year 2006-7.

While the demand for hydrocarbons has steadily been increasing year after year, the supply from domestic sources has not been keeping pace. Oil was struck in India way back in 1866, just seven years after the first discovery in the USA. However, for more than a century, the exploration activities were restricted to the north-eastern part of the country. Till 1953, India was producing just around 2,70,000 tons of oil per annum. By 1962, with the development of two large fields in Gujarat, production crossed the 1 million mark. It was only with the discovery of the huge Bombay High offshore basin that production took a giant leap to 10.2 mt in 1977. The crude oil production during 1997-8 was 34.2 mt and by the year 2001-2, it is expected to go up to 37 mt.

The extent to which the demand for petroleum products is being

TABLE 1: DEMAND OF OIL

Year	*Demand in mt*	*CARG (5 year period)*
1986-7	38.8	
		5.4
1991-2	54.1	
		6.9
1996-7	79.2	
		6.8
2001-2	113*	
		7.3
2006-7	155*	
		7.3

Note: *Estimated.

TABLE 2: PRODUCTION/DEMAND OF PETROLEUM PRODUCTS

Year	*Domestic Production (mt)*	*Consumption/ Demand (mt)*	*Percentage Self-reliance*
1990-1	33.02	55.04	56
1991-2	30.35	56.97	50
1992-3	26.95	58.90	43
1993-4	27.03	61.54	41
1994-5	32.24	67.45	45
1995-6	35.17	74.67	44
1996-7	32.90	76.17	39
1997-8	34.20	85.49	37

met out of indigenous production (the self-reliance index) has been declining over the years, and from 90 per cent in the mid-1970s is today only 37 per cent. Considering the levels of future demand and the present projections of indigenous crude availability, the index is likely to decline to 27 per cent by the end of the next decade.

To meet the shortfall in indigenous production, imports of crude oil and products are resorted to. With the consistent fall in the self-reliance index, imports are increasing. In 1990-1, India imported around 26.71 mt (net of exports). In 1996-7, this figure went up to 51.01 mt. By the year 2001-2, the imports are projected to increase to a level of 92 mt.

Currently India's import bill (for crude and products) is about US $ 9 billion per annum. Even with the somewhat subdued oil price, India's import bill amounts to 30 per cent of its export earning. This high level of imports could have serious repercussions on the country's balance of payments position. More importantly, it makes the country extremely vulnerable to a sudden spike in oil prices, which would result in a consequent increase in the prices of other commodities. Also, it has serious bearing on the energy security of the country.

NATURAL GAS

Natural gas is steadily gaining importance as a fuel for power plants. It is becoming increasingly apparent that just as oil has been the fuel of the twentieth century, gas will be the fuel of the next century.

Production of natural gas was a mere 6.3 million cubic metres per day (mm^3) during 1980-1. Since then production has increased to 72 million m^3 per day in 1997-8. After meeting internal

TABLE 3: SUPPLY AND DEMAND OF NATURAL GAS

Year	*Supply*	*Demand*	*Gap*
1997-8	57.6	95.5	37.9
2001-2	63.7	148.0	84.3
2004-5	68.0	188.0	120.0
2009-10	68.0	284.0	216.0

Note: Figs. in million m^3 per day.

requirements and shrinkage, the available gas for utilization was 57 million m^3 per day. Against this supply, the demand for gas is of the order of 95 million m^3 per day.

There are plans to increase the supply from domestic sources to 64 million m^3 per day by 2001-2. By that time however, the demand is likely to go beyond 148 million m^3 per day leaving a gap of 84 million m^3 per day. Thus, there is likely to be a massive shortfall in supply of natural gas that may have to be partly met through import of LNG.

RESERVES

Prima facie, from the point of view of reserves, the position seems to be comfortable. India has 26 sedimentary basins covering an area of about 3.14 million sq. km including 1.35 million sq. km in deep waters. However, of this, only about 16 per cent have been adequately covered through geo-scientific surveys and a reasonable number of wells have been drilled. The balance has been inadequately explored.

The country's total prognosticated reserves as on 1 April 1997 were 28 billion tons of oil and oil equivalent of gas. However, the proven reserves are only 6.5 billion tons, with the initial recoverable reserves being of the order of 2.3 billion tons. The reserve/production ratio is 23 years for oil and 27 years for gas. Thus, though the reserves are available, massive investments are required before they can actually be exploited.

INVESTMENTS REQUIRED

In order to meet the country's demand, phenomenal investments in this sector are called for. 'Back of the envelope' calculations suggest that the expenditure required in the oil and gas sector would be ranging between US $100 billion and 150 billion of which investments in the upstream sector alone would be of the order of

US $60 billion. Investments of this magnitude are clearly beyond the means of the national oil companies. The role of private capital, including foreign investments is therefore considered crucial and private players are being encouraged to invest in this sector.

MARKET STRUCTURE

The oil industry in India was operating as a free market till the mid-1970s and many of the multinational oil companies like Shell, Caltex and Esso had a significant presence in the market. Nationalization of the industry resulted in the private players being bought out by the government. Since then, state owned 'public sector enterprises' play a dominant role in this sector. In all these companies, government of India holds not less than 51 per cent of the paid up share capital. Both the upstream and downstream sectors are fully regulated.

Exploration and production (E&P) operations are mainly carried out by Oil and Natural Gas Corporation (ONGC) and Oil India Limited (OIL). Midstream (pipeline transportation and ancillary functions), and downstream (local distribution) activities of natural gas are handled by the Gas Authority of India (GAIL).

Seven companies manage the downstream sector. Of these three are integrated companies having refining and marketing operations. They are Indian Oil Corporation (IOC), Hindustan Petroleum Corporation (HPC) and Bharat Petroleum Corporation (BPC). IOC has a market share of almost 55 per cent and both HPC and BPC have a market share of 20 per cent each. IBP Limited is a pure marketing company with a 5 per cent market share. There are three refining companies—Cochin Refineries Limited (CRL), Madras Refineries Limited (MRL) and Bongaigaon Refineries and Petrochemicals Limited (BRPL).

The Oil Coordination Committee (OCC), set up by the government of India in 1975, provides support to the government in policy decisions and in their implementation.

In a sense, the OCC acts as a regulator. It plans and regulates the import of crude oil and refined products. Till recently, crude oil allocation to each refinery and its product pattern was also regulated by OCC. Product movement to various demand centres is governed by the industry supply plan. This plan ensures availability of products to all oil companies from various sources. Market shares of individual oil companies are controlled through sales plan entitlement.

The system has ensured the availability of products to all the marketing companies as per their sales entitlement irrespective of the volumes they themselves produce. The cost of the products made available to all oil companies at various supply locations is uniform irrespective of the source, ownership, and mode of transportation of the products.

The plan for development of infrastructure facilities is prepared on an industry basis, jointly by the marketing companies and OCC for approval by the government. This planning has not only facilitated development of facilities at an optimum cost, but has also ensured that there is no duplication of facilities created. Neither the lack of ownership of products nor lack of infrastructure facilities has affected the sales of a company.

The government through annual marketing plans decides development of the retail marketing network. Selection of the dealers and distributors is done through dealer selection boards appointed by the government. The government controls the enrolment of LPG customers, ceiling on distributors' refill sales, kerosene quotas and commissions for dealers and distributors.

Till recently, prices of most of the petroleum products were fixed by the government. Administered pricing mechanism (APM) ensures a fixed return to the oil companies based on a cost-plus formula. The 'price controlled products' include motor gasoline, diesel, kerosene, LPG and aviation fuel. Various oil pool accounts are maintained by OCC.

The APM achieves the following primary goals:

(a) Ensures availability of certain products like kerosene at subsidized rates to the economically weaker sections of the society through a system of cross subsidization.
(b) Ensures stable prices insulating the domestic market from the volatility of prices in the international market.
(c) Regulates returns to the oil companies at reasonable levels.
(d) Minimizes the cross haulage of products.

NEED FOR RESTRUCTURING

Over the last two decades since nationalization, the petroleum industry has made significant strides. However, it has also become one of the most regulated industries.

The industry possesses a number of strategic strengths particularly in the form of its experienced human resources and its massive infrastructure. However, fundamental weaknesses also exist. The non-competitive market structure has not encouraged efficient practices nor did it particularly encourage innovation. Therefore, the offerings are not based on customer needs. The customer has no choice. Moreover, there is a growing technological distance *vis-à-vis* the 'best practice technology' prevalent in the oil industry internationally.

It is therefore necessary to open the markets to full and fair competition so that the customer is given his rightful due and there is enhancement of customer satisfaction through delivery of better value. In other words, it is necessary for this sector to become consumer-friendly, internationally competitive and capable of global presence. In order to meet these objectives and to attract private and foreign investors, it is necessary to restructure the industry.

POLICY INITIATIVES ALREADY TAKEN

A number of policy initiatives have already been taken by the government of India. These are enumerated below.

DECONTROL OF LUBRICANTS

The lubricating oils were the first to be decontrolled in 1992 when the import of base oil for blending of lubricants was allowed. The international majors like Shell, Mobil, Exxon, Caltex took advantage of this and started marketing their lubricants in India.

PARALLEL MARKETING SCHEME

In February 1993, the private sector was allowed to import LPG and kerosene under their own arrangements and sell it at market related prices. No controls on distribution or pricing are exercised.

IMPORTS OF CERTAIN PRODUCTS UNDER SPECIAL IMPORT LICENSES

In addition to the products covered under the parallel marketing scheme, products like aviation turbine fuel, furnace oil, benzene, toluene and bitumen were also allowed to be imported against Special Import Licenses.

Opening of the Refining Sector

The government had opened the refining sector to private parties as far back as in 1983. In 1991, Indian oil companies were allowed to form joint ventures with foreign oil companies. As a result of this, licenses have been issued for substantial capacity additions in this sector. In the Budget speech made by the Finance Minister on 1 June 1998, he indicated that licensing requirements for petroleum products are likely to be abolished.

The present refining capacity in India is 62.55 million tons per annum (mt p.a.). Additional refining capacity of about 105 mt p.a. is likely to be created over the next few years.

Expansion of existing refineries	21 mt p.a.
5 new refineries under construction	42 mt p.a.
6 new refineries planned	42 mt p.a.

If all the capacities planned fructify, the refining capacity would be of the order of 168 mt per annum by the year 2006-7, which will be in excess of the demand.[1]

Programme for Dismantling of the APM

In order to comprehensively deal the matter of reforms in oil and gas sector, the government in 1995 had appointed a Strategic Planning Group on restructuring of the oil industry ('R' group) to make final recommendations for restructuring the oil industry. The 'R' group had recommended that dismantling of administered pricing mechanism (APM) in the petroleum sector needs to be implemented in phases and had suggested a 'soft landing' approach to reforms. An expert technical group was constituted in June 1996 to examine the impact on various sectors at different levels of duty structure in case of dismantling of APM.

Based on the recommendations of these two committees, the government has announced its intention to dismantle the administered pricing mechanism by introducing reforms in a phased manner. The deregulation process commenced from April this year and is to be completed by the year 2001-2. The plan envisages:

(a) Dismantling of APM in the petroleum sector in phases as per sequence given in the Appendix.
(b) Withdrawal of the cost-plus formula for indigenous crude oil

producers. The price receivable by oil producers will be increased to international levels in a phased manner.

(c) Abolition of the system of retention pricing for all (existing and new) refineries. Pricing of petroleum products at refinery gate level will move towards import parity. However, refinery gate prices of controlled products, viz., MS, HSD, kerosene, LPG and ATF will be fixed at adjusted import parity prices for the existing refineries during the transition period, and, all other products will be sold by the refineries at market driven prices.

(d) Moving consumer prices of major petroleum products to market prices. The price of HSD is now being fixed on the principle of import parity picking up to the ex-storage point level, and the prices of other major products, viz., LPG, ATF, SKO and MS will be moved towards the principle of import parity in a phased manner. The pricing of paraffin wax, bitumen, naphtha, FO and LSHS has been decontrolled.

(e) Imports and exports of all petroleum products, except crude (slop crude and crude condensate), NGL, ATF, MS and HSD will be decontrolled during the transition period. However, sourcing and import of crude will be allowed to joint and private sector refineries under actual user licensing policy.

(f) Duties on crude and petroleum products will be rationalized in a phased manner. The last budget presented has in fact taken the first step towards rationalization of import duties. Currently, while the duty on crude oil is 27 per cent, import duty on petroleum products ranges from 0-30 per cent. Effectively, this gives a negative protection to the domestic refineries. The budget seeks to reverse this and the import duty on crude was reduced by 5 per cent to 22 per cent. Excise duty on motor spirit has been increased from 20 per cent to 35 per cent. Simultaneously, additional levy of 8 per cent on product imports will result in a positive differential of 10 per cent between crude and product imports.

(g) Investments in the refining sector will be encouraged by providing reasonable tariff protection and making marketing rights for transportation fuels, viz., MS, HSD and ATF conditional on owning and operating refineries with an investment of at least Rs. 2,000 crores (US $500 million) or oil explortation and production companies producing at least 3 million tons of crude oil annually.

(h) Establishment of a regulatory framework to oversee the functioning of and enforcing a competitive framework in the hydrocarbon sector.

It is expected that these reforms will significantly contribute to promotion of efficiency in the oil sector and benefit the consumer by way of lower prices and better value. These reforms are also expected to give a clear signal to potential investors as a rational framework has been firmly put in place for gradually moving towards a market determined pricing system instead of the administered pricing mechanism as was hitherto followed.

Pricing of Natural Gas

As far as natural gas is concerned, prior to 1987, prices were fixed by the producing companies. Since 1987, the prices are being fixed by the government. The prices so fixed were, in general, lower than the alternative fuels such as fuel oil and naphtha. It has been decided by the government that from 1 October 1997 up to 3 March 2000, the consumer prices of gas at landfall point would be linked to the price of a basket of low sulphur heavy stock fuel oils. With the approval of the government, the price would be notified by GAIL for every quarter based on the figures obtained from Platts oligram for the previous quarter.

New Exploration Licensing Policy (NELP)

In February 1997, in order to attract investments for exploration and production of oil and gas, the government approved the new exploration licensing policy (NELP). This policy abolishes the monopoly of the national oil companies and makes E&P activities fully competitive. At the same time, it ensures that the national crude oil producing companies are also given a level playing field in respect of pricing of the crude oil and other financial aspects.

The salient features of this policy are as follows:

(a) There will be no mandatory state participation through ONGC/OIL nor will there be any carried interest of the state.
(b) ONGC and OIL will compete for obtaining the petroleum exploration licenses on a competitive basis instead of the existing system of granting them licenses on a nomination

basis. At the same time, ONGC and OIL will also get the same fiscal and contract terms as available to private companies.

(c) Open availability of exploration acreage to provide a continuous window of opportunities to oil companies. The acreage will be demarcated on a grid system and pending preparation of the grid, blocks will be carved out for offer.

(d) Freedom to the license holders to market crude oil and gas in the domestic market.

(e) Royalty payments would be at the rate of 12.5 per cent for the onland areas and 10 per cent for offshore areas. Half of the royalty from the offshore area will be credited to a hydrocarbon development fund to promote and fund exploration related activities, such as acquisition of geological data on poorly explored basins, promotion of investment opportunities in the upstream sector.

(f) Cess, which was earlier levied on crude production, has been exempted for the blocks offered under NELP.

(g) Companies will be exempted from payment of import duty on the goods imported for petroleum operations.

(h) There will be no signature, discovery and production bonuses.

(i) A 7 year tax holiday from the date of commencement of commercial production.

(j) The contractors have been provided fiscal stability during the entire period of contract.

(k) A separate petroleum tax code will be put in place to facilitate investors.

(l) A revised model contract has been prepared and will be made available to the companies.

(m) This regime will apply only against contracts signed under the NELP.

(n) Exploration and production sector has been given infrastructure status under the Income Tax Act.

Import of Natural Gas/LNG

The import of natural gas/LNG calls for large investments in handling terminals and transportation networks. Participation by private parties is therefore encouraged. Many private parties have already shown interest in these projects.

As one of the measures to bridge the gap between demand and supply of natural gas, Petronet LNG Ltd. has been promoted by GAIL, ONGC, IOC and BPC. These companies hold 50 per cent of the equity and the balance 50 per cent is being offered to financial institutions, strategic partners and the public. Petronet LNG Ltd. plans to set up LNG import terminals on the west coast of India. It is also participating in other initiatives to import LNG.

Pipeline Network

To develop product pipelines in India, Petronet India Ltd. will be a holding company and separate subsidiary companies will be floated for each pipeline. In the subsidiary companies, the refining company whose products are to be evacuated through the pipeline can take a major stake. The primary aim of this company is to develop a pipeline grid across the country and manage it on the common carrier principle. Five pipelines have already been taken up for construction with a capacity of 25 million tons per annum.

REGULATORY MECHANISM

With the gradual opening up of the petroleum sector to private players, the landscape that was hitherto dominated by public sector players is fast getting dotted with private sector companies. Even though the major players are still public sector companies, the private participation is likely to gain strength in the times to come. Therefore there is a need for an effective regulation of the markets.

Exploration

The Directorate General of Hydrocarbons (DGH) was formed in April 1993 as a regulatory arm of the government to deal with the upstream petroleum sector. The DGH has since carried out surveys for data collection to open up large unexplored or poorly explored areas of the country. It has also been monitoring the performance of various production contracts signed by the government, and suggesting measures for improving the productivity of various fields. However, DGH does not currently have any statutory status or authority. It is therefore envisaged that a new authority—Hydrocarbons Regulatory and Development Authority (HRDA) will be created by passing the necessary legislation to that effect. HRDA will be given the powers to act as an effective regulator for the upstream sector.

Natural Gas

The import of LNG will call for large investments in handling terminals and transportation networks. While Gas Authority of India Ltd. is expected to play a leading part in setting up these facilities, private parties would play a major role. There are certain proposals from private sector companies to import LNG at various locations. Besides, the developers of small and medium sized fields will have to make their own arrangements for the marketing of gas. Import of natural gas through pipeline and in the form of LNG is on the Open General License. In such a scenario, regulation needs to be introduced in the gas industry in order to encourage private investment and also effectively control the functioning of all parties. To meet this end, the government has proposed the formation of a regulatory board for the natural gas industry in India. Necessary legislation is likely to be introduced shortly.

Downstream Sector

In the deregulated scenario, it will be the duty of the government to ensure adequate availability to meet full demand of petroleum products at reasonable prices, in all parts of the country and to all sections of the society. Government would also need to ensure protection of consumer interests. Further, disputes could arise amongst different operators and there would be a need to ensure that all players follow the prescribed rules. It is, therefore, necessary that an empowered body be created to cater to these needs, in relation to the downstream sector. It is proposed to have a regulatory authority for the downstream petroleum sector.

RESTRUCTURING OF THE OIL SECTOR

Empowerment of the Public Sector Companies

The Parliament, as a custodian of the people's funds has a duty to perform in exercising the monitoring rights as far as the public sector companies are concerned. However, the current monitoring has more of a 'micro-management' angle than is optimal for best performance. The government exercises a control on all major decisions, including those on investments and personnel policies. Even though these companies are directly under the administrative control of the Ministry of Petroleum and Natural Gas (MOP&NG) only, other ministries also have a major role in the decision making process. Investment decisions beyond a point need to be cleared by the government. Purchase decisions in many companies beyond certain limits are to be approved by a steering committee appointed by the government.

All this was acceptable when the management of the national oil companies functioned in a suppliers market and did not have to worry about competition. However, today as the oil industry stands on the threshold of change, chief executives had better start to worry more about being customer focused. Realizing this, the government has recently announced that it will give freedom to a select group of well performing public sector companies who have the potential to become global players—the navratnas. Government has decided to grant substantial operational and functional autonomy to the navratnas. Proposals for nomination of non-official part-time professional directors for navratna companies are under active consideration. It is hoped that this will signal the beginning of a change towards a more 'macro-management approach'.

Organizational Alliances

Unlike the international oil industry, the Indian oil industry has a very distinct feature—There is not a single home-based fully integrated oil company. ONGC for instance only deals with the upstream and has no refining capacity, while IOC has no equity crude of its own and only does refining and marketing. Equally there are companies like CRL and MRL which are stand-alone refineries. GAIL is only a gas transmission company and has no access to equity gas assets. While ONGC, the only major gas producer, does not market gas. And then, IBP which is only a marketing company. The co-ordination amongst these companies is currently done through OCC. This co-ordination is feasible only when one single owner—the government owns all these entities. In future, there will be other shareholders and all these companies will be competing for increasing market share. Consequently supply/demand co-ordination by OCC is impossible.

In the era of free market prices, stand-alone refineries or stand-alone exploration and production companies will be exposed to greater risks with excessive uncertainties regarding their profit margins. These uncertainties can be dangerous for small companies and they may not remain viable. Hence, what is required is a re-organization of all these entities into fewer companies which are integrated but fiercely competing in the market place. Such vertical integration can be done through equity swaps, acquisition or mergers. The exact mode that will be chosen may vary from case to case depending upon each companies perception of where they can add value to their customers and consistent with their core competence. This would create a vertically integrated oil company whose size and potential capability is equal to some of the international majors. Such organizations would be of crucial importance to our country's energy policy and energy security. Such organizational alliances may be worked out in the future.

RE-ENGINEERING OF THE PUBLIC SECTOR COMPANIES

In a deregulated scenario, there will be tremendous opportunity due to the phenomenal growth in demand for hydrocarbons. On the other hand, the share of the existing players is likely to suffer due to the entry of a number of new players—many of whom will be international majors. It is therefore necessary for the existing players to gear up to face the competition. Oil companies are required to urgently take up restructuring—capital, organizational and business process re-engineering. Most public sector oil companies have appointed leading consultants for advising them and have started implementing the restructuring plans.

To cite an example—Bharat Petroleum realized how important it was to be ready to face and thrive in the emerging competition and is taking all steps to improve its operations and the levels of service that is offered to customers. In short, it is redesigning the organization with the prime objective of converting BPC into a learning organization—one that learns and changes faster than its current and potential competitors.

BPC selected Arthur D'Little to assist it with this exercise. An internal core group of 30 young managers from BPC worked full-time on this project. Massive visioning exercises were conducted with staff at all levels to understand their aspirations for themselves and for the company. The next task was development of the change plan. While the vision statement spelt out the aspirations of the employees, the current reality was the state of the situation as it then was. Identifying the gap between the two and the ways to bridge this gap formed the basis for creating the change plan—thereby completing the first diagnosis exercise.

Among the other changes suggested it was felt imperative that the organization be redesigned in such a way that provides a much greater focus on the diverse needs of BPC's different segment of customers. Therefore, the organization structure was so designed to be process oriented as against the then functional orientation. In addition a number of organizational design elements like vision and values, performance measures, new competency required to work collaboratively and holistically, rewarding mechanism—have also been addressed.

BPC also focused on the human side of enterprise and realized that in order that employees care for customers, they themselves must first be cared for by the organization. Steps were therefore chalked out not only to fully involve the staff in the process of change but also to truly and sincerely make them feel that BPC is a great place to work.

The change plan was put in place recently with the six strategic business units formed and the staff put in position. The company is confident that by this exercise it will gear up to face the competition.

Similarly other oil companies are also improving their operations. The results are already becoming visible to the consumer. In the lubricants sector, for example, fierce competition has forced companies to improve their offerings and price their products more competitively. In the retail sector, state-of-art petrol stations are sprucing up here and there, with modern convenience stores. Thus, the industry is slowly getting used to a new order where customer satisfaction and creation of shareholder value will be the real drivers of the business.

In conclusion, I would like to state that there are exciting times ahead for the industry. I see a vibrant and globally competitive industry developing over the next few years fully meeting the surging energy demand.

NOTE

1. In February 1999, the oil coordination committee decided to stop imports of high speed diesel after July 1999. This reflects the change in the patterns of petroleum products imports of India due to the commissioning of new refining capacity.

APPENDIX
DISMANTLING OF ADMINISTERED PRICING MECHANISM

Particulars	*Model*
Transition Phase	4 years
Year – 1 (1998-9)	
(i) Removal of cost plus formula and payment to crude producers as percentage of weighted average FOB price of actual imports	75 per cent
(ii) Products to be controlled during transition period	MS, HSD, Kerosene, ATF and LPG
(iii) Withdrawal of retention margin concept for the refineries and refinery gate prices for controlled products	Adjusted import parity prices to existing refineries and tariff adjusted import parity prices to new refineries
(iv) Products to be decontrolled	Naphtha, FO, LSHS, Bitumen, Paraffin wax
(v) Exim policy	Decanalisation of imports/exports of all petroleum products except crude (slop crude and crude condensate), NGL, ATF, MS and HSD
(vi) Sourcing of crude	Sourcing of crude to be liberalized and import to be allowed for joint and private sector refineries under actual user licence.
(vii) Customs duties	Rationalization done in a phased manner
(viii) Increase in prices of	
Kerosene (PDS)	30 per cent of existing ex-storage point price
LPG (domestic)	33 per cent of subsidy passed on
(ix) Freight and other under-recoveries	33 per cent to be passed on, in an equated manner
(x) Shipping of crude oil	Withdrawal of cost plus formula for shipping of crude oil and move towards market related rates.

Particulars	*Model*
Year – 2 (1999-2000)	
(i) Payment to crude producers as percentage of weighted average of FOB	77.5 per cent
(ii) Increase in prices of: Kerosene (PDS)	30 per cent of revised ex-storage point price at the end of year 1
LPG (domestic)	A further 33 per cent of subsidy to be passed on
(iii) Freight and other under-recoveries	A further 33 per cent to be passed on, in an equated manner
(iv) Rationalization of duties	to continue
Year – 3 (2000-1)	
(i) Payment to crude producers as percentage of weighted average FOB price	80 per cent
(ii) ATF	Deregulation of imports and pricing
(iii) Increase in prices of: Kerosene (PDS)	20 per cent of the revised ex-storage point price at the beginning of the year.
LPG (domestic)	Suitable adjustment in prices to reach subsidy level at 15 per cent of import parity
(iv) Freight and other under-recoveries	Balance subsidy to be passed on, in an equated manner
Year – 4 (2001-2)	
(i) Payment to crude producers as percentage of weighted average FOB price	82.5 per cent
(ii) Increase in prices of: Kerosene (PDS)	Suitable adjustment in prices to reach subsidy level at 33.33 per cent of the import parity
	Full deregulation
2002 onwards	Transfer of subsidy on SKO (PDS), LPG (domestic) and freight subsidy on supplies to far-flung areas to the fiscal budget of the government

APPENDIX
DUTY STRUCTURE FOR 2000-1

(in %)

Customs Duty	*Existing 1997-8*	*Proposed 2001-2*
Crude	27	0 to 5
HSD/LDO	32	15
MS	32	15
ATF	32	15
LPG	12	10
LNG	12	0 to 5
FO/LSHS	32	10
Naphtha/NGL	0	5
Kerosene	0	0
Bitumen	32	15
Others	32	15

Excise Duty	*Existing 1997-8*	*Proposed 2001-2*
MS	20	165*
LPG	10	10
LNG	10	10
FO, Naphtha and LSHS general use	15	15
FO, Naphtha and LSHS fertilizers	0	0
Kerosene	10	10
HSD/LDO	15	15
ATF	15	40
Bitumen	15	15
Others	15	15

Note: *Inclusive of surcharge.

Contributors

YOGINDER K. ALAGH is currently Member of Parliament (Rajya Sabha). He was earlier Minister of Power and for Planning and Programme Implementation with additional charge of the Ministry of Science and Technology. He has taught Economics at the University of Rajasthan, Indian Institute of Management, Calcutta, University of Jodhpur, Swarthmore College and the University of Pennsylvania. He has five books and over a hundred articles to his credit, published both in India and abroad.

PIERRE AUDINET is currently with the OECD's International Energy Agency in the Division for Asia-Pacific and Latin America. He was earlier the Director of the Centre de Sciences Humaines in New Delhi and spent ten years in various institutions. He has contributed many articles to leading international journals. Among his recent publications are: *Knowledge Transfer, Partner Selection and Contract Design with Foreign Firms in the Indian Biotechnology Sector* (co-authors: S. Ramani, M. Elraoui), SERD-INRA, 1999 and *L'Etat entrepreneur au Brésil et en Inde. Economie du sucre et de l'éthanol*, L'Harmattan, Paris, 1998.

GILLES BOQUÉRAT is a member of the Centre d'Etudes de l'Inde et de l'Asie du Sud, Paris, and currently affiliated with the Centre de Sciences Humaines, New Delhi. Among his foremost publications are: *SAARC: Economic and Political Atlas,* Pondicherry, 1996, *Les avatars du non-alignement: l'Inde et les politiques d'aide américaine et soviétique de l'indépendence à la conférence de Tashkent*, Paris, 1997, *International Relations in South Asia: A Directory of Institutions,* New Delhi, 1999.

GULSHAN DIETL is currently a Professor at the Centre for West Asian and African Studies, School of International Studies, Jawaharlal Nehru University, New Delhi. She has been the Director of the Gulf Studies Programme at her university; a Fullbright Scholar in-Residence; and a Guest Research Fellow at the Copenhagen Peace

Research Institute. Her publications include *The Dulles Era: America Enters West Asia,* 1985, *Through two Wars and Beyond: A Study of the Gulf Cooperation Council*, 1991, and numerous papers on domestic developments, foreign policy and security matters in the Gulf and West Asia.

GILBERT ETIENNE is Professor Emeritus at the Graduate Institute of International Studies, Geneva. His most recent publications include *Chine-Inde: le match du siècle*, Paris, Presses de Sciences Po, 1998, *Feeding Asia in the next Century,* New Delhi, Macmillan, 1998, *China, India, Pakistan, Disparities and Weak Links in Economic Performance*, Rajiv Gandhi Institute of Contemporary Studies, 1997, and *Rural Change in South Asia, India, Pakistan, Bangladesh*, New Delhi, Vikas, 1995.

EMMANUEL FAGESIS is currently working as an economist for *Electricité de France*. He has published extensively on the greenhouse effect, informal economy and the energy sector in the developing countries as well as on their integration in the negotiations on climatic change.

JOHN GALE is a Senior Consultant with the CRE Group Ltd, Cheltenham. A specialist on energy, he has authored/co-authored several books and a number of articles in specialized international journals.

FRÉDÉRIC GRARE is currently Director of the Centre de Sciences Humaines, New Delhi. A specialist on South and Central Asia, he was previously with the Programme for Strategic and International Security Studies at the Graduate Institute of International Studies, Geneva. He has authored four books and contributed articles to leading international journals. Among his recent publications are *Islamism and Security: Political Islam and the Western World*, Geneva, Programme for Strategic and International Security Studies, 1999, *Tajikistan*: *The Trials of Independence* (co-authors: Shirin Akiner and Mohammed-Reza Djalili), London, Curzon Press, 1998, *Le Pakistan face au conflit afghan: au tournant de la guerre froide*, Paris, l'Harmattan, 1997, *La Russie dans tous ses états*, Bruxelles, Bruylant, 1996.

SUJATA GUPTA is currently Dean, Policy Analysis Division, Tata Energy Research Institute. She was previously Research Consultant at the International Institute for Applied System Analysis (IIASA),

Laxenburg, Austria. She is also an Editor for *Environment and Development Economics*, and the *Global Environment Review*. She has published numerous articles in leading international journals.

S.K.N. NAIR is an ex-Civil Servant who, in his official career, worked for the Government of India in various capacities in the transport (railways), power and telecommunication sectors. Between 1993 and 1996 he was Consultant to the Ministry of Power, and Member of the Expert Group that compiled the 'India Infrastructure' (1996). His recent publications include chapters on power in the *India Infrastructure Report* (1996), NCAER, New Delhi, 1996, *Energy for Growth and Sustainability* (co-author: Rakesh Mohan), Allied Publishers, New Delhi, 1998.

NICOLE NORTH is currently a Project Manager in INFRAS which she joined in 1995 as a research assistant. She mainly runs projects on sustainable development and capacity building in climate change policy in India mandated by the Swiss Agency for Development and Co-operation. She has co-authored with Othmar Schwank and Thomas von Stokar, *Structural Transformation Processes towards Sustainable Development in India and Switzerland*, Zurich, Development Alternatives Delhi, IGIDR, TERI, 1996.

PHILIPPE ROGIER joined the Institut Français du Pétrole (IFP) in 1963 and has had more than 30 years of experience with the oil and gas industry, including petroleum exploration in Algeria, in India and in France, underground oil and gas storage, as well as environmental issues in Europe.

OTHMAR SCHWANK is Managing Director of the environment department in INFRAS. He has specialized in environmental management, environmental impact assessment, sustainability related research and international technology co-operation. His publications include *Long-Term Structural Transformation Towards Sustainable Development: Switzerland as a Model Case within a Global Perspective*, Proceedings of the 20th Annual Conference of the International Association for Energy Economics, 1997, and *Workshop Report in Study on the Potential for Hydrocarbon Replacements in Existing Domestic and Small Commercial Refrigeration Appliances* (co-authors: N. Shall and S. Hess), United Nations Environment Programme, Multilateral Fund for the Implementation of the Montreal Protocol, 1999.

P.R. SHUKLA is a Professor with the Public Systems Groups at the Indian Institute of Management, Ahmadabad. He is a consultant to the Government of India and numerous international organizations on energy and environment policies. His recent contributions have been in the area of technology and hedging strategies in the context of emerging global financial instruments and economic implications of global climate change agreements on developing countries. Professor Shukla is a lead author of several international reports of Intergovernmental Panel on Climate Change (IPCC) and United Nations Environment Programme (UNEP). He is co-author of eight books on energy, environment and climate change policies, and has numerous publications in reputed international journals.

LEENA SRIVASTAVA is currently Dean, Regulatory Studies and Governance Division, Tata Energy Research Institute. She was previously Vice President, Tata Energy and Resources Institute, Washington, DC. She has authored/co-authored six books and published a number of articles in leading international journals. Among her recent publications are: *Transition to a Liberalized Environment* (co-author: S.K. Sarkar), Tata Energy Research Institute, 1999, *Global Partnerships for Sustainable Development* (co-author: R.K. Pachaury), Tata Energy Research Institute, 1994, *Role of Innovative Technologies and Approaches in India's Power Sector* (co-author: R.K. Pachaury), Tata McGraw-Hill, 1991.

U. SUNDARAJAN is Chairman and Managing Director of Bharat Petroleum since 1994 and a member of the Institute of Cost & Works Accountants of India. He was appointed as Convener of a Study Group for developing a comprehensive long-term perspective plan for the Hydrocarbon Sector in India for meeting the challenges that will emerge by the year 2010. The report of the Study Group is now popularly known as the 'Sundarajan Committee Report'.

THOMAS VON STOKAR is a member of the management of INFRAS where he was previously a project manager, working on numerous environment, energy and telecommunication projects. He has co-authored with Nicole North and Othmar Schwank, *Structural Transformation Processes towards Sustainable Development in India and Switzerland*, Zurich, Development Alternatives Delhi, IGIDR, TERI, 1996.